About the Author

This book is the autobiography of the author who as a young child had a dream where God spoke to her about the long and emotionally difficult journey she would be travelling. The road was indeed long and strenuous but with God's guidance and protection she overcame all the obstacles.

Dedication

I thank God for His grace and strength provided in my life.

Maria Bezuidenhout

Jesus Said: I will never leave you nor forsake you

AUSTIN MACAULEY
PUBLISHERS LTD.

A CIP catalogue record for this title is available from the British Library.

ISBN 978 1 78455 950 2 (Paperback)
ISBN 978 1 78455 952 6 (Hardback)
ISBN 978 1 78455 951 9 (eBook)

www.austinmacauley.com

First Published (2016)
Austin Macauley Publishers Ltd.
25 Canada Square
Canary Wharf
London
E14 5LQ

Acknowledgments

The reason for writing this book is mainly to help women finding themselves in similar situations, that one can make a stand for yourself and you can make a difference in someone else's life. If home life is difficult to handle get something outside that will boost your confidence and will provide fulfilment, a reason to make that difference.

Contents

My childhood and marriage

By God's grace, I was sent to this earth on September the tenth, nineteen-forty-six. I was safely delivered in the old-fashioned way by a midwife and made my grand entrance into the lives of the two people who I came to love and respect with all my heart: my parents.

My Father was of French decent and from him I inherited a loving and caring attitude to all people, and patience. From my Mother, whose descendants hailed from Germany, I inherited the gene that dictated that all had to be perfect and on time. Although my Father spoke many languages, we all were raised as, and spoke in Afrikaans. Unbelievably, I was the ninth in a line of ten siblings.

Growing up I found confusing the fact that there were so many people in one house. To be exact there were four brothers, two sisters and another brother born four years later. There were two more children, a boy and a girl I believe, but sadly they passed away in infancy. It must have been a tremendously heartbreaking experience for both of my parents to part with two of their children. If the little girl was still alive, I would have been called Helena instead of Maria.

My eldest brother was twenty-one years older than myself, and at first I thought he was one of my uncles. My eldest sister was nineteen years older and there were only three years difference between her first child Ann and myself. Being by nature a very inquisitive little soul, always wanting to know the reasons for everything, I landed myself in hot water many a time. It was very confusing for a young child, as no one would tell me why there were so many people living in one house. Coming in at the tail end, so to speak, my presence brought little joy and no novelty and nobody deemed it important enough to try and explain, even if it was only to keep my mouth shut. Frustrating to recall as my hunger for knowledge was a driving force in my make-up and a cause of pain for the rest of the family.

Being in the British Commonwealth when World War II broke out, all able-bodied men in the British Dominions were called up for duty to fight against Hitler. My father was one of them. World War II started on September 1st 1939 and ran until September 2nd 1945: six years and one day the war lasted. On his return, jobs were few and difficult to find and my father decided to start his own brick-making business. It was also a blessing as it provided work opportunities. The most welcome part of it all was the trucks used for the delivery of the bricks, as one was used each December for our annual holiday, and for three weeks it was converted into sleeping quarters for my mum and the younger children, who were Anna, Chris and me, during a camping trip.

But as children, we did not like the weeks running up to the big event as my mother started in November preparing for the trip. That meant it also was biscuit-baking time. They were baked by the barrel full. During these times we were told stories about Mum's childhood. Her childhood years started in nineteen hundred and six. My grandmother, we were told, was one of the victims of the nineteen-eighteen flu epidemic and sadly left my grandfather and children bereft of wife and mother. At the tender age of thirteen, my mum, as the eldest child, had to take over the running of the house and raised her brothers and sisters. They were altogether ten children. Mum and Dad married on Christmas day nineteen-twenty-three, and two years on she gave birth to my eldest brother Gert and nine other children followed, the last one Chris was born in nineteen fifty. She not only raised her siblings but also eight of the ten children that she gave birth to.

The cookie recipes were all from her family, handed over from generation to generation and I am still using them. My children speak of the cookies that melt in your mouth. It just seems to disintegrate once it is quickly dunked in some coffee and placed in one's mouth. The month of November was always dedicated to baking these cookies for the immediate and extended family members.

Having God-fearing parents, all the children had to go to Sunday school every week, which I did not mind at all and actually looked forward to each week. This lasted until we finished school. We were afforded the opportunity to meet Jesus and He became the most important part of my life.

In the era I grew up, the saying "children are to be seen and not heard" was taken quite literally. Unfortunately my hunger for knowledge did not subside to the great dismay of my family and I landed in hot water more often than I care to remember. My father tried to give me answers, my mother was very tightlipped. She was far too impatient. As a young child, I was abnormally concerned with placing all brothers and sisters, uncles and aunts, cousins, nephews and nieces. I simply had the drive within me to know all the facts that link a family together.

In later years, my sister Anna and I, three years older than myself, became very close. As for the others, they were all grown up and the age gap too large. Some were married or working and did not have time to listen to a slip of a girl like me who strove to be a little miss know-it-all.

I must have driven my mum to utter distraction. When I was five, fed up with me, she sent Anna, my sister-in-law, to enquire about early enrolment in school. The pretext was that she could detect a high level of intelligence in me as I was reading my sister's Grade 3 readers. As it turned out, the head master was willing to do the tests and found that she was right and duly gave permission for me to be enrolled. I myself was dumbstruck for once. With seeming haste, I was dressed and speedily marched off to school. My mother must have sighed with relief. She would finally enjoy some peace and quiet, even if it was just for the morning.

As children certain rules were instilled in us: not to lie, what is right is right, and what is wrong is wrong. They were simple biblical principles that are so lacking in today's society. There was no place for grey areas, no justification for wrongful acts. Your character was judged by the way you lived your life.

My mother was the local "adjudicator" or "comforter ", so to speak, in our community. All the ladies with troubled relationship problems or in need of advice or perhaps just a shoulder to cry on visited Mum on a regular basis. Mum was never one to go out and pay visits. These ladies trusted her and knew that their problems would be a closely guarded secret. We all need someone we can trust. And she was a real homebody, happiest when she was left alone with her books for she was an avid reader. Unusually for those times, she could not knit. However, she crocheted a lot and loved embroidering and taking care of her family.

I excelled at school and my favourite subject was history. I could sit for hours just reading about the past. European History was on the top of my list. I could release all my energy at school in my quest for knowledge. I was a loner. People found weird the fact that having friends was never a priority in my life. I could happily occupy myself for hours, reading, and drawing. At primary school I was a member of the basketball team. Once we reached the regional finals but sadly lost. We each received an acknowledgement in the form of a certificate with the names of the team and a group photo.

Then my life took an unexpected change. One day I came home from school to find a very old lady in our kitchen talking to my mum. I found out that she was my great aunt and that she was in need of company at night. She lived alone in a flat in someone's back yard. Aunt Poppy wanted my sister to come and sleep there at nights. My sister refused and I got the job. It was during the time that I spent with my great aunt that a change occurred in my young life – something out of the ordinary for a young child.

One night I was lying awake and heard someone walking towards the bed. I was listening but was not unduly scared. I was very inquisitive by nature and my curiosity overwhelmed any fear I might have felt. I liked "out of the ordinary things". The steps fell silent and a man started to speak. At that I took fright and crawled under the blankets shaking like a leaf, my heart pounding. Yes I do like new experiences but this was a bit too much even for me. When I calmed down and thought about the incident, all I could remember was the sound of his voice and all he said was "dogter" meaning daughter. If anything else was said it was lost on me, as I was so overwhelmed by the sound of the voice which was so soft and calming, and also so beautiful, it was indescribable. I told my father, and he was a bit upset about it and wanted me to stay at home from then on, but with much pleading from aunt and myself, as I felt sorry for her, I told my dad that I do not mind sleeping there.

Aunt Poppy was very happy and relieved as all she could think of was the old age home her own children wanted to send her to. She really dreaded the thought of going there. What good could I do if something should happen during the night? I was only ten years old. But it was not long after the previous incident that I had a dream. I dreamt that I was walking, I did not know where I was going as my head was bowed. I wanted to lift my head but I was unable to do so. I came to a halt in front of a man, head still bowed. He was dressed in white robes, just like Jesus, and on his feet were the same sandals that the men wore in Bible times. Again I tried to look up, but I could not manage it. This man put his hand on my head and said: "Go child, it is going to be a long and difficult road, but in the end I will restore everything that was taken away from you."

The following day I told my father and asked him what it meant, as he was good at interpreting dreams. It was strange for me and I could not understand much, but I saw him shaking his head as he related the dream to mum and said to her: "this child is something else".

After that he called me and told me that it was God who spoke to me. He emphasized that from now on I will find that I will get messages. These will be out of the ordinary and not mundane messages. He said: "You will know instinctively that it is different, like a thought that suddenly comes to mind, especially if you were not thinking about it at that moment in time, just like in the dream you had. Hold fast onto it, do not waver. If you are asked to do something, it must be done. You are special, but at the same time you must understand that it is a great responsibility to have such a gift. You are very young, but just be obedient to God and it will be well with you."

At that age I thought it was weird, it scared me. I was trying to understand it all. What I did discover was that my hunger for God's word and my yearning to know more about Jesus increased so much more and there was a deep inner belief in love and righteousness. My father became very worried. Because of aunt Poppy's age, well into the nineties by then, he was concerned that she might die during the night, and he was worried about the impact this might have on me. But a solution appeared in the form of a transfer of my dad's place of work. We were to relocate to Bon-Accord, a small place north of Pretoria. My father must have been very relieved as he now had a valid reason to end this arrangement without feeling guilty or worrying about it.

The question was now: "what to do with our home?" Mum was very much attached to it as she had bought it under very trying conditions during the war years. Would they look after her house, and what to do with Anna who was attending high school? This problem was solved by the news that my third eldest brother was getting married and the newly wedded couple would occupy our house. It suited my sister Anna too, as she did not want to leave the school she was attending. Her nature was the opposite of mine. I would go after every opportunity afforded to me, and she would shy away from the challenge of the new.

Alas I was not going to be a flower girl, and I so much wanted to be one, but my sister was one of the bridesmaids. I was heartbroken, but it was understandable as I was a very cheeky little girl, and spoke my mind frequently. It was obvious that my sister-in-law-to-be was not so very fond of my outspokenness. If I saw something was wrong, I would tell a person, regardless of how old he or she might be. I got into trouble with my father many a time because of this habit, too. I think in the end he also realised that it was because of the dream I had had. I did not do it intentionally, it came naturally, and I could not help it, so to speak. I was not purposely cheeky or rude to people. I just could not handle unfairness.

The bridesmaids were my sister Anna and Evelyn, the bride's best friend. With her was her brother, the best man Ernie. I was only eleven years old when I saw him for the first time, and something in me told me that I was going to marry this guy. I looked at him. I was not interested in any boys and this was not a boy but a full grown man and I did not even know his name. What a weird idea I thought. At my age it was the last thing on my mind. I just shrugged my shoulders. I did not dwell on it as I was too busy playing with my cousins.

Back at our new home, the time arrived to enrol at a new school called "Heuning nes Krans Primary School," which was a small farm school. Relocating from Johannesburg to such a small community was something to get used to. My younger brother Chris and I had a lot to keep us occupied. As we stayed on a ten-acre smallholding, we had lots of things to explore.

Sadly the day arrived to enrol, something we were dreading. Apart from making new friends, we had to get used to new teachers. The school was very small in comparison with what we were used to. The worst of it was that we had to catch a bus to get to school. The school itself had about seven classrooms, the head master's office, teachers' room and a small school hall.

On the morning I was enrolled, the head master and my mother nearly came to blows. I was only ten going on eleven and in standard five, or grade seven as it is now known. He was astonished as he had never encountered a standard five-pupil of such young age – the youngest pupil in his school in standard five was twelve years old. He wanted to demote me to a lower standard. At this, my mother became very angry as he had the documentation from my previous school in front of him, all the proof he needed. Mother told him in no uncertain terms that if he dared to demote me, she would send me back to Johannesburg and my old school. I liked that idea but said nothing. He conceded defeat, but he was not happy at all. He told my mother that he would be calling for a full report covering the day I entered school up until the present from the previous school principal.

It was difficult being the new kid on the block. Because of all the fuss the enrolment had caused, most of the pupils stayed clear of me. Unfortunately one always comes across a class bully and I had the privilege of having her sitting behind me. I had long hair which was plaited according to school rules, and she decided to dip the tip of my plait into an inkwell. How old-fashioned that sounds now. Given today's technology where even grade two children go to school with an IPod, the inkwell really sounds as if it came out of Noah's ark. My school uniform consisted of a white school shirt and a navy blue skirt and it stands to reason that my mum was not very happy with the blue ink on my school shirt. So I got into trouble with Mum even though I tried to explain the situation.

The following day the same thing happened, but I was expecting it this time, and as soon as I felt a tug on my hair, I turned around and gave her such a smack across her face that she burst out crying. We both got into trouble, but at least that was the end of the inkwell episode. A rumour went round the school: "Don't mess with her, she might be small, but she comes from Johannesburg". In their opinion, people born in Johannesburg are brought up to be rough and contact with them should be avoided. I was never so glad to have the personality I was blessed with, being a loner, as everyone started avoiding me. Not having a yearning for friends, it suited me down to the ground.

Finally the reports were received, and the headmaster came rushing through the door without even knocking. To my dismay, and in front of everybody in that class, he shoved them into the hands of the teacher and very excitedly told him that I was indeed phenomenal, look at her reports, exceptionally clever, he said.

I groaned inside, I was already so "well liked", what now? As things would turn out, the real victimizing would come not from the pupils but from the class teacher, a certain Mr. Winterbottom. He reminded me of Miss Rottermeier in the Heidi classics. Whenever a lesson was presented in class and he started to ask questions, he would zero in on me and say: "You are the clever one, what is the answer?" He was tall and very skinny and reminded me of a wizard with his long crooked nose. Luckily I had learned by then to keep my opinions to myself. If I had said what came into my mind I would have been expelled. Was this the birth of wisdom in a child so young?

I found it most uncomfortable to be treated in this way and in such a vindictive manner. The whole class sniggered, enjoying every minute of my distress and for the first time the classroom became a very unpleasant place for me. I came to have nightmares of the class teacher coming after me in my dreams pointing his fingers at me and staring me down with his beady eyes. I started to lose interest in my schoolwork. It became a mission for me just to get up in the morning and to go to that labour camp. Thankfully my father received news a few months later that he was needed back in Johannesburg, to the relief of us all. My mother missed her friends who used to visit her, as she was also not one to make friends easily.

Back in Johannesburg, life progressed at the normal pace, and I graduated to high school. We all attended Die Burger, an Afrikaans high school. We were given a choice after completing standard eight (grade ten) either to leave school and go job hunting, or to continue and to complete our schooling hopefully with grades sufficient to meet university entrance requirements. We were given a list of subjects to choose from and it was expected that we would choose six that would be complementary to our chosen career. English and Afrikaans were compulsory and of the electives I chose history, accountancy, domestic science and typing. No computers in those days.

Our bookkeeping teacher, Mr. Van Der Merwe, was a very temperamental human specimen and when he wore his brown suede jacket, we all knew that *that* day would be one of those "wonderful" days again. On such days, we would have to be at our best behaviour as nothing we did or said would meet with his approval. We all hated his moody days. Needless to say, I still had the habit of speaking up when I did not agree with something. But the funny thing was that I was never punished nor received detention for it. I can only thank God for that. To me it meant that I did the right thing, stood up for justice but without overstepping my boundaries. I never took advantage of the fact that I could say what I liked and get away with it. I only spoke up when something was wrong.

On his bad days he would give us three to four exercises to complete in the two period sessions. One period was three quarters of an hour long. One exercise consisted of the opening of accounts, recording transactions and then extracting a trial balance and drawing up a balance sheet. It was his habit to leave the classroom for nearly the whole session and reappear again a few minutes before time was up. Before he left he would stand in front of my desk and point his finger at me saying: "Don't you dare tell them what to do if they should ask you."

Normally my tasks were completed long before any of my classmates. As a result, I become fidgety and bored. My mind needed to be busy at all times. To pass the time and try not to disrupt others, I would help those who were really struggling.

Writing the above reminds me of the day that I spoke boldly to my father. It was one Saturday afternoon when my mother developed one of her headaches again and, as usual, the shops had closed before she realised that she had no headache tablets in the house. When Anna and I were still in our early years which was back in the nineteen fifties, it was against the law to keep shops open after one o'clock on a Saturday. Even the shops in central Johannesburg had to abide by the trading hours set out by the government. But mother dear would then insist that we go around the back and bang on the gate to buy the tablets. At times Laileng, the Chinese shop owner, would overlook the rules and provide us with the tablets. In the apartheid era, the "non-white" population was not allowed to trade in the "white" areas and vice versa. But a blind eye was turned to those who did. The trading hours were from nine-to-five on weekdays and Saturdays from nine-to-one in the afternoon. Sundays they were closed. No trading on a Sunday or Public holiday. Lo and behold, that particular Saturday after one, Mum got one of her legendary headaches.

Anna, being older and more experienced, saw what was coming and did a disappearing act. As a result, I was sent to buy the tablets by the "back door", so to speak. I tried, but Laileng was not available and my mum could not or would not take no as an answer. I simply had to get her the tablets. To make matters worse, at that precise moment my father arrived home and she told him that I did not want to go and get her the tablets. One thing about Afrikaans families: a child may never talk back to his or her parents. I had not done so, but Mum made out as if I had. I could not tell my father that

11

Laileng had refused to come to the gate, and he believed my mother and the result was that I got a hiding. When he was busy hitting me with the belt, he lifted his hand up again to deliver another blow, I screamed at him "You can hit me until I am dead, but if Laileng does not want to come out and give me the tablets, there is absolutely nothing I can do." I cried. He stopped right there in the middle of the act and looked at my mother. He did not say anything and stopped hitting me and walked off.

Towards the end of the year at Christmas time my dad would take us to Central Johannesburg on a Sunday and would also stop for a while at Joubert Park. The gardens were beautiful with all the colourful flowers, trees and benches to sit on and even swings for the children. One could sit there and enjoy the people, even have a picnic. Across the road from the park was Hillbrow, nicknamed the 'concrete jungle' as there were huge apartment blocks built to accommodate the large influx of people coming in from the rural areas. They made full use of the park and had picnics there. It was particularly beautiful around Christmas time when the lights were displayed in the streets and parks. It was festive, and brought about a wonderful community spirit as well as many bright eyes staring in awe at the beautiful displays. Father Christmas was also there with presents for the underprivileged children. Anna and I also joined the queue to the horror of my father and he quickly came to yank us from the line.

Another building that was to my mind very impressive was the Johannesburg Library. I paid frequent visits to it later when I was finally old enough to catch a bus to town by myself. My mother was a compulsive reader. She was a member of the 'travelling library' that came to our area each Thursday of the week, and she was also a member of the Johannesburg Library.

One Saturday afternoon I was bored and decided to walk to my brother's home half a block from ours. Guess whom I met there. Yes, none other than the best man that I first saw at the wedding four years prior. We felt a mutual attraction, not a mind blowing "wow", but we started seeing each other on a regular basis from then on.

I was in grade eleven in high school. My dream had always been to study law, but with a shortage of funds and no loans available, I left school at the age of sixteen to the great disappointment of my father, but he also realised there was nothing we could do as the funds were just not available to go and study at university. I went job hunting and found employment. I was successful in landing a job at a branch of Standard Bank situated a block away from the Lower Law Courts.

Ernie came around on Wednesdays and weekends, which was the norm in those days. And anyway it suited him I guess as it would have been difficult for him to pay more frequent visits since he stayed in Troyville situated on the east side of Johannesburg and at that time we were living on the Westside.

Some weekends he gave some weak excuses for not turning up. I later discovered that he went fishing with his friends and my father would never have allowed me to go on overnight outings with him. Instead of coming out with the truth, he'd simply not turn up and later give some weak reason for not doing so. I was not too happy about this behaviour. I explained to him that the least he could do was to tell me straight out so that I could make plans with my friends instead of sitting at home waiting for him.

On the weekends on which he was free, so to speak, we would go dancing, mostly in a group consisting of members of my family. Sometimes his brother Eddie and sister Evelyn would join us. In those bygone days the dress code was somewhat different. It was actually show time, all the more so for the ladies with their fancy evening gowns. I must mention that, at these occasions, Ernie seemed very pleased that I was his fiancé and very proud of having me by his side. In my simplicity, 1 found it encouraging. The world out there is not as safe as one thinks it is and I was learning fast. However, at that time I was still somewhat naïve. I was used to the love, truthfulness and commitment that I was exposed to by my parents, brothers and sisters.

"Boykie", as he was known by his family, a nickname that was bestowed upon him by one of his uncles for some unknown reason, decided it was time to introduce me to his family. He came from an English-speaking family, and I had a purely Afrikaans background. I was nervous and not really looking forward to it, although my English was not that poor. It was very likely that there would be a stark contrast in values, particularly given the fact that his family was not familiar with the Afrikaans language. These facts dampened my hopes. As anticipated, the introduction did not go well. His mother Polly, as she was known, did not approve of the courtship at all. I told him that I was very disappointed. I felt that neither his mother nor his brothers and sisters approved of me at all. The only comment he made was that I should not take it so seriously. This was of little comfort to me to say the least. Marriage was a very serious matter to me − it is a union between two people that should last a lifetime.

The main reason that I was so upset was that he showed no concern at all. If it was not for the fact that I was shown by God on the day of my brothers' betrothal that Ernie was the one I was going to marry, I would have not have given it a further thought. Knowing that this was where God wanted me, I acquiesced as He had promised that He would be with me at all times. I felt that it was similar to the marriages that took place between members of the Jewish nation of old, the bride was chosen and she had no say in the matter. I felt that way: chosen.

There was no doubt in my mind that Polly would never come to accept me into her family. That thought was very discouraging and it really hurt me. Little did I know that this was just a foretaste of what was still to come. Comparing my introduction to his family to the manner in which my sister and brothers-in-law were made welcome in our family, I felt devastated. I consoled myself with the thought that at least I knew what I was up against. Yet I received that all too familiar feeling within me that this was the man I was destined to marry. Many negative warning signs screamed out at me but this feeling persisted. I recalled the message: "I will be with you Maria".

My sister Anna got married, and soon enough she was expecting her first child. I was so excited yet envious as I loved children and saw myself surrounded by quite a few of them. William Junior was born on the twenty-first of May 1962. We were very relieved as she had had great difficulty giving birth. He was a hefty little chap weighing in at over ten pounds. This was not very surprising as his father was a big man and six feet, seven inches tall. We thanked God for the new life that had entered our lives. In spite of the fact that this was not the first time I had become an aunt, it was the first birth giving that I had actually been caught up in. I danced the baby to sleep each night. That was the highlight of my day. I was filled to the brim with the dream of an own child, so much so that I felt as though I could burst from the mere pleasure of the thought.

All of a sudden Ernie became very anxious for the nuptials to take place and he mustered enough courage to ask my father for my hand in marriage. My father grudgingly gave his consent. He felt that Ernie was not the right choice for me. Our wedding plans took on a new momentum, and it looked as if Ernie was really enthusiastic about it too, as if something was pushing him. We talked about where we were going to set up our first home. Obviously I wanted it to be on my side of the world, close to my parents. Polly's unhappiness about the pending nuptials was obvious and she took every opportunity to tell me so. I found this very offensive.

One Saturday morning, Ernie phoned and told me he was on his way to pick me up, and that he had a huge surprise for me. After everything that had happened thus far I was overjoyed. I liked surprises and coming from my future husband it gave me hope that things might just change for the better after the wedding. I was in for a gigantic surprise indeed. Polly arranged a rental of a two bedroom, dingy little semi-detached cottage in Troyville about fifty metres away from her home. That was not the end of it. She took it upon herself to buy the most dilapidated secondhand furniture she could lay her hands on. The worn lounge suite came with her assurances that it would be recovered as Ernie was an upholsterer by trade.

I was flabbergasted to say the least. How insensitive of him to allow his mother to interfere to such lengths, I thought, and I asked him just that. The answer he gave me was a shrug of his shoulders. Polly just stood there with a huge grin on her face. The place was dirty and dark. Because of my disapproval, I was labelled selfish and ungrateful. Needless to say, I cried myself to sleep that night, but I made a vow that I would replace each piece of furniture in that place. I learned that it was useless to go up against Polly. I would just have to go around her. Sadly, as it turned out, the lounge suite was never recovered. At that moment I again felt that I should turn on my heels and run, but the nudge came again and I breathed deeply, closed my eyes and silently asked for strength to be obedient to the call I received at the age of eleven. I kept faith as Jesus said He would be there with me every step of the way.

The date of the marriage was set for the twenty-eighth of December 1963 and preparations took on a new momentum. My parents wanted to meet his mother, but she refused out of hand and would not have anything to do with my side of the family. It turned out in the end that I had two wedding receptions. One good thing that came from this union was the opportunity it gave my father to walk me down the aisle. He was never more proud and it showed in his beaming, smiling face. Both my sisters had married in court, robbing him of this opportunity.

Unfortunately in November, a month before our wedding, Anna's son William Junior suddenly became very ill and was rushed to hospital. My father told my mother to prepare herself as Junior was not coming back again. At his saying that, I became both very sad and also angry. Like me, my father was one of those people who had premonitions that were almost always right. I hated these premonitions and unfortunately, it seemed to me, certain individuals are "blessed" with such a gift for life. For the first time I became fully aware of our total dependence on God, Jesus and the Holy Spirit to help us through situations like these.

The doctors could not determine what had made him so ill and they tried everything they could to help him. However, alas, he was taken from us four days later. According to the doctors, it was an unknown virus in the kidneys that caused him to have these severe kidney attacks that were very painful. They were at a loss, but still worked around the clock to try and identify whatever it was that caused these violent attacks. Unfortunately, William Junior could not be saved. It was so sudden and we were heartbroken by this event. How can one describe a death, any death, let alone a little boy just six months old? The doctors told William and Anna that Junior was the fourth child in the world that had contracted this illness and that they were in contact with overseas medical personnel, but they were also at a loss. It was terribly sad to look into the empty cot and when one did this, the truth seeped in that he would never occupy it again. I would not be able to dance him to sleep every night any longer. My heart went out to my sister and brother-in-law. They were shattered and Anna looked so forlorn and lost.

The funeral was held and I arrived early, before anyone else, and found the little casket lying there waiting for the last farewell. There was etched on his little face the pain he felt just before death. I thought Ernie would join me but there was no sign of him, another disappointment. Not a word of condolence was received from Polly or her family. I was to learn that to them it meant nothing as everyone has to die.

Because of the unwelcome tragedy, though the wedding would still take place, the reception on our side would only be a quiet and subdued affair. Polly showed no remorse for her cold heartedness and without a care in the world carried on with the arrangements for the wedding party which in the end she could not stop happening for her side of the family. I just could not understand these people and I just prayed for strength to get through all these things that were happening around me.

My marriage celebrations were marred not only by the death of my little nephew but mostly by the insensitivity of the family I married into. That evening instead of me lying lovingly in the arms of my husband, he was drunk and passed out and lay there next to me snoring. The dream came back to me that I had had seven years prior, and again I was reminded that the road would be tough. "It is going to be a long and difficult road but in the end everything taken from you will be restored." However, from all that I could tell at that point, there appeared very little hope of any happiness and a bit of me died that night. I could not help wondering what God wanted from me other than faith and submission to His will.

New beginning – Troyville

It was, indeed, a new beginning as we started our married life together as husband and wife. It was an adventure for me and I was still optimistic, even with the absence of support from my future husband and his family during the mourning of William Junior. In spite of this, I looked forward with excitement to what was to come. The hope that Ernie would change and become a responsible husband was still a dream I cherished. Unfortunately, I was in for a very rude awakening as the next morning when I woke up, hubby was gone. I looked through the house but he was nowhere in sight. I tidied up a bit and after having a strong cup of coffee, I decided to wait awhile but alas there was still no sign of him. I then walked to Polly's house, and there he was together with the rest of his family, enjoying breakfast and discussing the wedding reception. I was given a sideway glance by way of acknowledgement. Thereafter I was totally ignored as they carried on discussing the wedding and continued eating their food. I really felt like an intruder. After sitting there for a while as no one made any effort to invite me to join in, I felt so out of place that I got up and left. I was devastated. After yet another hour passed, Ernie finally made an appearance in our new home and immediately started to yell at me.

"How dare you just get up and leave, you did not even have the decency to say goodbye!" he yelled.

At first I just looked at him in total disbelief.

"What do you mean? When I woke up, you were gone. I wondered where you were. You did not even have enough decency to wake me up to go with you. Nor did you leave a note to say where you had gone. I decided to go looking for you and found you at your mother's place having breakfast, and to crown it all, when I walked in, I was not even greeted by anyone or asked by either yourself or your mother whether I would like to join you. What kind of people are you? None of you show any hospitality or manners," I responded.

He just stood there, gasping for air like a fish on dry land. He did not know how to answer me. I was dumbstruck to say the least. I just could not believe it. What did this family think of me? Did they think that I would just be a walkover?

It became crystal clear to me that I would need all the help possible from God and the Holy Spirit to keep me going. This would be a very long and emotional battle indeed. For how long only God knew. I would have to keep believing. I knew with certainty that this was where God wanted me and that I would actually have to learn how to walk in faith and to rely on God for strength and guidance. I had not foreseen at any point that people could be so unsociable and that Polly would go to such lengths to demonstrate her dislike for me. I would have to run this race with the understanding that one must not rush towards the finishing line. At first I would have to take one day at a time. It was no good crying about yesterday and worrying about tomorrow or trying to find solutions on one's own. This would be a total waste of energy. I accepted that this was a spiritual battle and that without God I would not survive.

"Take one day at a time and you will be shown what to do." This was the message I received in my Bible reading during that period.

In my spirit I was again reminded of the dream. I was also urged never to take my eyes off Jesus. He would never leave or forsake one. "You will see that at the end of the race you will stand amazed." That was a new revelation and it provided me with a new boost of energy that I so desperately needed.

Ernie had no desire to try to build a relationship. I had a niggling feeling that I was used by him for some reason, but at that moment I had no evidence to support it. The question did arise in my mind as to why Ernie had all of a sudden become so keen to get married? It was strange as every time I had brought the topic up, he had tried to postpone talk of it. Towards the end, however, he actually pushed for it more than I did. After that heated exchange of words on the first day of our marriage, which had left him without wind in his sails, he had just stormed out of the house and I only saw him later that evening.

After an unsuccessful attempt at running his own business had failed, Ernie had joined the Johannesburg Transport Department three months before our marriage. There was no leave due to him and he had to report for duty the Monday after the wedding. I had a week's leave so I set about unwrapping all the presents we received. There was absolutely no interest from his side to see what we had received. With all the energy I could muster, I started to clean the house the way I was taught and to make it as homely as I could. As Ernie was on day shift, he was due home at five in the afternoon. With the fiasco of the day before behind me, I started to prepare our evening meal. As I progressed, I became more relaxed as I was thinking of our first meal together as husband and wife.

I had set the table and was pleased with myself as it really looked good. I gave myself a pat on the back. I waited and waited and it was now fast approaching six o'clock and still Ernie was nowhere in sight. At half past six he strolled in and looked at all the preparation I had made, and looked at me and said: "I have already eaten at my mother's place."

"How could you? Who are you married to, your mother? Is she never going to let go?" I said.

He just shrugged his shoulders and went and sat on the front porch. He left me in the kitchen with all the food I had prepared and without as much as an apology. He came in again and told me to come outside as he wanted to introduce me to a family friend. There was no sign of regret shown for what had just happened. She was not a family friend as such, but he was friends with her brother as their mother was Polly's neighbour.

After the formality of exchanging names, I offered Mara coffee and she accepted the offer. Ernie left again to visit his mother. There was an immediate bond between us which I cannot explain. As we talked I found myself telling her all that had happened thus far and all about Polly's behaviour towards me. It felt so good to unburden myself, as I did not realise how tensed up I really was. I also told her that when I cooked our first supper as husband and wife, he did not even bother to come home first, but went directly to his mother's house and had supper there.

"My girl," she said, "do not allow that family to walk over you. I know she is your mother-in-law, and I know you are going to say that you must respect her, but with this family you will have to learn to stand your ground. The sooner you do that the better. I suggest that when you start cooking tomorrow, cook for yourself only. When he arrives from work and if he has the decency to come home first, send him to his mother's place to eat, as it seems that your cooking is not good enough for him. I repeat, do not let them walk over you."

Taking such advice would be totally against my upbringing and a new experience for me. However, all is fair in love and war, as they say, and I thought it was worth a try. The following night I did just that. Made myself something to eat and then I went and bathed and got into bed with a book. To my surprise he did come home first and wanted to know what there was for supper.

"Sorry," I told him. "There is no supper. I am afraid you will have to go and eat at your mums again."

He was not in the least happy with the situation, and stormed out of the house and went to his mother. I think he might have regretted introducing me to Mara. Another thing was that she knew the Bezuidenhout family very well, and I became quite enlightened by her tales about them. The sad thing in a way was that I had never been exposed to such behaviour and was shocked to say the least. My parents had never interfered in their children's marriages. If there was a problem, it had to be solved by the couple themselves. No running to mummy or daddy.

Mara's advice worked wonders. Whatever was said that night at his mother's house, I will never know. But from that day onwards he came home for supper. I knew then that we would never agree on most of our values. However, the ice was broken and perhaps there could be a real truce between us. After that unfortunate incident, Polly was more accommodating towards me. This experience also taught me to be more assertive. I knew I could be, but again because of my background, I automatically showed respect for all elders. But desperate times call for desperate measures.

They did complain about my friendship with Mara, especially Margery, Ernie's sister. Mara was not their "class" and I should not lower myself by associating with her, I was told. I totally ignored this advice because Mara was the only one I could speak to. They did not include me in anything. I felt uncomfortable when I went to his mother's place, and Ernie hardly ever asked me to go with him. If I should go there of my own accord, they would all leave the room and busy themselves somewhere else. It was not a nice situation to be in, always feeling rejected, only three months into our marriage.

As time went by Mara and I became close friends. I told her about the dream I had at the age of ten. "You are extremely blessed, you might not consider it so important now but keep on walking the way God directs you."

Mara also said that I must remember that there was a vast difference in the upbringing of Ernie and I. I was raised in a home where God was at the centre of everything. Polly, on the other hand, was not religious and hated God. What disturbed me the most was that Ernie did not really care how his family was treating me or how hurt I was about the situation. He never suggested that we should go out for a movie or a meal. I told Mara, too, that I had this feeling that he married me not because he loved me but for a reason I could not yet understand. I also expressed my questioning of why God would put me into this situation. "Only time will tell," Mara offered by way of trying to comfort me.

The eating at mum's house had stopped but something new emerged. Every Saturday afternoon Ernie disappeared. I asked him where he was and his answers were always so evasive. He was helping his mum with something or somebody's car broke down and he had had to go and give a hand. Apart from Maurice, no one made an effort to speak to me. At that early stage of our marriage, it was difficult to find out the true reasons for his disappearances. I actually hated going to his mum's and avoided visiting as much as I could without being rude.

I put Mara in the picture about his latest habit and she just shook her head and said: "You are so young and loyal, Ernie and his family are not what you deserve. All you do is work, come home and see to his every need and he spends every free minute of his time at his mother's house. It is not right and only you can put a stop to it. Your life is passing you by. As I told you before, even if you dislike confrontation, you will have to fight this family with all you have or do what Polly wants, divorce him."

I decided to investigate the next time he went missing. On the next Saturday afternoon, as was his new habit, he arrived home from work, changed his clothes and went to his mother's house. This time I confronted him and asked him where he was going and the answer was the same as usual, that Polly needed something to be fixed. I offered to go with him which he quickly declined. I found that very strange. I waited for a while and walked to Polly's house and when I entered I could see the amazement on their faces. They did not know what to do or say. I asked them where Ernie was, and there was silence. I threatened to stay there until he returned if they did not tell me. Most of them disappeared, and it was his brother Eddie in the end that actually came out with the truth. He told me Ernie had accompanied a family friend to the local cinema. Did this news hurt? Yes, indeed. I felt crestfallen.

I told Mara what Eddie had said, and she told me she had suspected as much. She also said that the "family" friend's name was Elizabeth and that she was the one that his mum wanted Ernie to marry. She was a divorcee and had two children. The sad thing of it all was that she was the ex-wife of one of Ernie's best friends. Everything became much clearer to me. The most cruel and hurtful thing was that it was now obvious that he had married me to avoid being forced into marriage with her. He wanted his bread buttered on both sides. How self-seeking and cruel could a person be? Divorce was out, I could never do that. With this new information, I would, indeed, need all the wisdom and patience in the world to help me walk this long and lonely road.

When he finally got home, I asked him where he had been. I told him that it would be pointless for him to lie to me as I already knew the truth. He stood there with a smirk on his face and said that if I knew the answer, then why did I ask him? The sad thing was that he did not even try to hide it. I expected at least some remorse, or "I am sorry, it will never happen again". His attitude was that what he did outside the home had nothing to do with me. It was not long after this incident that Polly started telling me that I should divorce him before there are any children. I told her that marriage in my family is a binding agreement and that there would be no divorce.

"I will not run away from my responsibilities, although it seems that none of your children possess that unique quality."

Polly was not happy with my answer. Nevertheless, from then onwards a kind of truce arose between us. I knew more than ever what I was up against and I decided to live, as the Bible teaches, one day at a time. The doors would open. Trusting Ernie was not a viable proposition, as he lied like a trooper and depending on him for support whether emotional or financial would be wishful thinking. There was only person that counted in his life and that was himself. I did carry the hope within me that God would actually touch his life, and I prayed for this every day.

Regrettably, he would only consider family if it would benefit him. It was also with sorrow that I found that even his mother was not on his list of priorities even though she would support him in any way she could. He complained to her that I took all his money and she was highly disgusted with me and told me in no uncertain terms that it was his money as he worked hard for it. He liked the fact that she would readily give him alibis whenever needed. But he had little affection for her. I started to feel quite sorry for Polly. He was just one selfish monster and I, for one, had to deal with that fact the best way I possibly could.

To my great benefit and relief, I really discovered the power of prayer. It gave me energy and peace to continue the struggle in the knowledge that God was in control all the time. Four months into my marriage had shown it to be but a mockery of that holy institution. How could one person be so insensitive to another? How could anyone be so selfish? Only God could be my refuge and the source of my strength and my everlasting hope in survival. He would give me all that was necessary; on my own, I would certainly perish. Unfortunately, Ernie realised that my attitude to marriage as a sacred and inviolable institution could be used against me. As a Christian, divorce was out of the question.

He liked the idea as in his mind it gave him the freedom to continue in his old ways which I had no knowledge of before I married him. He could continue to pursue woman, without taking responsibility for his exploits. He was now untouchable by the whims of Polly and especially other woman who might have landed in trouble through him. It turned out that he could not be relied upon to take responsibility for anything. He was a womanizer and there was nothing I could really do save divorce him, but he knew also that my Christian values were too important to me and I would not go so far as to file for a divorce.

I prayed for some kind of miracle. I just wanted to get away from his family and from that dingy house we stayed in. I just could not make sense of their way of thinking and the way they treated people. It seemed that they had absolutely no regard for anybody but themselves. Polly herself told me that one must take from life whatever makes one happy, regardless of the pain and heartache it might cause another person. That included Ernie's lust for woman. According to her, it was his life and he must do what makes him happy.

Amazingly an opportunity arose to buy a house. My eldest brother, who was in the police force, had resigned after accepting the post of Chief of Security in South West Africa for a diamond mining concern, the Oppenheimer Corporation. I told Ernie about it. My brother had given us the first option of buying as he knew our circumstances. My parents had told him the conditions in which we lived, and he was not happy about my situation either.

By this time I knew exactly how to pull the strings to get Ernie to do things. I told him about the house my brother wanted to sell and that he had given us first option. At the same time, I told him that he would be the first one owning a house in his immediate family. This prospect was extremely flattering to him.

As I hoped, his ego went into overdrive. We applied for a home loan and we were successful. I also urged him not to tell anyone as I wanted to surprise them. I wanted the deal signed and sealed before letting the cat out of the bag. I knew that if Polly caught a whiff of what was happening she would immediately try to put a stop to it. The papers were submitted and duly finalized and I was overjoyed as I knew freedom was in sight. Not freedom from marriage, of course, but we would be residing in Greymont which was situated on the West side of Johannesburg, miles away from Polly.

Ernie knew that I liked to attend church and he promised that he would go with me the next Sunday. Sunday came and he was summoned home and I told Polly he was not available that day as he had promised to go to church with me. Before I knew what was happening, she flew through our front door screaming at me. She said that I must not think that I would ever take her son to that bloody place. "Church," she screeched disparagingly, "there is no God. Do you understand me? There is no God."

Ernie stood there with a big smile on his face. He was now exempted from going with me as there was no way that he would act against his mothers' wishes. He was actually enjoying the attention he received. Sadly, the result was that I went to church on my own and my unfaithful hubby went to his mum's for breakfast. But before I left for church I told Polly with a very big smile on my face: "Did Ernie tell you the great news?"

"What news? Don't tell me you are pregnant."

"No not yet, but we are moving at the end of July."

I knew it was vindictive of me, but I so much wished that I had a camera in my hand. Her face became contorted with the shock of the news. She stood there rooted to the spot, mouth half open and for once she had nothing to say. So I continued the onslaught:

"And you know what, there is nothing you can do about it. But I am going now, I do have a bus to catch and I do not like being late, especially not for church." I felt a bit sorry for her, but for my own sanity I had to put some distance between Polly and myself.

As I left, she was still standing there in our lounge, dumbstruck. For the first time since we had gotten married, I felt free and happy. I actually felt completely relieved that at last I had really stood up to her, and she was completely lost for words. Most of all, I took pleasure in the fact that we would be miles apart. That alone was a great relief. Visiting her would only happen on special occasions like birthdays and public holidays.

Purchase of our first property

Before I left for church, I told Ernie to go with her as she was in shock and not looking too well. I assume she never thought that he would consent to moving away from her side of town. She looked so forlorn.

On my return, Ernie was not at home. I waited a while and then decided to tackle the bull by the horns and I went to their house. On entering I was immediately verbally attacked not just by Polly but also Margery.

"How dare you buy a place in the slums of Johannesburg?" Margery demanded.

"I beg your pardon," I retorted. "I was born and raised there. I am proud of my heritage. I have no reason to be ashamed of where I was born and raised. Why don't you do yourself a favour and take a very good look around you. Even you do not want to be associated with these surroundings. Let me tell you another thing, I unfortunately overheard a conversation of yours where you tried to conceal where you were actually staying. Talk about double standards. It is sad thing, too, that all of you are ashamed to say that you attended Troyville High School. What is the matter with this family? After settling here, Polly no longer had to search for a permanent place to stay, and you cannot even appreciate the fact that your step-father Maurice took you all in under his roof. At least show some appreciation for what Maurice has done for all of you. I can also tell you that if I should die at this moment in time, and it so happens that I am buried here, I will take my own bones and march off from this black hole posthaste. Now I will give your brother an ultimatum. Either he moves with me or he stays here. The choice is entirely his to make. You see as a husband he is spineless, and that does not reflect well on his upbringing, does it now?"

The atmosphere had become so thick one could cut it with a knife. There followed a deadly silence, and no one opened his or her mouth. After standing there waiting for a reply which was obviously not forthcoming, I turned around and marched off, leaving them all in a state of shock.

I went to Mara and related the whole saga to her. She was jubilant when she heard that I had actually stood up to them and gave them a taste of their own medicine.

"It is so sad to think that we have to move house under these circumstances, Mara. I just do not understand these people. I have never in my life encountered the likes of them. They are really vindictive. Then to make matters worse, I retaliate in the same manner as they do, which to me is worse. It is degrading, and I am just not used to it. We were taught to respect our elders and not scream at them in the manner I have just done. That is not who I am. I have never known or encountered anything like this. I know this is the road I have to travel, but blimey, I will need all the strength and wisdom that the Almighty can give me. I do not want to think what would happen to me if I should try and do it on my own. I would not be able to withstand the onslaught. I expected confrontation, but this is total insanity even coming from them. I cannot understand why they dislike me so much, why they cannot just keep an open mind. On the other hand, I feel a bit guilty, as I did not discuss our intention to buy this house with her. But I also knew that it would have been fruitless as she would have tried to nip it in the bud."

31

"My girl," she said. "I am sad that you are moving, but believe me it is the best thing that you can do as their small mindedness will never stop, believe me. We have known that family for quite some time. When the time comes, I will come and help you to pack. That way we can turn it into an adventure and not a disaster. Just promise me that you will hold onto your faith as I am sure you will make it. Hold on to God's hand and it will be well with you."

I left for home and I went to the bedroom and prayed.

"Father, I ask that You give me enough strength to face each day and to do what is right in Your eyes. I am looking forward to this opportunity to move to better surroundings. Forgive me for all I have said to them today, also please help me to become more tolerant. I really do feel bad and so discouraged. Father, please keep me safe as I take refuge in You."

I could not say when he came home as I fell into a deep sleep. The following day it was work as usual. Ernie was on early shift so he left at five in the morning. I did not bother to get up to make him breakfast like I normally did each day. He had become accustomed to breakfast in bed, but I did not have the energy to do it that morning. He left without saying goodbye.

We only had four days to arrange for our meagre belongings to be transported to our new home. I did not apply for leave with the result that the packing had to be done at night. When he arrived home that evening I asked him what his intentions were. Was he going to get someone to take care of the move, or was he going to do it himself? All that was needed was a little help with transport. I did not really foresee any one of his family members helping me in any way with the actual packing of the crockery, linen and so forth, but I needed to know what plans he had made, if any, in order to plan things properly. He went to the lounge and sat down sulkily, staring into space.

This was new but I was getting used to his different ways of trying to make people feel sorry for him. I took the opportunity to unburden myself while I had the chance and I told him that I felt like a complete outsider.

"Your mother is on my case again about divorcing you, urging me to do so before there are any children as she has been doing since a month after our nuptials. What hurts the most is that you do not make any effort to defend me nor give me any moral support. If you want a divorce, go ahead, you have my full support, I will not contest it, but I will not file for a divorce," I said.

"Let me make something else also very clear to you," I continued. "I am not in any way dependent upon you for help. You have proven again that you will not take any responsibility for this relationship. This you showed clearly when you admitted that you only married me to get away from being pushed into a marriage with Elizabeth. You are free to go. I know that it is what Polly wants. You have to make a choice here and now. You either give me some support or I will move with the help of my brothers. I also have family as you may have realised, and they are just waiting for me to ask them for help, as they will not interfere unless I ask them or it is life-threatening. They are just a phone call away and they will be here like the wind to load our meagre belongings. I am not that reliant on you or your family. You might as well understand that now, the sooner the better. The previous six months have been an eye-opener for me and I know full well that I will never be accepted by your family. I have no expectations in this regard anymore. I will make a life for myself as you have done. Make up your mind to either arrange for a pickup truck or you leave me no choice but to phone my brother. I am tired of your delaying tactics," I concluded.

He had not foreseen this angle of attack. He was too used to everyone dancing to his tune. He had never encountered retaliation and he was at a loss as to how to react. He opened his mouth as if he wanted to say something, but then he closed it again. He looked at me again with such a ridiculous expression of unbelief on his face.

"Did you think that I would be a pushover? I might be only eighteen years old but one thing you must realise right now is that I am not scared of you or your mother. I will show her the necessary respect due to mothers, and she is my elder after all. But you can rest assured that you will never be able to control me. As a Christian, I have faith in God to protect me at all times. God made that promise to me at the age of ten. There will be no way that you will ever lift your hands to me or reduce me to a whimpering fool, and neither will your family dictate to me how I must run my life. I give you five minutes to decide whether to go back to your mother or to help arrange transport of our belongings to our new house."

I left the room and went to the kitchen to make a cup of coffee. It was not long before he came to the kitchen where I was busy packing. I just kept out the utmost essentials − some crockery and cooking utensils, the rest of the stuff I was packing in boxes. I looked at him and I could see that he was not at all sure of what to say to me. I was sure there would be no apology for the way his family treated me, as by then I knew that the word sorry did not exist in their vocabulary. Anything that went wrong in their lives was always somebody else's fault. Also, it would be the first time that he would be separated from Polly by any real distance.

Ernie looked very uneasy, and I asked him if he had made up his mind. He told me that he would make the arrangements for transport and I would not have to phone my family. With that he turned around and left the house. I continued with the packing. I was determined that if there were no signs of any arrangements made by the coming Friday, I would phone my brother. It was sad and hurtful to accept the fact that one's husband was totally untrustworthy. The sadness was threatening to consume me again, but I filled my mind with the knowledge that God is in control. I took a couple of deep breaths until the sadness subsided. It was still light outside so, I went across the street to Mara for a much needed cup of coffee and a pep talk.

When I came back, my thoughts went out to the little old lady living next to me who was the mother of Polly and I wondered why they were not talking to each other. I did ask Eddie once and the reasons he gave held no water, made no sense. All I had managed to pick up was that there existed a lot of bitterness between them. She sometimes peeped over the fence to see what I was doing, and once nearly fell off the dirt bin she was standing on as she was such a short and frail lady. We were never actually properly introduced to each other. There was no family unity in the sense that I was used to.

Eventually Friday arrived and everything was in place and ready for the next day's move to our new house. Ernie's brothers Eddie, Alan and Clive helped him with the furniture. I would transport the rest of our worldly possessions by car. Come Saturday morning, Mara was standing on her front verandah waving us off to the disgust of the Bezuidenhout family, or "B family" as I had come to refer to them. I felt extremely relieved that we were leaving this dark hole but on the other hand extremely sad as I would miss Mara. I promised that if and when I visit the B family, I would pop round for a lovely chat and nice cup of coffee.

Greymont

Sadly I did not go to Polly's home to say goodbye, I just did not have the energy. After everything was packed, I let Ernie deliver the keys of the house to Polly as she had made all the arrangements in the first place so she could hand the keys back to the owner. Arriving at our new home, I found that my sister-in-law Anna had left all the curtains for me, with a note saying that they all wish us well in our new home. What a difference it made. I would not have to worry about making and hanging new curtains. This gesture was a real Godsend.

Ernie's brothers were actually very impressed by the house, as the light streamed in through decent-sized windows, and being high up against a hill, one had no obstructions and could see for miles. There were many rooms: an entrance hall, lounge, three bedrooms, a kitchen and a scullery. No painting to be done, everything was so neat and clean.

My thoughts went back to the dark and dingy little house I had left behind, and my heart soared with gratitude for this new opportunity to turn a house into a home. There were also two verandas, one in front and one at the back. This made a huge difference. Outside there were the servants' quarters, a garage and a garden in the front with ample space for children to play should we be blessed with any. All these facilities had been sadly absent from our rented house in Troyville.

Eddie, Alan and Clive left soon after everything was offloaded. Ernie brought all the things that were in the car into the house and promptly got into the car and disappeared for the rest of the day. If I had had any expectations of his help with unpacking, I was in for a rude surprise. I supposed that I should count my blessings, as the actual furniture had found its way to where I had wanted it, but as for the boxes, they had all been dumped in the entrance hall.

I had learned a few lessons since I first made my acquaintance with this family six months before and one of these lessons was to accept the things one cannot change. The move was a great moment for me and it was with much pleasure that I started to unpack the boxes. I washed everything and was busy placing the last bits and pieces in cupboards when I heard the car enter the yard. The sun was about to set and I was busy making myself a cup of coffee. When he stepped through the door, I did not ask him where he had been. However, Ernie could not wait to tell me. He informed me that he had gone to visit a few of his colleagues who happened to live in the vicinity as they were all bus drivers on the same route.

"Yes and you left me to do all the unpacking while you were socializing? I could have done with a little bit of help from you and a bit of enthusiasm, too." I said, but he took little notice and continued his tale. I did not offer to make him coffee and went to sit on the front veranda where it was pleasant even though it was still officially winter and a bit cold outside. It helped me to cool off as I felt very tired and hot, and also I was feeling very upset and trapped in this marriage. Was it so wrong of me to expect a bit of help from him? It was his house, too. What is the matter with this man? I wondered.

He ignored what I said and followed me outside and continued to tell me about his colleagues. I was tired and I really did not have the energy to hear about his new circle of friends. I was actually waiting for him to give me a reply as to why he did not stay to help. No apology was forthcoming so I cut him short and asked him to go and buy something to eat as I was definitely not going to cook. As he left, I felt more drained than before. I think he was actually glad to escape at that moment as he sensed that I was not at all impressed by his behaviour. I could not see the point of him going to visit his friends while I was working myself senseless to get some order in our home, not just for myself but for him, too. He did not even drop a remark like: "Wow, the house is looking good;" or: "Fantastic." He showed no sign of appreciation whatsoever. His reactions made me feel even worse. It would have made a huge difference if he merely showed a little gratitude. It would have given me a sense of self-worth.

What I should have done was to leave everything until he returned and roped him in to help, but that was not the way I was raised. I was very upset as I could not accept his insensitivity, the fact that he was so thoughtless as to leave me to do the unpacking by myself. It was really hurtful. What on earth was he thinking? How did they grow up? All these thoughts were going through my mind and I really felt disgusted towards all of them. I honestly could not understand the Bezuidenhout family, period.

This time somewhat surprisingly he did not take hours. I was grateful as I was famished. We sat and ate our supper in silence and he even offered to make tea. I was so taken by surprise, I nearly fainted. But I decided to keep my mouth shut. After I washed up the dishes, I was again surprised when he dried them. I went and bathed and crawled into bed. I was so tired − sliding into bed was an absolute pleasure.

Sunday morning arrived too soon for my liking. I was a bit disorientated waking up in new surroundings and, once I was fully awake, I pulled myself into a sitting position in bed. It was with joy that I took in the sun streaming in through the windows as the main bedroom was east facing. I was at last free of that dingy house in Troyville. No more in-laws breathing down my neck. Ernest was not on duty today due to the move, but he was gone, nowhere to be seen. I had thought that after moving away from his mother, he would not disappear as he did before. So where could he have gone to this time?

At first I thought he might be outside, investigating the outbuildings. I really was so naïve as to think that the most natural thing to do for a man was to show some interest in his new surroundings. The garage he never previously had, for instance. He might be there. It was supposed to be a man's domain, as they say, a man's pride and joy. Besides, there was the garden, too.

Being the beginning of August, there was not much to do as yet in the garden. However, in my innocence, I really thought that he would show some enthusiasm for getting his hands soiled, so to speak. I was told he was the gardener in the family. Was that also one of their illusions, or were my expectations too lofty? Was I really so stupid as to set my hopes overly high and to think that he would busy himself in the garden or the garage? Alas, he was nowhere to be seen.

There were no cell phones in those days and although my brother did not cancel the landline when he moved (for which I was grateful and arranged to have the phone written over to me), I did not want to phone Polly to ask whether he was there, as I had come to expect lies from them and besides that, I did not want to give her the satisfaction of learning that he had deserted me on this first morning, or to admit that I did not know where he was. It was a horrible situation to be in and due to their lying all the time, covering up for each other, I was getting into the habit of doubting everyone else, too.

To keep myself busy and my mind occupied, I rummaged through the cupboards and rearranged them again, sorting out the cutlery drawer. As for the crockery, I assigned a place for everything. The pots and pans were packed on the ample shelving space in the scullery together with the groceries I had. I needed to buy fresh bread and milk, but walking the distance to the shops was not a priority at that moment. I just wanted to relax and take it easy for the rest of the day.

The only drawback the property had was the distance to the nearest shop; it was situated far from the shops and, and due to a steep incline on the road towards Twelfth Street, walking was difficult. It would be really very difficult carrying bags of groceries from the shop home. To go to the nearest decent-sized grocery store required a car. Unfortunately for now I would have to rely on Ernie and my hopes were not very high as his commitment to household chores was absolutely zero. There was a small café on Ninth Street and the bus stop was situated across the street from the shop. It was good exercise for one to walk all the way to Twelfth Street, but definitely without any baggage. It would surely keep me fit as I would have to walk the distance each day going to work and back.

I had to figure out which bus I needed to board, at what time, and how long it would take to get to the centre of Johannesburg and get to the office on time. The banks opened at nine in the morning and we were expected to be at our work stations at least fifteen minutes before opening time. I had applied for a transfer to the Braamfontein Branch of the bank which was pending approval. It was still far off but accessible by public transport. There were branches closer to our new address, but one would need a car to reach them. If only I had a car at my disposal, I said to myself, it would be so much easier.

On that first Sunday at our new home, Ernie re-emerged several hours later. I did not ask him where he had been but I did ask him to take me to a shop so that I could buy some bread and milk. I also suggested that we stop at my parents' house just to say hello and to tell them we were now settled and looking forward to visiting them more regularly. We had not once visited them since we were married and had lived in Troyville. My parents had visited us once to have a look at the dismal place we lived in and I could tell that they were not impressed, even though they kept their disapproval to themselves.

He obliged and I, ever hopeful, interpreted this as a good sign. I also asked him about the bus schedules and he told me that there was a bus from the terminal on Ninth Street at seven and half past seven in the morning and that I should try both to determine which one would get me to work on time. The traffic could also play a huge role at that time of the morning.

Was the hopefulness due to the dream I had had? Over the years, people have asked me why I stayed with Ernie as he showed no affection or regard for me. It has always been difficult for me to explain and whenever I mentioned the dream, many thought me crazy. Those things only happened in Bible times, they would argue. But it is not so, it is still very relevant and happens even today.

The only one that ever understood the situation fully was my father. It must have been heartbreaking for him to witness what was happening to me and yet be helpless to do anything about it. One day at a time. I felt like Father Abraham, walking with the incontrovertible assurance that God was with me.

My sister Anna and husband William were still living with my aging parents. There were no children in the house except my younger brother Chris, who was still at school. All my other siblings had flown the nest. My mother's health was declining. This was due, I believed, to a long hard life as well as giving birth to and raising so many children. Although she was only in her fifties, she looked much older.

During that first visit, Ernie had to content himself with the company of William. Because of my father's disappointment in my husband's behaviour towards me, he ignored Ernie completely. Mum, Anna and I had a good long chat. Six months was a long time, and we had a lot of ground to cover. While in Troyville, Ernie had not wanted to visit my parents on the pretext of the distance we would have to travel. Anna had joyful news. She was pregnant and the child was due in January. I was so happy for her, especially after the loss of their first baby, William Junior.

En route home we stopped at the corner café and bought the necessities; we would do a thorough shopping the next day when we could get to a supermarket, which would be cheaper. Arriving at home again, I started preparing supper, and for the first time in our marriage, Ernie was with me in the kitchen and talked to me while I was cooking. It felt so good. I really felt happy and contented.

It did not take long before Ernie's sister Margery came on behalf of the family to inspect the new abode. The brothers Eddie, Alan and Clive must have given their comments but she was sent to confirm their findings. She seemed impressed but would not admit it. When we went to visit his family afterwards, I was curious to hear their opinion of her impressions, but nothing was said. As usual I was totally ignored and the realisation sunk in that there would never be anything I could do for the betterment of the two of us that would ever find favour in their eyes. I felt let down and out of place and was sad as I would have liked to have been accepted as part of their family.

On the whole, our life on the opposite side of town was much happier and I saw hope for a better future. I never tried to keep him away from his family. He never liked visiting my parents although he had made contact with my one brother, Rolf, and visited him frequently. We often went to see friends – both his and mine. He appeared to be enjoying the new way of life that we were leading. It was not something he was used to.

Nevertheless, in spite of some changes for the better, money was still an issue. His mother continued to stress that he could do as he wished with the money he earned. It became obvious that he took this view to heart and he was happy to play house without contributing to running expenses other than paying half of the mortgage instalments. I was amazed at her seeming insistence that Ernie bore no responsibility for the success of his marriage, seeing that she had not succeeded in getting any money out of her ex-husband and father of her eight children. Having divorced an irresponsible husband, she might have known better.

With my earnings I'd replaced all the threadbare furniture. He wouldn't do so because he was quite satisfied with the dinginess we'd lived with since moving into our first home. I suppose it stemmed from his childhood days, it was something he had grown up with. Although my new possessions were not extravagant, the house now looked cosy and it was a pleasure to have friends and family around without feeling self-conscious. I cannot recall his mother ever visiting us.

Occasionally, when Ernie was not working over weekends, we'd join my brother and his family on camping trips. This was an opportunity for him to experience family unity. He also introduced me to his Uncle Richard, who was known as Dick, and Aunt Hetty who did not live far from us. I loved Aunt Hetty as she was also Afrikaans and we bonded from the moment we met. As for Uncle Dick, I found him uncompromising and selfish like his nephew. He was a really bombastic type of character who demanded perfection at all times. Aunt Hetty I found had a very soft nature and was almost always in tears when we visited them. Uncle Dick completely undermined her confidence.

From them I learned a bit more about Ernie's back ground. It became clear that he'd never had much happiness in his life. Their father had been an alcoholic and cared very little about his family. At a later stage when Eddie came to visit more often I asked him about their upbringing. I learned that they had spent most of their early years in fear as their father always arrived home intoxicated and started arguing and physically abusing their mother and them, and they often went to bed hungry.

Although he appeared to enjoy the comfort of a secure and loving home, he was not prepared to give up his bachelor lifestyle which only occasionally included me. Everything had to be laid out for him without any input from his side. Coming from a family where my father and mother worked together, and my mother was a stay-at-home mum, it was difficult for me to come to terms with the way that Polly impressed upon Ernie that he did not have to support me or his family. I found it very odd that a woman who went through so much hardship herself would impress such a thought upon Ernie, and the sad thing was that he followed her directions. I wondered many times whether she would act the same way if he was married to Elizabeth.

The first Monday in our new home, I barely managed to catch the bus leaving at seven o'clock. The bus went through Greymont and I was very happy to see that it passed my parents' home. The bus route to the centre of Johannesburg went through a number of suburbs I was not familiar with: Roosevelt Park, Emmerentia, past the Johannesburg gasworks, then through Braamfontein where the University of the Witwatersrand is situated, past the Johannesburg Railway Station situated on Harrison Street which was the last stretch before the driver turned into Loveday Street. Eventually, after an hour, we turned into the terminus that was situated on Loveday Street, a block away from the Town Hall. From there I still had a twenty minute walk to the bank and I managed to arrive just on time. Clearly, the early bus would be the best choice when commuting to work. Life seemed to flow peacefully for which I was thankful, as the stress of the first six months of marriage in the shadow of the B family had been unbearable. I felt that their presence had whittled away at my self-confidence. I was recovering nicely.

Polly phoned one evening and unfortunately Ernie was not at home as she wanted to talk to him. She pointed out that she had not seen him since the day of the move. She invited us both for lunch the following Sunday. After I replaced the receiver I became very upset with him as he should have been home already. Where was he? Thoughts of what had happened in the flashed through my mind.

We were hardly together on weekends, that is, if we were not off fishing which only happened occasionally. Where was he then? I felt angry as Polly might think that it was me who was keeping him from visiting her. When he failed to come home after his shift had finished, I automatically took it for granted that he had gone to visit his mum.

Ernie had taken to not coming home directly after work, and now his mother was phoning me. It made me feel very unsure, and many thoughts crowded my mind: was she trying to sow discord by making me feel insecure or had he established a new harem again? How I hated the things that they have done to me thus far and now they were causing me to doubt him. I confronted him when he eventually arrived home. I was afforded a side way glance, but that was all. He took his paper and went to the bathroom without answering me. That annoyed me even more.

"Your mother invited us for lunch on Sunday," I shouted through the bathroom door. Luckily it was his weekend off and if he had been planning something else just for himself, his plans were now foiled. He did not comment and went to bed soon after.

We did go to his mum's for lunch and it was actually very pleasant. I had not been looking forward to it and had no or very low expectations. It turned out to be good and I really enjoyed it. It seemed that the separation from them had worked wonders. I could look at things from a different perspective. However, the experience was marred later that afternoon when Polly called me to her bedroom. It seemed there was something that she wanted to show me. Instead, however, I was told in a very unpleasant and hateful manner that I must divorce Ernie before there were any children. This put an end to my hopes and expectations. How was I to live in peace with this family. I was sadly mistaken to even think that there would be any harmony between us and I was really shocked to find out that lady Elizabeth was still lurking, waiting in the background. I actually felt sick, and told her that if she wanted us to divorce so badly she should kindly tell her son to file an application. I would not contest it.

I got up and walked out of the bedroom and left her there. With all my hopes dashed once more, I was on the verge of tears and asked Ernie to take me home. Everyone looked surprised at my request and although he was not very happy about it, he was very familiar with my body language by now, and hastily got up, said his goodbyes and we left. I was hurt and angry with myself for being so gullible and allowing myself to think that there was a flicker of hope of trying to build a relationship with this woman. Polly was just the most unpleasant person I had ever had the misfortune of meeting.

Once in the car, I told him that his mother had asked me once more to divorce him. He just looked at me with a grin on his face, shrugged his shoulders, and gave no answer. It seemed that the discord between mother and wife flattered and amused him at some level.

It struck me with sudden force that he really did not care about my hurt feelings. I was just there for his convenience. With much pain I realised that I was only a safety net of sorts. When he disappeared it was for his own pleasure. He had a string of ladies who were happy to meet his sexual needs. He was not only extremely good-looking, but he could charm the pants off anyone. I remembered an argument we had had earlier in our marriage when we lived in Troyville and he disappeared most Saturday afternoons. I accused him of marrying me only for his personal convenience and pleasure. He smiled and said: "*A man has to do what a man has to do.*"

This statement would be repeated many times during our marriage. To him, this sentence concluded the conversation. I felt so lonely and disregarded, so soiled thinking that I would have to stand on the sideline waiting my turn. There were just no words to describe the humiliation I felt. The sadness was also beyond words. I felt trapped because of my beliefs as divorce was not permissible. One makes a promise before God on the day of one's wedding: "Until death do us part". My mind was in turmoil as few people would or could understand the situation I found myself in. I had never dreamed that the road God placed me on would be so full of pain and heartache. I had felt His closeness on a daily basis and therefore in faith I continued. He promised that in the end all that had been taken from me would be restored. Through His strength I would survive. I became more aware of God's guidance in my life, and I learned to rest upon His love for me. There was a kind of protective blanket over me. The dream I had had when I was ten was starting to manifest itself as I was experiencing exactly the beginning of my life with this man; it had been revealed to me at the age of ten that the beginning would be difficult.

But I had not in my wildest dreams ever foreseen that any person could be so cruel. Just the actual thought of this long and lonely road that was lying ahead of me was enough to send shivers down my spine. The only saving grace of the situation was that I would have the protection of my Father in heaven which was a great comfort to me.

The chances that he would file for a divorce were very slim. For him, the circumstances were ideal and could not be better. He would cling to this marriage with all his might. Apart from a capacity to lie through his teeth to save himself, he also possessed the power of persuasion over people and had a talent for self-representation as an innocent victim of circumstances and could depict all others as unfairly against him.

I was mentally exhausted and to think I would have to endure this type of mental torture for who knew how long, it was just unbearable to take it all in at this moment. As these thoughts ran through my mind at breakneck speed, Ernie was happily driving and looked very satisfied with himself. Life could not be better indeed at this moment in time for him.

We were home earlier than I thought we would be, and he dropped me off and left again soon after. I was exhausted and crawled into bed. I felt utterly discouraged. I must have drifted into a deep sleep and when I awoke I felt a bit refreshed. I reached out for the Bible for some reason.

After reading for a while, the following verses caught my eye. It was a great encouragement and I felt stronger mentally and physically. I knew that I would regain the strength to continue this journey. Also I needed to draw closer to God and I was not to let the circumstances undermine my faith in God.

Deuteronomy 31:6

Be strong and courageous. Do not be afraid or terrified because of them, for the LORD your God goes with you; he will never leave you nor _forsake_ you."

Joshua 1:6

Be strong and _courageous_. Do not be terrified; do not be discouraged, for the LORD your God will be with you wherever you go."

Psalm 3:3

But you are a shield around me, O LORD;
You bestow glory on me and lift up my head.

After reading these verses and with my strength renewed, I got out of bed to run a bath. There was still no sign of Ernie, but I did not care. I would live my life in a Godly manner and be contented. In other words, I would continue to make a home for Ernie as I was taught and which he never really had. I also decided to employ a domestic as I just did not see myself working all day long and still come home and to do the washing and ironing of his clothes which he did not appreciate anyway.

The cooking I would do as I really enjoyed this task. Visits from me to the in-laws would be restricted to special occasions only. I was not going to expose myself to such insensitive behaviour again. Another task I set myself was to become mobile. I would get a car. I did not expect any financial help from Ernie, but I would make sure that he at least paid his share of household expenses.

Ernest Junior's arrival and mum's death

After some soul-searching and decision making, and after I have taken a bath, I went back to bed again as I was in no mood to wait up for Ernie, the next day was a working day.

What time Ernie arrived home that night I could only guess. I knew he had to leave at five thirty in the morning to be on time for his shift. Performing my wifely duties, I got up at half past four to make him breakfast. No lunch pack as he was due home at ten when the first part of his shift ended. Whether he came home I could not tell, as the next shift started at two and finished with his last run from Johannesburg at five in the afternoon. The bus depot was situated in Ferndale, and he would be home around six thirty, by which time I'd be back from work.

My timing improved and I managed to arrive on time for work each day. I even had time to enjoy a cup of coffee in the staff room before going to my desk. Banking hours those days were heavenly for any "penpusher". On week days, the bank opened at nine in the morning and closed at three except for Wednesdays when it closed at one. On Saturdays the working hours were from nine to eleven o'clock. I often wondered why they even bothered to open, and why I ever left the bank.

The only time we worked late was when one of the tellers could not balance. When a discrepancy occurred, it had to be checked and corrected before anyone could leave the building. The bank's reputation was at stake. Failing to record a client's transaction, especially if it turned out to be a deposit, was the priority.

Every document had to be individually checked when accounts did not balance. A typical cause was that one of tellers had failed to pass a transaction through to the debtors' department and the paperwork was still in his or her booth. The tellers had to record their transactions by hand, and their combined totals had to balance with the debtors' daily printout. There were always three tellers on duty during the day and when it became busy or near closing time a fourth teller would be called in. No luxury of computers in those days.

On such occasions the atmosphere was unpleasant and tense. Those of us who were travelling by public transport and if one missed the last bus would have to get home by taxi.

Due to the lovely hours we worked and in spite of the travelling time, I was home early enough to prepare a nice meal for my husband. I made sure that each meal was special. It kept me busy and I enjoyed it. It gave me a sense of satisfaction. In this way, I also regained a little of the self-respect which had crumbled under the weight of disapproval of mother-in-law and the errant behaviour of her son.

Before I got married and still lived with my parents, I used to cook on Wednesdays. My father really enjoyed it as he always commented on how nice it tasted and that it was the highlight of the week as he never knew what to expect. There was always a surprise waiting for him. Mum, after giving birth to ten and raising eight of her own children, not to speak of grandchildren, was understandably in a rut. She cooked the same meal practically every day.

Mum never bought bread from the shop. Dad called it "spook brood" which means "ghost food". There was no substance to it and it was not filling. She baked six large loaves of bread every Monday morning. As we children grew older, each one in turn was given the task of preparing the bread dough. How "grown-up" I felt when it was my turn. Soon I realised, however, why the other siblings had been so keen on stepping down as it was a laborious task. It was hard work to knead dough until it had the right consistency and no longer stuck to one's hands any longer. Roelf, my brother, hated it when the dough stuck to his hands, and so did I. It felt like hours before I was able to satisfy my fussy mother. The excitement soon disappeared into thin air and I could not wait to end my turn. The question was to whom I would hand over? I was second youngest and the youngest, Chris, being the baby of the family, escaped the task, lucky devil.

I was immensely relieved when released from this awful task once I started high school. Six loaves were baked together with a batch of "vetkoek", a traditional Afrikaans dish from the Voortrekker or pioneering time, passed on from generation to generation. Every morning without fail my mother was in her kitchen at four in the morning, each and every day of the week including Sundays. One could not blame her for running out of steam, and she never had any extra help. She cleaned the house and washed all clothes by hand. I was in standard one when she got her first washing machine. It consisted of a washing tub and mangle or wringer. In addition, she did all the ironing. In those days, shirt collars were still starched. Even our dresses, from the waist down, were also starched. A glutton for punishment, she was.

At least my cooking was the one thing Ernie really enjoyed, as his mum was the same as mine. With my mum it was a stew, each day, plain or curried. With Polly it was rice with mince most of the time until Ernie's stepfather, Maurice, took over the cooking as he had a very early shift and was home long before any of them. Like Ernie, he worked as a bus driver. Maurice had mastered the recipe for making mayonnaise that no shop bought could exceed. One could eat it by the dessert spoons full. He also made great parfaits. He was always so willing to please was little appreciated

On Wednesdays I made a point of visiting my mum and sister. The three of us, Mum, Anna and I had a wonderful time together and I could catch up on details of her   progressing pregnancy, after the loss of her child. My sister looked so radiant and I could not wait to fall pregnant.

To my surprise I fell pregnant sooner than I anticipated. I was so very young, just turned eighteen, and our child was due in July, two months before I would turn nineteen. Getting married young did not worry me, but being pregnant at such a young age scared the living daylights out of me.

Of course, I was overjoyed, and so was Ernie. His enthusiasm and joy was short-lived, however, as Polly expressed her disapproval. Fortunately she said very little as she knew there was nothing she could do about it. Oddly, however, when she spoke to others about the coming grandchild, she seemed delighted. However, with me she didn't show any pleasure. Again I had the feeling that I could do nothing to please her. It was a ridiculous situation. Why could she not just accept me? Why could she not stop perpetuating the conflict between us?

I had tried being friendly during visits, but her only reaction was to avoid me. She had resolved never to give me a chance. I felt like an intruder. I started to get along with most of Ernie's seven siblings. Eddie and Gladys were fine. Even Evelyn was showing signs of acceptance. Alan and Clive were no bother either. They were at high school and very much into soccer, and the youngest one, Heather, was still at primary school. The younger ones took everything in their stride as they were too wrapped up in their own childhood worlds. Ernie's only elder sibling, Margery, still did not accept me, however.

Pregnancy was difficult for me. I suffered severely from morning sickness and often my appearance was very pale. The bus driver on our route was an elderly man by the name of

Tom. He knew Ernie, but how he had come to know that I was his wife remained a mystery to me. Being older than Ernie and having a few kids of his own, he had made an informed guess as to my condition. I must admit that at times I felt that I was not going make it to work, as the movement of the bus during the first stage of my pregnancy upset me terribly. Tom had seen me waving each morning to Anna as the bus passed my parent's home and he asked me who she was. I told him that my parents lived there and that she was my sister. From then onwards, whenever he concluded that I was not fit for work, he would promptly stop in front of their house and order me off the bus to the great amusement of the other passengers.

I felt myself lucky to receive such pampering from my family and from a stranger who made an effort to help me in my discomfort. It made me realise afresh that there were good people around. Ernie's comment was that I must stop being such a baby and pull myself together. I think Tom told him what had happened, and Ernie must have felt embarrassed as it had not occurred to him before to notice such things. I could not stand the smell of cooking food, especially meat. The result was that I cooked for him but did not eat. I knew it was not good. I thought it a waste to eat as I would throw it all up in five minutes anyway. I could not handle the process as it left me weak and trembling.

The kindness that Tom showed worked wonders with Ernie as he started to take notice of my poor state. That evening he stood next to the bed trying to encourage me to eat. Suddenly he became a caring person and my hopes soared again. Thankfully, the nausea stopped after a few weeks – but so did his interest. My hope was again short-lived. "Why am I always so desperate for him to show kindness when I know deep down that it will never last? Please, Lord, help me not to go insane," I prayed.

When giving birth, it was traditional amongst the Afrikaans population in those days to use a midwife with a doctor on standby. This I was planning to do. I wanted a homebirth. Private clinics would later be very much in demand, but at that time tradition reigned. Polly, however, did not agree. She insisted that I should go to the Queen Victoria Maternity Hospital as it was subsidized by the government and this service was offered free-of-charge. I was totally beside myself and asked Ernie if his mother planned to control my life. I was told by him to that his mother knew best.

I spoke to my mum, and she said that I must comply with Polly's wishes for the simple reason that it was my first child and that I was so very young. Polly was jubilant as she must have thought that she had scored a victory. The hospital was situated in Braamfontein, opposite the Johannesburg Children's Hospital. Call it providence. My transfer to Standard Bank Braamfontein branch became a reality, and I was to start there the following day. At least after the initial registration at the hospital, I would be able to walk there for the monthly checkups.

I was also delighted as it reduced my travelling time by twenty minutes. The only drawback was that I had to leave my friends that I had made at the old branch. I was pleased to discover, however, that joining a smaller branch was fantastic. I felt at home from the first minute that I stepped through the door. I soon found out that there were four of us in the "family" way. The accountant of the branch commented that we should start a maternity ward in one of the offices, it would save time and money, instead of getting replacements when one of us gave birth. However, we were all due at more or less the same time. By law we had to take three months maternity leave. Unfortunately, it was unpaid leave and with four of us gone, the department was left seriously understaffed.

Although I was apprehensive about the actual birth, as one hears such horror stories, I could not wait to wear a maternity dress to show the world that I was about to become a mother. To my disappointment, I was carrying very small, so much so that Mister Accountant asked me whether I was really pregnant or whether it was a figment of my imagination. I was then seven months' pregnant and I assured him that I most definitely was not imagining it. I asked him whether I should go for monthly checkups to make certain. After looking me up and down, with smile on his face, he quipped: "I was just wondering where you are hiding it, in your ear?" I gave him a dirty look and at lunch time I went shopping for my first maternity dress.

I found out to my horror that the Queen Victoria Hospital was also a training facility for students studying to become obstetricians. I was a unique case according to *their* Professor, who happened to be *my* physician during pregnancy, as I had had trouble with my kidneys on top of the fact that my tummy was not "expanding". There was no place for the baby to move and it could become a serious matter as the baby would not be able to breathe. I was scared out my wits and to top it all my examination turned into a lecture as I was used as a working example of what they could expect in a complicated pregnancy. I did not tell my mother what was happening, as she was frail and ailing. There was actually nothing she could do about it but worry and that was the last thing she needed at that point.

It was so humiliating and embarrassing that I resolved never to allow this to happen to me again. All of this mental torture for "free". My dislike of Polly grew in leaps and bounds as she continued to insist that I go there on the grounds that Ernie had no money to waste. In so doing, she overlooked the fact that Ernie's medical aid insurance would cover such costs. The worst of it was that he agreed with her. At times I felt as if I was going to go totally mad. I wept and begged the Lord to give me strength enough to get through this ordeal with some of my dignity intact. On one visit to the hospital for a checkup, I asked Ernie to accompany me as I was scared. I needed some support. Sadly his response was abrupt and hurtful: "You go, you must grow up. I do not have time for nonsense". I just could not understand this man. He showed no sympathy whatsoever for me and sadly no support was forthcoming.

Thankfully the nausea stopped after a few weeks, but so did his interest. He began again to disappear over weekends. Once, leaving the house in his driver's uniform, he returned in casual clothing. My despair returned. I suspected Polly of being up to her old tricks again, encouraging him. When I confronted him he explained away the deceit by saying that he had had to help his mother with some cleaning up and therefore had to change clothes.

"You look neat and tidy, what did you help your mother with?" I asked.

He shrugged as usual and stared into space. The penny dropped. I realised that the transformation into devoted husband had only been temporary.

Admittedly, I was young, but I had been raised to believe in Christian morals and values, unlike Ernie and his family. They seemed to believe in the survival of the fittest.

During the first year of our marriage, I was still fool enough to think he would change. Even moving away from the in-laws hadn't helped. Now that I was expecting a child, I could not go to my parent's home since both my father and mother were frail and ailing. My father would have helped if he knew the situation, but because of their condition, I could not burden them with my problems. I could not speak to my sister about my feelings as she not only had the task of caring for them both, she had her baby to look after, too. Anna told mum that she was worried about me, but she reassured her that everything was fine.

I really wished Ernie would just take his things and leave. He was no help to me at all, just an added burden. However, he was deeply rooted and far too comfortable to leave. If he left, he would lose the comforts he had come to enjoy: work clothes set out for the next morning; breakfast in bed; supper ready and waiting for him upon his return from work.

Because of his strong attachment to his mother, making demands or showing anger would also have had adverse effects. It would perhaps have resulted in the same sort of fighting that he had been steeped in as a child and I certainly didn't want my child to be raised in such an environment. If I was certain that I would get the house, who knows, I might have kicked him out. I needed security for my child and myself. But given my parent's situation, and Ernie's refusal to change, there was really nothing I could do. I even thought that God was making it impossible for me to leave him. And after all, God had pointed him out to me at the age of ten as my future husband.

I recalled my father's pep talk before we married – that this was a lifelong commitment. So I decided to hang on and try to make the best of a bad situation, one day at a time. I started speaking to God on a daily basis, at times silently, but when it became intolerable, I would speak out loud. It became such a habit that I started to have these conversations with the Lord on a daily basis.

Our relationship was also adversely affected by poor finances. He contributed less and less to household expenses, encouraged by his mother, it seemed. Having walked this road herself, I was amazed that she didn't expect her son to take more responsibility for his home. If he contributed anything at all, I considered myself extremely lucky. When I questioned him about his salary, and what he did with it, I was told that it was no concern of mine. At least he was still paying the bond and the lights and water, as he knew he would be homeless otherwise.

His interest in my pregnancy evaporated and he no longer enquired about my monthly checkups. We continued to visit his family over weekends and still he would not come to see my parents with me. My father was given to believe it was because he was doing shift work, or that he was tired after working hard all day. They had no idea of the type of person he really was and that he didn't show any real interest in me or his future child.

Dad and Mum were both unwell. Dad had asthma and Mum seemingly just gave up on life. She lost a lot of weight and was more in bed than out. The doctor recommended that she be hospitalized but she refused. He commented that if she did not go to hospital, Gabriel would come for her before the year was out. He was trying hard to convince her of the seriousness of her illness. He was an Indian doctor and Mum would not let anyone else come near her. She firmly believed in Abdulla, but disliked hospitals.

"Then so be it," she said. This loss of interest in life was very much unlike her. She used to be in her kitchen at four in the morning. Now she stayed in bed. We were all worried about her, especially Dad. At that point, they had been married for forty-two years, and my mother was only fifty-eight years' old.

The saving grace for me during this period was such preoccupation with work and getting to know my new colleagues that thoughts of self-pity seldom crowded my mind. After supper each night, I kept myself busy preparing for the new baby. My sister gave me a cot for the new arrival and I bought baby clothes, napkins and all other necessities for the big event. The only exception was a chest of drawers I wanted so desperately and could not afford. I asked Ernie to buy it as he otherwise hardly gave me any financial support. As usual he ran to his mother or Polly to discuss it with her. Needless to say, both of them reckoned that it was a waste of money, and he came home that afternoon with a cupboard Poppy had given him. It was about one and a half feet high, and was supposed to have two doors, but one was missing. In addition, one of the shelves was dilapidated. In sum, it was in such a poor state, I would have been ashamed to give it my house help.

I can hardly describe my feelings. To top it all, due to my negative reaction to this gift, I was branded as the most ungrateful creature on earth. Polly was trying her best to please me and all I could do was complain about her. The only one that understood me was Evelyn, Ernie's sister, who told her mother: "All she wants is a chest of drawers, not that piece of rubbish." Polly just ignored her completely. None of her daughters would have accepted this piece of furniture. Why should I not only have to accept it, but appreciate it, too? Miracles never cease, however, and the next event nearly caused me to faint. Coming home from work one day, I found a brand new chest of drawers in the baby's room. I still do not know how it got there, but who was I to complain? I knew it was not Ernie or Polly and it was definitely not one of my own family members. I guess it was either Evelyn or Eddie.

I became more reliant on God and started having long conversations with Him, and it helped me so much. There were times when the family drained me to an extent that I became extremely angry with God. I always received an answer in scripture, or in my dreams, and even from the preacher during the Sunday service. I know Jesus was there all the time, a "crutch" as Polly called Him. I regularly attended the Central Methodist church in downtown Johannesburg. It was more convenient for me as I only had three blocks to walk to the bus stop in comparison with a mile and a half to the nearest local Methodist Church. Following each service, I returned home feeling uplifted, positive and able to face the week ahead.

Two days before the expected childbirth on July the first, 1965, I started to experience the most hideous pains imaginable. I had been told about them by my sister. This was the onset of labour and I was rushed to hospital, and literally dumped there by Ernie. He did not even wait or help me through the procedure of being admitted and transferred to the labour ward, where I spent the next forty-five hours in agony with the professor and four of his students. This was not only embarrassing but also frustrating for me. While I suffered severe pain, he relentlessly explained each procedure to students. It was the same group that had accompanied him each month during my routine checkups.

Judging from the expressions on their faces, they were completely unprepared for what was about to come. Two of them left halfway through the procedures on the first day. Mercifully I was eventually given a sedative, which helped me to fall into a half sleep. This was a slight relief as after nearly two days of labour, I was totally exhausted. The birth was difficult because the baby was too big for my small frame. I wanted to scream at the professor and ask him if he had ever heard of a caesarean, but to him it was clearly an opportunity not to be missed, tutoring his students. My comfort was of no concern to him. I was just a means to an end, a tool in a demonstration.

My son was delivered with the help of instruments, and finally arrived at twenty past two on the afternoon of July first, exactly as predicted, weighing in at eight pounds ten ounces. To my horror, he had carrot-red hair. During the pregnancy, I'd vowed that if any of my children was born with red hair, the same as my father's hair in his younger days, I would dye it black. I had hoped that he would have my colour hair which was auburn, or his father's, which was black. In spite of the hair, the baby was gorgeous and simply perfect. I was so glad that this ordeal was over and that my child was alive after everything that he had to endure. I could not thank God enough for His grace and protection. Not just for me but for Ernest Junior, too.

Afterward, I wanted to ask the professor doctor why he had not performed a caesarean section, but I never saw him again. I asked one of the nurses and was told that this procedure was only followed when the birth became life-threatening to mother or child. Well, I said to myself, I will keep my peace. Again I vowed that this place would never see me again, regardless of the free service.

After being moved into the general ward with ten other mothers, I was given some medication and a host of other tablets, among which there must have been a sleeping pill as thereafter I slept for nearly eighteen hours. It was Saturday when I woke up and then only had the opportunity to hold my son in my arms for the first time. Yes, indeed, he had red hair, but who cares? I said to myself. He was just perfect and the tears came rolling down my cheeks as I tried to take it all in. I was so proud I cannot describe the feelings this little man stirred up deep within my heart.

Whether my son's father had come on the Friday, I could not know. According to my roommates, no one had come. One of them told me I should not worry as she was in the same boat − her husband never bothered to come either, so I was not the only one. This made me feel a little better and less embarrassed as I watched some other fathers cooing over their offspring. You could see the pride written all over their faces. Also, love and appreciation shone in their eyes when they looked at their wives. Yes, once more I was both disappointed and sad, as I was seemingly not destined to enjoy the privilege of an appreciative husband. I nevertheless counted myself lucky to have survived the ordeal of childbirth. I was still alive and was fit enough to tell the story. I was so proud to hold my little boy in my arms. At the same time, I felt extremely exhausted and emotionally drained.

I received a message from Polly via the front desk that Ernie had been called away by the army to attend a three-week camp, hence his absence. I looked at the nurse in shock. I just could not believe it. She must have seen the hurt in my eyes and said: "I am sorry". I managed to smile at her and assured her that it was not her fault.

What were they taking me for, a complete idiot? For goodness sake, what did they think? Or better still, if it was the case, why had he not told me so himself? Why send a message via his mother? Surely the birth of his child was more important than an army training session. I knew that after the initial mandatory training had ended, he had signed up as a volunteer to take part in occasional military exercises.

I had not seen any call-up papers, but I supposed his mother would claim that these had been sent to her address. What about his work? Surely he had had to notify them well in advance? It was all a pack of lies, I concluded.

Polly fervently covered up for her son. However, she could not convince me. He had not come to visit me in hospital even once, had not sent flowers or a card. Not even a phone call to the front desk to enquire about our wellbeing. This was all the more surprising given the fact that this was his first child, his son. I really did not know what to say or do. I felt so empty and at the same time so disgusted at the lack of interest from his side. So many emotions were floating around inside me, and so many questions for which there were no real answers, and there was no way to resolve the riddle.

But miracles do not cease. There came an unexpected surprise: a card from Polly. At that moment I could muster no positive feelings for that lady and I did not appreciate it one bit. Why would she send me a card? Was she feeling guilty? It just did not make any sense. I tore it up and threw it into the dustbin.

The level of my blood pressure was going up and down and I was not allowed out of bed. I even had to use a bed pan which I hated. I used it only because I felt so weak and at times my legs felt like jelly and I was very shaky. Unfortunately, I was unable to produce any milk and little Ernest was bottle-fed from the very beginning of his life. In those first days in hospital, mother's milk was donated to us by the other ladies in the ward who produced more than they needed.

At night they would take all the babies to the nursery. One particular night I could not sleep and went for a walk to the nursery and I could not see Ernest, another shock to the system. Fortunately, one of the nurses saw me and came rushing out to tell me that Ernest was fine and that there was nothing wrong with him. Apparently he had been crying and had woken the others, so they put him in the nurses' room.

She showed me and after I saw him I became convinced that there was nothing wrong with him I went back to bed.

My poor little chap, I thought. You must feel your mother's grief deep inside. I was by now well-trained and kept my feelings to myself. Who could I speak to? Not my family. Mum and dad were too poor in health, and as for Anna, she had both my parents plus the new arrival, a little girl six months before, to deal with each day. Humanly there was no one, but spiritually there was God. I poured out my soul to the Lord silently in my mind, and mercifully fell into a deep sleep, at least this time without a sleeping tablet.

Ernie never came and yet I still hoped that he might. At visiting hours I found myself staring at the door. Midweek I had this particular and overwhelming urge to see my mother. I cried nonstop, but they would not let me go home. I begged and pleaded. I even offered that Ernest stay there while I pay a short visit to my mother. The doctor told me that I was not fit enough to be discharged yet and that they were considering keeping me in hospital until the following week. That upset me even more.

I had no choice. I tried very hard to calm down. On the Friday night of that same week, my brother-in-law William, came to visit and as he entered the ward, the first thing I told him was that I knew what he had come to say. My mum had passed away. He looked at me with a shocked expression on his face and asked how I knew. I could not explain it as the words had just came out of me without thinking. I told him of wanting to go home on Wednesday and that the doctors had refused permission for me to go.

He asked me if Ernie has been to visit. I told him the unlikely story I had been given and he, too, could not believe what he was hearing. He told me that he would come to fetch me the next morning. The doctors had not given instructions for me to be discharged, but the matron managed to obtain permission for me to leave.

"Dear God, I ask that You have mercy on me, give me the strength to cope with everything that You have laid across my path. I cannot do it on my own strength. I know that through the help of the Holy Spirit, I will manage. I ask it in Jesus' name."

Thankfully, I had little Ernest to keep me focused, because in my grief I was unable to concentrate on anything else. They gave me a sedative as I was a hair's breadth away from collapsing. With Ernie not there, the horrible professor using me as a guinea pig, and now my mum gone to be with the Lord, I asked myself what else on this earth could go wrong? I just could not make any sense of it. All the shocks to my system were just too much and yet through Christ I kept on going.

I felt bereft, lonely and defeated and asked God: "Why now, God, why take her now, one day, just one day, before my discharge from hospital? How could you let this happen when she hadn't even seen my child?" I sobbed.

William and my sister Anna came to pick me up from the hospital. There was no sign of my husband. The first stop was my parent's house to be with my father and to show him his grandchild. All of us were trying to be brave but our sadness made it difficult to speak. After a union of forty-two years this was a very difficult time for him.

On the day of the funeral, the in-laws sent a card conveying their sympathy. My husband came but just said: "I'm sorry to hear that your mum passed away," without giving any sign of warmth or regret. No member of his family came with him. He was dressed in normal civilian clothes and I asked him how it had been possible for him to obtain permission from the army to come home that day to attend the funeral, since it had been impossible for him to be there for his son's birth. He gave no answer. Then I asked him when he was due back at the military base.

"I am not going back," he said.

I looked at him and said: "But the three weeks are not over yet, you have another two weeks to go. You said a week ago that it was compulsory, but now after the birth of your son, it is no longer an obligation for you to be there. It does not make sense, does it?"

He realised his mistake, and with a splutter, as he did not know how to answer me, and a shrug of the shoulders, he turned around and walked off to join rest of the family.

The reality of my mother's death was almost too much to bear. The sight of the gaping, cold black pit finally hit home, and as the coffin disappeared into the grave I felt deserted and grief-stricken. Instead of the sympathy I expected from my husband, he told me to behave myself.

My eldest sister asked me for my share of the cost of the flowers that she'd bought for the funeral. Not having any money on me, I asked Ernie to give her the money. Although it was not a large amount, he refused, saying that he didn't have money to waste. I was speechless. His insensitivity continued to surprise me. I felt so hurt at the thought that we had to leave my mum lying in that gaping hole and that I would never see her again. It was too much for me and the grief became overwhelming. This knock, together with the birth and dealing with a hardhearted husband, was just too much for me to handle. All I could focus on was getting home and crawling into bed.

Not one of the in-laws bothered to attend the funeral. Their attitude was that she was not a relative of theirs and, besides, we all have to die at some point. I also could not get used to their double standards. They seemed incredibly heartless to me. As if that was not enough, Ernie decided to visit his mother after the funeral as she wanted to see her grandson. I was furious. All I wanted to do was go home and seek some closure, but no – we had to go to the other side of Johannesburg to visit his family. How insensitive could one be?

On arrival nothing was said to me. Baby started whimpering and I went to feed him in one of the bedrooms. Following the suggestion of my mother-in-law that she made before the funeral, l was not to breastfeed baby Ernest while I was sad because it would cause him to be upset. But I was not breastfeeding him as I had no natural milk. I bottle fed him. She obviously noted this fact and, instead of speaking to me herself, she sent her son to ask me why I was not breastfeeding my child. Upset, I told him the reason and added that I didn't have enough milk to breastfeed anyway and that it had nothing to do with her... He stormed out. He was back in a flash to tell me:

"Mum says that's utter nonsense. The funeral is now past and you must get on with your life."

I'd had enough and told him off in no uncertain terms. I then demanded to go home. He complied with my request, intuitively understanding that I'd been pushed too far and had reached my limit. The in-laws understood this, too. I can only be pushed so far before exploding. We left soon after and I felt enormous relief to be back in my own domain, away from the strife that always seemed to be present in their house. He was upset that I had refused to follow his mother's instructions. I told him that his mother was a control freak and she would have to learn that I was no pushover.

"And while you are here for a change, I want you to listen, and you must pay attention. You know me by now: I will only take so much and no more. You have overstepped the boundaries as a married man by a large margin. From now on, you will have to take responsibility not only for me but for your child, too. You will see to it that there is food in this house, and that everything is paid for from your salary. It is not your money, it is our money. Another thing: you must make sure that you come home when you are done with work each day. This habit of disappearing must stop. If you do not comply with this demand, you will find your belongings on the pavement. I want to handle the family budget. I must make sure that everything is paid, and I know now that I cannot trust you to do this. I have three months unpaid maternity leave. My job is secure at the bank and will be there once I'm ready to return. But just remember this: right now I have no money. If there is no money, there is no food."

He just stood there with his mouth open, gaping like a fish out of water, as per usual when he was lost for words or when he knew he had messed up again

"I've had more than enough from you and your mother who is forever trying to dictate to me what to do. Do you understand or must I repeat myself?" I continued.

He did not know what to say, but after regaining his senses he told me that there was a parcel from his mother on our bed. After months of rejection and secondhand offerings, what could it be? I opened the parcel which was fairly large; I found all kinds of baby stuff for Ernest Jnr. Blankets, baby grows, baby powder, oil, soap, and even a lovely blue towel for him more or less the same as the last time together with a couple of cards congratulating us on the arrival of our son. First the utmost hostility, then mixed signals, and now this? I phoned her and thanked her for the gifts, but I was not effusive.

The hopes and dreams I'd had when I moved away from my in-laws had come to naught. It was not that I didn't value her input. If she'd shown some sympathy for my loss, a bit of care or interest in me at this sad time of my life, it would have been welcome and a help, but instead all I had received was open animosity from her. The fact that she'd never accepted me into the family stood out like a sore thumb, once again. It seemed that there would always be this antagonism between us.

After the call, I lay on my bed and thought about all the events that had taken place these last two weeks. When I rose, I was surprised to find Ernie still at home. I was even more surprised to find that he had actually cleaned out the garage and was busy tidying up the backyard. He also watered the flowers in the front garden. Unfortunately, instead of hope rising up within me, I skeptically wondered how long this miraculous behaviour would last. Would he continue with it? They had robbed me of my trust, not only in him and his family, but in everyone. It was a horrid realisation.

After we had supper, I asked Boykie

"Why is your mother so negative towards me? What have I done to her?" As always, he just stood there staring into space, shrugging his shoulders, his usual reaction when he didn't want to answer my questions.

I asked him again: "If you knew she was so dead set against our marriage, why did you marry me? It seems that you don't want to be married, to me or anyone for that matter. You prefer being a bachelor as your behaviour clearly shows. You do not show any interest in this marriage. Are there too many complications related to being married? Tell me what you want from this marriage. Marriage is a commitment, a beginning of a family, a new generation."

He truly looked baffled, as if he didn't have the foggiest notion of what I was saying. I may as well have been speaking a foreign language as far as he was concerned. At that moment, I became so annoyed with his noncommittal approach that I screamed at him.

"I asked you a question. Why did you marry me and for once, give me an honest answer."

"To spite my mother," was his reply. "She wanted me to marry Elizabeth and not only did she have two children, she had also been married to my best friend."

I was hurt and shocked by his selfishness. I asked: "Why me? Why should I have been the lucky one?"

"You walked in while I was visiting your brother and I thought you were respectable, beautiful and naïve enough to influence and control. Also, it would keep my mother at bay," he said, and to rub salt into the wound he added with a smirk on his face:

"I was right, wasn't I?"

With eyebrows raised I asked: "Did you honestly think that it would be that easy? Your luck lies in my Christian faith. Because of it, I will never file for divorce. However, in the end, you will pay for this, not by my hand, but by God's. Someday you will reap what you have sown. You may quite rightly point out that I am too young to be married, but believe me, I am not a pushover and, moreover, I am also not naïve. Sorry if this disappoints you, but I can see right through you, and I know exactly what you have been up to. Apart from Elizabeth lying in wait, there a few other ladies, too, who receive your attentions. I really feel sorry for them."

He could see that I knew all about his extramural activities. Shock and disbelief were written all over his face. As usual, whenever he could not face up to a situation, he quickly withdrew and disappeared.

"Yep, Lord, the road going to be long and difficult. At least I know that You will be there and You will guide me as you promised in the dream I had," I prayed.

"Why, Lord, Why?" I could not resist asking. It felt to me like a lifelong sentence, dwelling in the wilderness like the Israelites. I seriously thought of divorce, but I knew that this would be both wrong and that I'd be worse off financially as he'd never pay maintenance and I was not willing to give up the house as I had nowhere else to go. I would get more out of him if we remained married. I missed the comfort and advice of my mother. I had no choice but to take care of Ernest Jnr and wait until my maternity leave was over. Then I could go back to work so that I could earn money to take care of myself and my son.

The following weekend I asked Ernie to drop me off at my father's house as I wanted to visit him, but he refused. He told me I could walk there if I wanted to see him so badly. I did and on arrival I found him in bed suffering from one of his asthma attacks. He told me he wanted to talk to me and I sat down and put Ernest Jnr on the bed next to him. He told me he'd had a disturbing dream about my mother the previous night; she was upset as she could not rest as you were crying so much.

I was astounded, because my dad had no idea how much I cried. How could he have known? I had kept it from him. Even my sister was not aware of my crying and could not have told him. I said that I'd try, but it hurt a lot because she had never seen my child.

That night, near midnight, I awoke and saw a very bright light shining in the room. I assumed Ernie had put the lights on when he had come in from his night shift, but he was fast asleep beside me. Then I saw that the light came from the end of the cot. Someone was standing there looking at the baby. The being, then moved across to the foot of the bed, as if preparing to lie down. The next moment it disappeared and we were in darkness again. I felt an inexplicable calmness fill came over my whole being.

Ernie seemed to be in some sort of coma. I vigorously shook him to wake him as I wanted to tell him my mother had been present, but he slept on soundly. Just as well, I thought, because he would not have understood and would have responded with ridicule.

I must have fallen asleep. I woke in the morning and felt that the intense broken feeling I had been enduring was gone. My mind became clearer and I could function normally again. I had the comfort of knowing that no one could take my memories of my mother away from me. Thank God for giving us the capacity to remember, as one can always recall the wonderful times shared in life. It gives one a warm feeling around the heart and brings a smile to the face. Death is so sad and so final.

It was absolutely clear that I would not be a stay-at-home mum. When the three months' maternity leave were up, I went back to work. Martha, my brother's wife, offered to look after Junior until I felt comfortable to leave him at home with the domestic help who worked for me. This was the norm in those days. There were no day care centres. Most mothers stayed at home to take care of their own children. I was not so fortunate.

We could easily afford for me to stay at home. However, Polly insisted that I go to work as soon as possible. In addition, it was the only way for me to gain some measure of independence. It was always a mission to get Ernie to pay for anything. I found begging him for money intolerable. It did not dawn on Ernie to take responsibility for supporting his family and there was no encouragement from Polly for him to do so. Over the three months of maternity leave, I had had to ask for money for food and baby things on a daily basis. Most of the time, these sessions escalated into arguments. My father, who believed a woman's place was in the home, had accepted the fact that I had to work. He knew the man his daughter had married was not a family type.

Life continues – Greymont and father's death

It was a harrowing three months. I fought on a daily basis for money just to buy the basic commodities. Although he enjoyed the security of our home and having a wife clean and cook for him, he still hankered after freedom. I so much wanted him to walk away from our union on his own accord, but I was out of luck. It never happened.

Discussing marriage with him and what it entailed was a waste of time. As usual it only led to promises that were never kept. He also started making fun of our discussions, and tried to break me down mentally. He also began making fun of my faith in God, made horrible remarks and lashed out at the churches and the "holy polics", as Polly called the people attending church. Polly told me that she and her children did not need a crutch as they had enough stamina to face life.

I had given up hoping that he would attend church with me. I told him again that, because of my faith, I trusted in God and that He would never leave me nor forsake me and that He would continue to give me the strength to persevere until such time that He called a halt to my suffering. Perceiving that I would no longer give him the satisfaction of allowing his remarks to upset me, he lost interest and left me alone.

However, his ceaseless lying still infuriated me immensely. When he was caught lying and failed to give a satisfactory explanation, others would be blamed, or he would try to justify his actions. When all his attempts failed, his difficult youth was then brought up once again to garner sympathy.

"You must understand," he would say, "I don't really want to do these things."

He acted like a naughty child caught in the middle of a mischievous act, but did not learn from his mistakes. I asked God to give me the strength and perseverance necessary to deal with this most multifaceted and complicated person. I needed to learn how to put up with all this and still retain my sanity, if that was at all possible.

Another tragedy transpired on my side of the family. My father, who suffered from asthma, was taken to a hospital in Hillbrow. After my mother had passed away, he seemingly gave up on life and had been continuously on oxygen support. Needless to say, I visited him alone, walking from the bank in Braamfontein during my lunch hour. It was dangerous for women to be out alone after sunset, but there was no other choice.

The afternoon before his death he sat on his bed, surprisingly without the oxygen mask. He told me to promise him that I would look after myself and bring up Ernest Junior to know God. I promised him that I would do so, little knowing that it would be the last time that I would see or talk to him. He died the following day, seventh October nineteen-sixty-six, only a year and three months after my mother had passed. It was comforting to know that he had gone to join my mother and that his last words to me were of God. He had pointed out a bougainvillea in bloom, hanging from a wall outside his window, and said how good God is, supplying us with so much beauty, how wonderfully He had made the earth and everything in it – but he never once mentioned Ernie, my husband.

My father and I were very close and his death was very painful to me. I mourned in private, mostly at night, because I'd learned to hide my emotions from the Bezuidenhout family. As before, there was very little sympathy from the in-laws, although they did send a card. As was the case when my mother died, they did not attend the funeral. I was surprised to see Ernie there. Now that both my parents were gone, my sister and I became very close and she shared my pain and tribulations with the Bezuidenhout family.

My father and I used to visit my mother's grave, but he had put off erecting a gravestone, almost as if he knew it wouldn't be long before he joined her. They were buried in the same grave. Before he died he showed me a simple gravestone with a marble framework filled with white stones, saying that he wanted that type of stone, a simple one that did not require a lot of upkeep.

My elder sister by twenty years took it upon herself to choose a gravestone and had it erected without discussing it with us. I had told her what Dad wanted, but she had decided upon a two-slab marble set, one slightly smaller than the other, and a monstrously large slab of stone to cover the grave. It was too elaborate. Dad wanted a simple memorial with only their details embossed upon it.

I was shocked when I saw it and made the remark: "You indeed made sure they would not escape from this grave." Of course, I was not popular after making this remark, but I could not help myself, I was so upset. She had no right to decide upon the stones, particularly after I had told her what our father had wanted. I felt that the least she could have done was to include all of us in selecting the stones. After all, we all had to contribute financially to the cost of the burial and stones. I asked Ernie if he would help. Again I was told that he did not have money to waste. I just left it at that.

Three years down the line. It was back-to-basics living, survival is another way to put it. Due to the lack of support, consideration and honesty of my husband, I felt robbed of love and dignity. I had lost all respect for him, and found I could not trust him at all. Once his truly selfish character was revealed, my former love for him was replaced by a deep feeling of sorrow and disgust. This proved to me that a life without God is no life at all. God is love and if you don't have love you have nothing at all. Without love he had nothing to bring meaning into his life. This feeling was foreign to him. Love and caring for others were non-existent in him. There was just one person in his world and that was Ernie himself, and unfortunately Polly endorsed everything he said or did.

It seemed that he grew tired of pursuing woman and his restless spirit led him into another direction. One of his friends introduced him to canaries and he decided that it was just the thing he needed to keep himself busy. I agreed and was happy that he had a hobby with which to occupy himself. I had no trouble filling my hours with cooking, knitting, crocheting and, believe it or not, writing short stories. Mostly love stories because it was my way of experiencing the love I was denied. It helped me to dream, apart from God giving me the strength to keep on going. It helped keep my spirit alive and prevented me from falling into depression.

Ernie devoted all his energy to the new pastime. He bought a number of cages – my husband didn't believe in small beginnings – together with all the feeding and water trays. As I watched him assemble all this paraphernalia, I wondered where he was going to put the cages because he made no attempt to clear space for them. I was amazed at the amount of money spent on what he wanted. Whenever I had asked him for any money, he had always declared himself penniless.

He told me that the spare bedroom in the house would be perfect for his bird cages. I nearly had a heart attack. The arrogance of this man was beyond belief, to say the least. It was beyond my wildest dreams that he could even consider having an aviary inside the house. There was just no end to this man's capacity to shock me with his suggestions. How could he even consider converting a bedroom into an aviary? Birds were messy creatures and also a health hazard especially considering the toddler. I felt as if I was going to choke.

"I promise it will only be temporary, until I build the outdoor aviary," Ernie said.

"Over my dead body will you turn this bedroom into an aviary, even a temporary one. Build the aviary first, and then get the birds. Knowing you, once they are in the house you will forget about moving them. How did you grow up? How were you raised? You just don't seem able to tell right from wrong. I am telling you now that you will not under any circumstances bring those cages into the bedroom. If you must start now and don't want to wait until your aviary is built, leave your car outside and use the garage for your birds."

He was most unhappy because he had arranged to collect the birds the following day and the garage was in an unbelievably bad state. There was not a chance that it would be ready by the next day. There was no foresight in this mortal. What future planning he did exhibit took the form of hoarding everything that might be of use "sometime in the future", a circumstance that rarely if ever occurred in practice.

When I arrived home that evening, a very unpleasant surprise awaited me. Mister had completely ignored me and the birds, in their cages, were neatly installed in the bedroom. I flipped my lid and another argument erupted. More promises were made. The aviary would be built within the next two weeks.

Soon, the room began to smell bad and the house started to stink. Needless to say, the embarrassment one felt when people came to visit was unendurable. Ernie could not have cared less. He was insufferable and would have driven any psychiatrist insane. I certainly couldn't figure out why he didn't realise that what he was doing was totally out of the norm. His selfishness was beyond any human reason. He seemed to have no self-respect, no pride, and – to crown it all – showed no consideration for his family. However, there was no way I'd allow myself to be dragged down. When, after a month, no material arrived for the aviary and there was no indication that he was going to build it, I lost my patience and threw the lot out of the house. To top it all, Ernie was beside himself with indignation when he arrived home that evening. To him, living with animals was a run-of-the-mill practice. It was beyond his comprehension to understand that no one should even consider doing such a thing. He paid no regard to Ernest Jnr or me.

"You're lucky I did not open the doors of the cages and set your precious birds free. Do not even think about bringing them into this house again. If you do so, I will not hesitate to give them their freedom. It is a disgusting and embarrassing situation. There are no words to describe my disgust that you would stoop so low as to actually bring them into the bedroom. Have you got no respect for yourself or for your child and me? I did not grow up in such filthy conditions. You might be used to it, but I am not. One canary in a cage as a pet is fine, but you've got far too many cooped up together in each cage. It looks like a pet shop with cages one atop the other. Your selfishness extends beyond all reason. It is unbelievable," I said.

Worse than Ernest's anger was mother-in-law's. She was very upset with me. Why did I not allow her poor son his hobby? As usual she justified his actions.

"Ernest needs some sort of distraction. He works so hard to keep up his family," she told me.

What was she thinking?

"What about your grandson's health and mine?" I replied, "I have nothing against him having a hobby, but surely he could have planned it properly. How did you raise your family? How can you possibly think that it's all right to erect an aviary in a bedroom? As for your remark that he is keeping up his family, he is doing no such thing. He pays the bond, yes, and the electricity, but as for food, it is I alone who buys the food and he is quick to eat it. The responsibility for supporting his family rests solely on the man's shoulders, whether his wife is working or not," I retorted.

Apart from her usual gestures of hunched shoulders and staring into space, the way her son acted, she did not reply. After this incident, the aviary was built in double time and peace was restored, for a while. All his spare time and energy was spent at home, tending to his birds and aviary. At least he was at home and Ernest Junior had the chance to bond with his father. The child had started to walk and they spent wonderful hours together looking at the birds, with Junior even trying in his own way to feed them.

One night Ernie came home excited with news of a meeting he had had with an old friend with whom he'd lost touch. They had done their three-year military training together. After that, the friend, Richard, had left the army, while Ernest had continued voluntary service until the unit had been dissolved. We were invited to visit his friend's home in Potchefstroom, where we spent an enjoyable weekend.

Soon after this visit, Richard, who worked for a bank, was transferred to Johannesburg and had to find a place to stay. Dear generous Ernest offered him and his family temporary residence at our home while they looked for permanent accommodation near to the new place of work.

Meanwhile, Ernest's sister Gladys and her husband Paul, who had been living with mother-in-law, had a family argument and had left the maternal home and had moved in with us. The Bezuidenhout family philosophy seemed to go that if you agreed with them on everything, you were accepted. If you contradicted them in any way, you were banished.

Richard and Martie subsequently also moved into our house. She was not working and offered to do the cooking, which I found very helpful. They had two sons. When we had visited them in Potchefstroom, I had noticed that there had been a lot of drinking. I was not one to drink and did not join them. After moving in, the drinking began. Every weekend they ended up drunk. It was not long after that that Gladys and Paul decided to return to her mother's house while they waited for their bond on a house in Kensington to be approved. Gladys told me she was going back to her mother's house. I was surprised and queried her.

"Why don't you wait until the bond is approved?"

She was a bit evasive at first, but then told me the reason. We had been invited to a party held at one of Ernie's colleagues and we had all gone there together. During the party, Paul, Gladys's husband, had seen Ernie and Martie in a corner kissing. His hands had been where they should not have been. Martie had, according to Gladys, also made advances on her Paul.

I told her that I knew about Ernie's weakness for women and was not shocked at her revelation. He usually didn't have "affairs" – just one-off encounters, then, "Thank you Ma'am," and he was back on his bicycle again. Gladys said she would tell her mother about his unacceptable behaviour and in due course she did try, but Polly refused to believe ill of her son. What I could not understand was why he did this to his best friend? Had he really no scruples?

"Boykie," as his mother called him, "would never do a thing like that."

Paul told her that he saw it with his own eyes and that resulted in her increased dislike of Paul. She conveniently forgot that she had arranged dates previously for Ernie with the lady she wanted him to marry, and that she had done so even after we had married. I wanted to scream "Hypocrite," when I heard this, but let it go. People with double standards have rules only they can understand.

Andy, a friend of Ernie from school days who stayed in the house behind us, invited us one day for a visit. This was an unusual thing for him to do. For some reason, he started talking about their younger days, when they were still bachelors. One of the stories that came out was that whenever they had "needed" a girl they would go to the nurse's residence where some of the nurses were reputed to go out with the boys. Ernie was very good-looking and had no trouble attracting women.

One Saturday night he was challenged to "have" a different girl each night for a month. He accepted the dare – and won, concluding that he was "Mr. Wonderful". Andy shook his head as he related the tale, but Ernest beamed with pride. I wondered why on earth he was relating all of this now. Was he trying to tell me something or other but did not want to speak openly as he did not wish to cause trouble?

As his house was higher up on the hill than ours, he had a bird's-eye view of our property. Had he seen some shenanigans between Ernest and Martie while Richard and I were out working? Ernie was home between ten and three o'clock each day and that set my mind racing.

I confronted him about his sexual advances on his friend's wife at the party. He was disappointed to have been caught out, but made the excuse that I didn't give him enough attention. I just shook my head in amazement. In actual fact, it was I who was in need of attention. Unfortunately, I must admit the degrading fact that I was only considered when there was no one else around to satisfy him. This was, indeed, a bitter pill to swallow.

"Father God," I cried out again, "Help me. Why am I still in this situation? My mind tells me to take my things and run, but why do I feel I have to stay in this relationship? This is not a marriage. It's a joke."

Of course, there was no verbal answer to my prayer, but I had a deep conviction that I should remain and recalled again the dream I had had as a child of ten, when God put his hand on my head and told me that everything would work out in the end.

One day after work I boarded the bus to go home and who should be on the bus but Martie. "Hello, what are you doing here?" I asked.

"I felt like getting out of the house." She said, "Do you know that the bus driver fancies you?"

"I beg your pardon. I certainly don't need another man in my life, thank you."

Although I hadn't discussed what I'd heard had happened at the party with her, I got the feeling that Ernie had mentioned something. My instincts told me that this was a set-up. However, it went on for about a month. One day she told me to wait until all the people had left the bus because the driver wanted to speak to me. In a way I felt flattered and felt that a little flirting would do no harm. After Martie left the bus the driver spoke to me, but I let him know that I was not at all interested and left. Nevertheless, the flirting had lifted my spirits.

Martie called me a prude and seemed disappointed in me and we walked home together in silence. Eventually, human nature being what it is, the interest continued and eventually the bus driver and I chatted every afternoon and then kissed. Not long after, as we were kissing goodbye, the bus inspector knocked on the door and wanted to know what was going on. I was so embarrassed I didn't know where to hide my face.

Two days after the incident on the bus, Ernie came home and screamed at me for having an affair with one of his colleagues.

"How do you think I must feel?" he yelled at me. This was when he arrived home after his late shift. I was not even properly awake and had to gather my wits before I replied.

"I'm not having an affair. I kissed a guy and what's wrong with that? I'm not making passionate love to my best friend's wife each and every day, am I? In any case, my gut feeling was correct. This was a set-up by you and Martie with the aim of dragging me down to your level. Sorry, but you just blew it as the two of you will never succeed."

"And isn't that what Andy was trying to tell me the other day? Hadn't his wife seen you and Martie when you came home each day while I was at work? Have you no shame? You hadn't the decency even to wait until you were in the house before you started making out. Now, just get out."

He shut his mouth faster than he had opened it. His bravado disappeared into thin air and, mercifully, silence descended. The cheek of the man. I felt dirty for doing what I had done, but I felt cheated, too, as I pondered over what these two had tried to achieve. They had not achieved the desired effect. Mother-in-law was duly informed of my infidelity and my undervalued shares plummeted even further, if that was possible. She did not confront me. However, she did feel even sorrier for her son.

Ernie was very quiet for a couple of days – licking his wounds, I suspected. Soon after that incident, an apartment was found and the boarders departed. Once more I had my house to myself.

Occasionally we visited Richard and Martie and were invited for supper one night. As usual, alcohol flowed freely. Richard had the flu and excused himself after supper and went to lie down. The "love birds" suggested I relax while they washed the dishes. They took much longer than was necessary, so I went to investigate. I caught them red-handed, so to speak, making love. I picked up my sleeping child and walked out.

The journey home took about an hour and at one o'clock in the morning it was no joke but I survived. Ernie came home the next morning at about eleven, said nothing and sat working in the aviary for most of the day.

Around this time he took to slapping me. The first time his excuse was that I swore in front of his sister. Soon after the first incident, at five in the morning as we were all preparing to go for a picnic and were loading the car, mister decided he wanted breakfast. I refused to make it as it was an unreasonable request at that moment. The only reason he demanded it was that he wanted to show his authority.

The third time occurred when he was brought home by Richard the morning following the supper I had left early with Ernest Junior). After Richard left and we were in the house, he started accusing me of being unsociable. He began screaming at me and asked me whether I realised how embarrassing it had been to explain to Richard why he had stayed there without me. I sat on the bed listening to this tirade. When he paused, I retaliated by calling Martie a loose woman. For this, he slapped me.

The saying goes that one sees red when one is very angry. I can vouch for this: I was very, very angry. I lost all composure and grabbed him by the throat. I lifted him against the wall and began hitting him with my fist. I don't know how long it lasted to tell the truth. When I regained my senses, I found him sitting on top of me holding my hands.

"Let go of me," I screamed, and he quickly complied.

Ernest Junior was beside himself, jumping up and down on the bed, screaming. After pacifying my child, I turned my attention again to the hero who was still as white as a sheet. I said to him that he must never, ever lift his hands to me again.

"I swear to you, the next time it happens, I might kill you. I'm not like your mother."

He quickly dressed and left the house.

When he arrived home from work, he asked Ernest Junior whether it was safe to come into the house. This was a stupid question to ask of a three-year-old toddler who could not possibly understand the arguments of his parents. However, I repeated my threat that I could not be held responsible for my actions if he ever tried to hit me again.

At a celebration at his mother's house the next weekend, I told her that he'd hit me again, as I had mentioned to her on each of the previous occasions. She usually justified it on the grounds that he'd been tired or had worked long hours. This time she asked me with a smirk on her face:

"What did you do about it?"

"I hit him back and I swear to you I did a good job of it. Rest assured he will never lift his hand to me again."

Her face was a picture to behold and she raised the question of divorce again. For the first time since I'd known her, I lost my temper.

"On numerous occasions I have told Ernie to pack his clothes and leave, but your son doesn't want to go. I wish he would. He doesn't care for Ernest Junior or me or contribute to any of the expenses unless I force him to do so. He was never taught any sense of responsibility and is totally selfish. It seems I'm just a safety net so that you can't marry him off to your darling Liz, or so that any other lady can't sue him for maintenance. Please do me a favour and tell him to file for divorce. Perhaps he'll listen to you and make us both happy."

She was speechless and, lucky me, she didn't speak to me for months afterwards. After that, visits to the in-laws became fewer. Ernie didn't seem to like visiting them on his own accord, preferring to spend time with his friends.

Among my happier memories are of Sundays. I would take Ernest Junior to the Central Methodist Church in Johannesburg. It was a pleasant outing for the two of us. His father was not interested in church and was busy pursuing his own interests. I didn't have a car and the hour long bus ride each way was exciting for the three-year-old, who enjoyed the scenery along the way and being in the big bus. After church I focused on my own family and visited my sister.

With the breakdown of the relationship with his best friend, he had no external female interest, so he had to satisfy his needs by turning to his wife. It was around this time that I fell pregnant again.

Derek's birth and Australia

I started to focus on my own family and visited my sister every Sunday after church. Ernest Junior and his cousin played happily for some time before we walked home. The two of them really enjoyed each other's company as they were born only six months apart. I was then pregnant with our second child.

During this time it was quiet. There were a few extra-marital excursions by his lordship as the pregnancy progressed, but nothing very spectacular. Polly, who was not very happy about the pending birth, started up again about divorce. I told her that I was getting really tired of this ongoing saga and that she should speak to her son about filing for a divorce. Perhaps he would be obliging this time, knowing that there was another child on the way. I had anyway accepted the fact that the responsibility for the child would rest on my shoulders. Ernie would not or could not care for another being. He needed someone to take care of him and he found that person in me. I could not see him leaving me as he felt secure in his situation. A place to sleep, everything laid out for him, his clothes, his supper and he even had breakfast in bed. Personally I was not happy as my real role as a mother and wife fell well short of what it should be, but it was not time for us to part yet. When he was not working, he spent his leisure time on his hobbies, or with friends. He did not feel the need to spend time with us. He had all the freedom in the world. Why would he get a divorce if he could enjoy the life of a bachelor?

He had perfected the art of making people feel sorry for him. He was always the underdog and he was not allowed to do anything. A real "hen-pecked husband" was the impression he succeeded in putting across.

Once again Polly mentioned divorce. I told her that she might as well give it up as he would never make a good husband for anyone. Liz was actually very fortunate as she had survived one bad marriage, and another one to her son might well have been worse than the first. I also added that I wished I could persuade him to go and get professional help, as there was something seriously wrong with him. He was blocking something, who knew what. I did not know much about his background, apart from a few snippets that I had caught from her and the family. As far as I was concerned, he could leave at any time he pleased and that to do so would be a huge favour to me. I had survived thus far and I would in actual fact be better off if he would leave. However, it appeared that he had found the security in marriage that he had lacked in childhood. I also told her that my faith was in God and I knew beyond a shadow of a doubt that I would live through this ordeal.

I discovered that, apart from being a convincing liar, Ernie was an attention seeker. He also expected people to automatically cover and lie for him, even when he was in the wrong, which was the case most of the time. He had to prove his manhood. He even suggested that we should go to a "wife-swapping" party. This idea I found appalling. Not only did it prove that he had no respect for me; it also showed that he had no respect for himself.

At times he would arrive home with various new items, which he could ill afford, but felt he must possess. His desire for an item gave rise to his right to have it, so to say. When I asked him about it, he would grow angry or worse, he would lie and claim that it had been a gift. What made it even worse for me was that, though I supported him fully in our family matters, even when he had hit me, he continued this behaviour behind my back. I wondered in the presence of Polly whether this would be acceptable to her if he had married Elizabeth and had made her as miserable as I was Polly's response was silence. Not a word was uttered by her. I felt a deep sorrow for this lady. I wished I could help. I really longed for us to become friends.

I had met Ernie's aunts, uncles and cousins. Polly had three brothers. My favourite couple was Uncle Bill, the eldest brother, and his wife Aunt Lucy. Then there was Aunt Hetty, who was married to Polly's second eldest brother Richard (called Dick) and the youngest brother, Benjamin, and his wife, Aunt Emmy. Dick, I admit, I was never really fond of. To me he was a very domineering type of person. It was seemingly the only way he knew how to conduct himself, just like Ernie. But there was no way that Ernie would get the chance to turn me into the meek person that Aunt Hetty had become. We started spending more time with them because of the family hobby, keeping chickens. It was then that I discovered that Dick, like Ernie, was a womanizer. Aunt Hetty was a real "softy". Most of the time she was in tears, because of Uncle Dick's ceaseless bullying.

Nothing she ever said or did was good enough in his eyes. In addition, he spoke in a sergeant major voice, barking his orders. Tea had to be ready precisely at ten in the morning, and heaven help her if she was a minute too early or late. We paid many a visit to Uncle Benjamin and Aunt Emmy. I found them very caring and I felt at home there, too. In addition, they accepted me and were always very friendly and kind.

When visiting Uncle Bill and Aunt Lucy, I found I was at peace. They had the capacity to make one feel at home and were always friendly towards me and sympathetic when Ernie drank too much. He did not drink at home, though. He was a social drinker. He only drank when he was in the company of others, family or friends.

Uncle Bill and Aunt Lucy made a perfect couple. They reminded me of my own parents. Their relationship, too, had been warm and they had shown respect for one another.

And then there was Granny Lancaster, Ernie's grandmother, who had lived next door to us in Troyville. I found it very strange that mother and daughter stayed half a block from one another but were not on speaking terms. I asked Eddie why this was. I received an official Bezuidenhout family explanation placing all the blame on Granny Lancaster. I had learnt not to trust these biased explanations that also had the tendency to change over time.

Sadly, Granny Lancaster died in a tragic accident. While she was waiting at a bus stop after visiting her eldest son, Dick, she saw the bus approach and to make sure that the bus driver would see her and stop, she stepped off the curb into the street and waved to him. He did not see her in time. He slammed on the breaks to stop but it was too late and the bus hit and killed her.

While the above was taking place unbeknown to us, Ernie and I were out on a short trip, something we rarely did. We were not far from our home when I suddenly felt an urgent and inexplicable desire to return home. I asked him to please turn around and go home. He wanted to know why and I told him that I could not explain it to him, but that we needed to get back to our house. In addition, I told him that I felt that his sister would come there before the day was out. He looked at me quizzically and did not argue for a change. He just turned the car around and we went home.

We were not home for long when Evelyn stopped in front of the house; Ernie just looked at me with eyes as big as saucers. She brought the sad news that granny had been killed in a bus accident about an hour ago. Here again I witnessed with sadness the unforgiving spirit of the Bezuidenhout family. Neither Polly nor any of her eight children showed any real sorrow. Even at the funeral I was struck by the lack of emotion. All that they seemed to worry about was what was going to happen to all her belongings.

Life took its normal course and I became pregnant with our second child. Roelof, my brother and his wife, Martie, invited us to go out for a night's dancing as we used to do. Ernie agreed although I was near the end of my pregnancy with Derek. I did not really wanted to go, but I needed to get out of the house. I knew I would do little dancing. Not only because of the pregnancy, but also because of the humiliating experiences of these occasions. I normally ended up sitting alone at the table while he was dancing the night away with anyone who was willing.

On arrival, as usual Ernie would dance the first dance with me. Not long after the first dance, mister disappeared. The next thing he was waltzing past our table with all the flair and pomp he could muster, giving me one of his sarcastic grins. I felt so humiliated and, to crown it all, Martie saw it. She looked at me, and all I could do was to smile but I said nothing. Roelf returned to the table after getting drinks and I heard her telling him what had happened. He looked at me and one could sense his unhappiness.

As fate would have it, Ernie and the lady came dancing past again and this time with a bit more flair, pausing long enough to tell me "the closer to the bone, the sweeter the meat". Taunting and humiliating me. He was a bit brave, I thought, as my brother grabbed him by his arm and told him that we were going home now, and that if he wanted to come with he should get into the car now.

He had no choice but to leave the floozy there, otherwise he would have to find his own way home, and he seemed to have managed to get a bit drunk already. My sister-in-law, nearly hysterical, told me to get him home as soon as possible as my brother was now beside himself, and she could not say what he might do. On arriving home, a fight erupted between us. He told me to jump in the toilet and pull the chain. .

That put an end to our social life for a while. He could not change the way he behaved. Every time we went out, whether to a house party or to a dance hall, it was the same. He did not have much to say when we arrived home. Often he was too intoxicated and out of the car and passed out before he got to door of the house. I would leave him there and would go to bed. I could never say when exactly he would come into the house.

Later that week he came home in a foul mood. As I liked cooking and loved to experiment, I often tried my hand at making new dishes. However, on this particular night, I decided I would prepare what I thought was a favourite dish Mother used to make − curried mince with rice. It was a plain and simple dish and did not require much time to prepare; heavily pregnant and lacking energy, it was also not a demanding dish to make. On his arrival from work, he seated himself, looked at the food, pushed it away with disgust and remarked: "You call *this* rubbish food?"

He pushed his chair back, grabbed the newspaper and stormed off to the bathroom. Exasperated, I yelled at him: "You ate it at your mother's house and you will eat it here." I was in no mood to take his nonsense and I took the plate of food and scraped it into the dog's dish. When he came back he started looking for his food. He gave me a look that told me he was angry enough to beat me. However, he seemed to think twice about it and changed his mind. Perhaps he remembered the last encounter when he had slapped me and I had struck back.

"You can eat with the dog as I gave it to her," I said. Something in my tone of voice told him that he was treading on very thin ice and he left the house and did not return until late. I must have been asleep, as I did not hear when he came in.

Ernest Junior was happy to have Mum at home. When he was born, I bought a rough collie, the *Lassie* type. We called her Lady. As a pup, this dog went in the baby pram with us everywhere when Ernest Junior and I went for our walks. The pup would lie at the bottom end of the pram, as Ernest Junior only reached halfway down. It was one of the Queen Ann prams with enormous wheels and was easy to push and was higher than the regular ones. The height was convenient as one could stand upright instead of bending down attending to the baby's needs. There was ample space for madam to lie at the bottom, well away from him. When Lady was fully grown, she became very protective of Ernest Junior and me. However, she did not take to Ernie at all. My father told us never to underestimate any animal's intelligence as they could sense danger or sadness. An animal might act to protect one in situations it considered dangerous or potentially harmful. My child and I were the ones in our household not to be messed with as far as Lady was concerned. I was amazed at the instincts animals possess. As my time neared to give birth, I noticed increased attention paid to me by Lady who would watch my every move. She followed me everywhere. The nearer it came to the time to give birth, the more attached the dog became. There was no way that anyone could show animosity towards Ernest Junior as Lady would defend him with her life. She let it be known, through growls and stare-downs that she would not hesitate to attack if she deemed it necessary.

Perhaps this was why Ernie acted with some restraint with me or Ernest Junior. The dog showed no affection towards him at all. But then Ernie also knew I would not tolerate any violence. He had experienced my wrath, and he knew that any threat uttered by me was not an idle threat. He had physical proof of this. He was well capable of violence, but I believe God protected me and my children. Ernie picked up all these signals, and as a result stayed well clear of us and did not raise his hand in violence again.

Because of the bad experience in the hospital with the birth of Ernest, I decided that I would have my second child at home. This time Polly did not interfere. I had a midwife who visited me at home and there was a doctor on standby. At last the day arrived. Like Ernest's birth it was a difficult one, but thankfully with no audience. After a long period of labour, our second child was born on January the seventh, nineteen-sixty-nine. There were complications as the umbilical cord was wrapped around his neck and he was blue in the face due to lack of oxygen. The midwife was quick to remove the cord that was strangling him and actually sucked the muck off his chest. It sounds so horrible, but she was wonderful. He survived for which I thank God. For some time it was touch and go.

He weighed in at eight pounds and ten ounces. Like Ernest, Derek was also too big for my body and actually a bit heavier. Because of this, my hip was dislodged and it had to be pushed into position again, which was not a pleasant experience. Nevertheless, thankfully, the experience was not comparable to the treatment I had received at Polly's hospital. But we made it by the grace of God. It was much better than the first time. I was in my own environment and with a person I could trust and who was caring and understanding.

I was told after the birth that no one could enter the house or leave it because of Lady, our faithful guard. She had lain down at the back door and would not let anyone in or out of the house. They had had to use the front door. When the birth was over, she had come into the house and walked down the passage. She had then stuck her head through the bedroom door. She had looked at me as if to assess the situation, and then turned around and left. The midwife had been impressed. Seemingly the dog cared more about me than my husband, who again was nowhere in sight. He was still on the same shift and should have been home at ten as usual, but there was just no sign of him. But Lady was satisfied, it seemed, so she freed the backdoor for anyone who wished to enter or leave. When Ernie did come home he was in and out so fast, I hardly registered that he had been there before he had once more disappeared. Again, he had not attended the birth and I received no flowers or a card from him. However, Polly did send a bouquet and a card, and she also bought some clothes. It was with caution that I assayed her interest. I did not know what to think of it. In a way, however, it was a comforting thought that she had made the effort and that at least there was peace between us. I determined not to get my hopes up, though.

He was named after his second cousin, Derek Lancaster, and his uncle Alan. That evening I experienced the same vision I had had with Ernest Junior. The light appeared again, hovering at the end of the cot, but this time stretched itself out over the bottom end of the bed and then disappeared. I felt good and contented and at peace. I thanked God for his safe arrival and that he was also perfect, and thanked Him for helping me through the ordeal of giving birth.

I was looking forward to being with both of my sons for three months. I felt happy. One highlight was that this time I had saved some money and I would not have to beg for any, but Ernie was not aware of this. The only thing that saddened me was that, although I managed to learn to drive, I did not possess a car and could not afford to buy one which meant we could not attend church. But I had become so used to my conversations with God; it now came quite naturally to me and helped me tremendously when I needed some encouragement or strength. To stay close to our Father, my bible was always at hand. I kept in touch at all times, and it truly saved me.

After Derek's birth, I decided it was time for a change of job. Salaries in smaller companies were higher than the ones offered by the large corporate banks.

I applied for a job at Avalon Stationers as an assistant bookkeeper, and I was invited for an interview and then offered the job. I accepted. Avalon Stationers was situated in Jeppe in downtown Johannesburg and this meant that I had to board two different buses to get to work. However, financially it was more viable for both my two boys and me.

I had also embarked on studying all aspects of accountancy through the College of Accountancy at which I had already successfully completed and obtained a diploma with a recommendation for further studies. On the home front, nothing had really changed, and occasional visits to the in-laws were the only diversions. Social outings were also few. Ernie took to going fishing often on his free weekends. This new hobby was more important to him than spending time with us. Around that time, I came across this poem and it made me think and brought back the memory of the dream I had had when I was ten years of age:

Here we stand at a crossroad again like you said, in time the seasons change; looking back we recall the blessing and the pain, But now we turn our hearts toward what is still to come, We want to dream again. Lead us, Lord, into a life of fruitfulness, Prepare our hearts to risk again, And as we trust, taking simple steps of obedience, We know that you will lead us, Lord.

I was fighting depression at times but by staying in the Word, I was able to overcome the urge to give into despair. I could not conform to their ways and by wishing Ernie would leave me of his own accord was wishful thinking. Anyway, things were not that unacceptable any longer, as I had become accustomed to their ways. I was still on the outside looking in but with a bit more experience. I was not prepared to make compromises when it came to the lessons of my upbringing or my beliefs in any way. My faith in God was deeply established and with His guidance I knew I would succeed; also, I felt the conviction that it was not time to go yet. The words from the dream came to mind again and the memory of God putting His hand on my head and how He had told me that it was going to be difficult road but that I would receive directions within my spirit and that I had to obey them, regardless of circumstances.

I could not conform to the ways of his family. For example, it was difficult for me to say or agree with things about people of whom I knew nothing, but in the Bezuidenhout family, you were expected to automatically agree with their opinions no matter what, and this I refused. One reason they held me in contempt was because I believed in God, and according to them there is no God. Growing up, we had a rule in our house that if you cannot say something good about someone, you should hold your tongue.

In addition they did not agree with one another. There was a lot of animosity amongst them, too, and this was so tiresome. I simply could not understand it. As much as I tried, it was just beyond me. Since our marriage, I had not been given any option other than of spending Christmas with them and never with my own family. This selfishness brought a lot of ill feeling between the "in-laws" and me. But in order to make peace, one just had to suppress one's own feelings and in that way avoid any unpleasantness.

At least Edwin and I got along well. His family's outlook used to aggravate him, too. It was he who had told me about Liz every time she made an appearance, but this always happened after her visits. I asked him once why he only told me afterwards and not when it was actually taking place. He laughed and said:

"We wanted the house to stand, and you would have demolished it."

Uncle Dick and his family moved to a plot in the non-urban Walkerville area. As he was very involved in his hobby of keeping chickens, staying in a suburb brought a lot of complaints from the neighbours. He had quite a few incubators and not only did he hatch his own chickens, but he also presented them at the Rand Easter agricultural show, which took place each April. There were also the local club shows, which he also never missed.

We visited them quite often. I was very fond of Aunt Hetty, but not Uncle Dick. He reminded me of Polly − selfish and single-minded. Aunt Hetty, also a born and bred Afrikaner like me, was a really soft-natured person and we became very close. The two of us could relate our sorrows to one another and in this way we found release, strength and renewed energy.

I think that what we both found most difficult to accept was being snubbed. Both of us suffered because of it. Uncle Dick I found was the same as his nephew. He always had to impress other woman. I could not change Ernie's ways, but he knew where he stood with me. I told him at times in a gentle way, hoping it might sink in. At other times I completely lost it. Aunt Hetty was too timid, all she ever said was: "Yes Dick" and never retaliated.

During one of our visits to the Bezuidenhout family, Eddie, Ernie and I were talking and Eddie mentioned that he had itchy feet again, he wanted to travel. His Australian friends that he had met during his time in England wanted him to come over to Australia and explore possibilities there. Ernie piped up: "Why don't we go all together?" I nearly fell off my chair. Then: "why not?" I thought. At least it would be an adventure if nothing else. None of my family had been overseas except for those who fought in World War II. Plus it was something he wanted to do, so it would not be like "pulling teeth" and he became more willing to part with his money whenever his pleasure was part of the equation.

We came to a decision, one we made jointly and without outside interference. This in itself was a miracle. For once, his mother did not have to think for him. In due course we sold the house to my brother Roelf (he has since passed on, but his son still lives there). We moved and stayed with Moira and Tommy Quinn, friends of the family, for a couple of weeks while awaiting our departure for Australia. I resigned from my job, and with all the paperwork done, we were booked to leave from Cape Town harbour on the 27th March 1971 on the Ellinis, a passenger liner belonging to the Chandris line owned by Aristotle Onassis.

When dear mum found out about all this, there was a bit of a fuss but nothing to stress out about. I wiped the sweat off my forehead. I left my beloved dog Lady with her. I think she was pleased, but she did not say anything.

We travelled to Cape Town by train, which was an experience not only for me but also for the children. Born the second last of 8 surviving children, my parents were fairly elderly when I was young and we had never travelled outside the Transvaal area, so this was all new to me. My elation dipped as we left Johannesburg: would I ever see my family again? I wondered. But, I reminded myself, this was an opportunity that I'd never had before and might never have again. I saw parts of our country that made me realise how beautiful South Africa really is. The Karoo which is barren and flat as far as the eye can see. Suddenly, though, as soon as one enters the Hex River valley as the train enters the mountains, the scenery changes completely. It was beautiful. It reminded me of the pictures I had seen of Switzerland. Of my siblings, I was the only one blessed with *wanderlust* and a sense of adventure.

At last we arrived in Cape Town and we stayed at the Lord Nelson Hotel for two nights while we waited for the ship to dock. We had the opportunity to explore Cape Town. It was a pleasant experience since it was our first visit to the province. Ernest Junior was nearly six years old and Derek was two and a bit. The only thing I disliked with a passion was the rain. Within minutes the rain would come pouring down, and just as quickly the sun would peep out and say: "Hi, it's my turn now." Little did I know at the time that I was destined to settle in the fair Cape in my old age. We visited the Jan van Riebeeck Castle, the Botanical gardens, but we did not go to the top of Table Mountain as I was afraid of heights.

It was a wonderful sight to watch the Ellinis approach the harbour. I became quite choked up with emotion. Only then did it really dawn on me: I was actually leaving my country. However, it was too late to have second thoughts now. The children's eyes were shining with anticipation. They could not wait to board the big "boat" even when I tried to explain to them that it was a ship. We were to board the following morning. Ernest Junior and Derek were filled with such excitement it was only with great difficulty that I managed to persuade them to go to bed.

The following morning we went through the boarding procedures and were shown to our cabin. I had a nice surprise waiting for me. The people with whom we had lodged had sent us a beautiful bouquet of flowers wishing us well. As a family we had a fantastic cabin on the "A" deck. It was like a small flat. There was a double bed and bunks for the children, a bathroom and a lounge. Poor Edwin, as single man, was banished to the "hole" – just a bunk and a cupboard on "D" deck.

We all went back onto the deck to await the actual departure from South Africa. With the backdrop of Table Mountain, it was an impressive sight. I could not help shedding a tear or two. A lot of thoughts went through my mind. One of them was whether I would ever see my own family again? But thankfully the two boys distracted me as they were waving like mad as we drew further away. It was a heartrending yet exciting experience. Where are You leading me Father God? I whispered. Again the words that Jesus had said came to mind: "I will be with you always.

After we became familiar with the procedures on board and had had supper, the children were exhausted and it was not long before they were both fast asleep. Ernie and I went out for a stroll on the deck, taking in all the beauty of the night sky which was like a huge black velvet cloth that filled the expanse of the universe. I had never seen the moon so bright and the stars scattered all over, indeed too numerous to count. Ernie announced that he was tired and needed his sleep and I was a bit disappointed. Dreamer that I am, I had been hoping for a little romance, but it was not to be. Soon we joined the children. It did not take me long to fall into a deep sleep, too.

The following morning we were looking forward to our first breakfast on board. To my disappointment, I found myself alone with the children. Ernie was nowhere to be seen. I helped the children to dress and we left to look for the dining room as the children were famished. I found Ernie already at the table. A group of eight people were allotted to each table for the duration of the journey. The children had their own section where they met little fellow travellers in the hopes that the children would develop friendships as the journey would take two weeks. I found that, indeed, the world is small. At our table were seated two elderly ladies in their seventies who came from Kensington, Johannesburg the very same suburb that Polly and her family came from.

The journey would take two weeks, but each day was packed full of activities and there was no time to mope as the children occupied my attention. During the day we saw very little of Ernie. He spent most of his time at the swimming pool. At times we would go with him and enjoyed it tremendously until the crowds came. Then the children and I were in his way. Ernie would start chatting to everyone and totally ignore us. So it was up to me alone to take care of the children. There was a kindergarten on board but only during the mornings, so in the afternoons I would divert their attention to something else and avoid confrontation with Ernie. At least in the mornings I was free while the children developed new friendships in the kindergarten. But I felt lonely. Eddie had made friends and never went to bed until three in the morning, so he slept most of the day and one would see him around lunchtime, and then again in the evenings. I joined in the activities on board. I saw a lot of movies and went for Greek dancing lessons or just lazed around the deck, reading a book and relaxing. Ernie did not attempt to join me, and if I approached the swimming pool area, he would find another place to go. Sadly it turned out that my hopes for this journey would not be realised. I had actually hoped that we could perhaps learn to reach out to one another during the cruise.

Unfortunately I was the one who did the reaching out. I again tried to explain to him how important it was for the boys that there should be some harmony between us. However, my attempts met with no success. Actually the only time he talked to the boys, or played with them, was in the cabin. Each morning he used to pick them up, looked through the porthole and said: "I looked through the hole, and what did I see? I saw the sea". They enjoyed that and still remember it to this day.

At night after bathing the children and reading bedtime stories till they drifted off to sleep, we would go up on deck and watch the moon. This was an awesome sight. Romantic, yes, but alas my husband was not that way inclined towards me, try as I may. He would stay a while and then disappear to continue with his favourite pastime of partying. His single-minded goal was clear: have as many one-night stands as he could.

There were also different events that took place at intervals. When the halfway mark on the journey was reached, a party was organised by the captain of the ship to mark the occasion. When we docked at Free-mantle, Western Australia, there was an informal farewell celebration as some of the passengers would disembark the following day. After Free-mantle we docked at Melbourne where we went on land and visited the Melbourne Zoo. There we saw a platypus for the first time. Later that afternoon we left for the last leg of our voyage to Sydney. There Eddie's friends had arranged a rental of a basement flat in Bondi for us. It was three blocks away from the famous Bondi beach and the beautiful Pacific Ocean. Back then they were still busy building the Sydney Opera house.

Arrival and return to and from Australia

The flat was quite big with two bedrooms, kitchen, lounge and bathroom. The thing that amused me most was watching people's feet marching past as I stood at the kitchen sink washing the dishes. Being a basement flat, one might expect it to be dark and gloomy, but not so. We bought the necessary furniture. We bought it secondhand as we first wanted to make sure that this was the place where we would settle. To me it was still very strange to be so far away from my family. One thing I did was to put aside enough money to return home in the event that things did not work out as planned.

We were lucky as Ernie found a job very quickly, but as for myself, I did not even try. It was still too strange. We were still trying to get accustomed to the new country and figuring out how best to arrange things. For example, who was going to look after the children?

I found Australians on the whole very friendly. Unfortunately, they were not so friendly towards South Africans during the era of apartheid. I placed Ernest in a Catholic School in the hopes that he would make friends. One day I stood at the gate and watched him during playtime. Ernest would run after the children and as soon as he wanted to join them, they chased him aside and said that they would not play with a "nigger killer". It broke my heart, as the child clearly could not understand what this meant. It made me very angry, as it was so unfair. We were trying to make a new life without the apartheid stigma and we were not being permitted to do so.

In Australia I found groceries very expensive. Other items, such as household furniture, cars and clothing were, on the other hand, cheaper than back home. I would have thought that the food would be cheaper. We spent a lot of time on Bondi beach as we could walk there, but again I spent most of the time alone with the children. On other occasions we went to the Sydney zoo and other places of interest. I loved to visit the churches, especially the old ones. There was such a sense of peace to be found within those walls, and I could feel the calmness while sitting there. One thing that kept us very occupied was the television as we were not accustomed to it. Ernest and Derek enjoyed it the most. Eddie, who was still looking for a job, and I joined them with the result that we became a bunch of couch potatoes. The Flintstones were the children's favourite.

To make things worse, the South African Springbok rugby team was due for a tour of Australia. What a fiasco. There were demonstrations against the tour in all the main centres of Australia. Sydney was the worst, one of the slogans they chanted was: "Paint them black and send them back." If you came from South Africa, you were branded. Everyone ignored and avoided us, yet they knew very little about our country. For example, many thought Johannesburg, where we were from, was a coastal town. Ernest got an infection and I needed a doctor. Edwin's friends recommended a doctor they thought was very good. He turned out to be a South African by birth. He immigrated to Australia ten years before. When he found out that we were also South Africans, he went off like a trooper, blasting the Australians. He felt that they were a bunch of hypocrites. They had their own history of racism and ongoing problems in race relations. Taking a "holier-than-thou" attitude, they had banned all postal services coming from South Africa due to the Springbok tour.

"Who do they think they are? I have been staying here for ten bloody years, and where are their Aborigine friends? All in the outback." I found out that day that there were no Aborigines staying in regions like Sydney, Melbourne or Fremantle. But it was good to get someone else's opinion of Australians, and yet it was funny the way he carried on. I must admit I found their attitude much like the Americans, bombastic and loud. I found that he was a good doctor and the infection disappeared very quickly after only one injection and the medication he had prescribed. But then I understood why the children did not want to play with Ernest. The parents had indoctrinated their children: Australians were good, South Africans were bad. Thinking about what he had said, I pondered over the fact that the only "black" people I had thus far seen in Australia were four American soldiers on leave from Vietnam. At that time, the Americans were still busy fighting that senseless war over there.

Ernie, Eddie and some Australian friends went to watch the rugby match in Sydney between Australia and South Africa. The field was cordoned off with barbed wire to keep the demonstrators away. I saw on the news that in Western Australia the rugby fans had surrounded the demonstrators and they were forced to abandon their efforts to disrupt the match.

I felt so lonely at times. I could have conversations with Ernie. I felt very sorry for myself. There was also a shortage of money. I should have been used to it, but here I was not working and again as before in such circumstances, he failed to provide sufficiently. Most nights he spent in the pub, and to crown it all, I fell pregnant. It was July and in a way I was happy, but being in a strange country for the first time in my life I felt hemmed in and panicky. What's more, being South African in the block of flats where we were staying seemed to be somewhat of a crime. Neighbours refused to acknowledge us. The only friendly person I came across was the lady who owned a shop where I did my daily shopping. She wanted to know where we came from and so forth. We had pleasant conversations. But on the whole, I felt desperately lonely. I told Ernie that night that I thought I was pregnant and he actually looked pleased.

His reaction seemed strange. Then again, perhaps not as strange as my falling pregnant did constitute a pretext to return to South Africa, a good excuse. He also could not make friends, a new and troubling experience for him. So after only four months we decided that it would be best to go back home. The children were lonely. We tried to enrol them in a playschool and the application was rejected because of their nationality. In a way I was sad, as I would have liked to have made a proper go of it, but not under these circumstances. Being a foreigner there meant one had no government benefits. Ernie could not join a medical aid scheme. Eddie was not very happy with our decision, but he understood the situation. It could only get worse for us.

We were booked on the Achilles Laura, an Italian liner, to leave Australia, via Singapore. I was glad, for it would certainly turn out a memorable experience as we were to sail through the Malaysian Islands. Watching the boat people staying in actual boats around the islands it amazed me that the little children, three, four years of age, could balance on the edge of the boats without ever falling in the water. I would have had a heart attack if I had to stay in such surroundings.

When the ship docked in Singapore, we had almost a day to explore the country. We found it "unnaturally" clean and duly were told that one could get a fine of up to five hundred Singapore dollars if one dropped as much as a match stick on the ground. The gardens were fabulous, and being on the equator, it was extremely hot and humid. They sold litchis as big as the old half-crown. They were packed on ice and were so delicious one could not stop eating. Orange juice was freshly squeezed. The oranges were also stored on ice in a glassed covered stand, with two holes for the vendor's arms to go through to prepare your drink. For passengers it was a divine deliverance: none of us were accustomed to this kind of heat.

The gardens were picture perfect, as all Chinese gardens are, with lawns that look like carpets and the most colourful arrays of flowers. There were benches to sit on and absorb all this beauty. This was a heavenly experience. I would always remember it. To this day, after many travels since, I can still say it was the best I have ever seen. We did a bit of shopping and I bought my dear mother-in-law a beautiful hand-embroidered tablecloth. In retrospect, I should have kept it for myself. I never saw her using it, and whenever I asked about it, I was told that it was "somewhere".

But alas at the end of that day we had to return to the ship. We were joined by a regiment of British soldiers. For economic reasons, Britain had decided to withdraw its troops from Malaysia in stages. It was actually very moving as the remaining soldiers, still awaiting their turn, started singing: "Now is the hour, that we must say good bye..." while the ship was disembarking from the harbour. I do not think that there was a dry eye on that deck that evening. I still feel emotional just thinking about it.

Well now we were truly "homebound" as the next stop was Cape Town. As we sailed around the tip of Africa, we ran into a storm and as I was lying in bed and listening to the raging elements, and the ship's creaking, I started praying like never before. Funnily enough, I later discovered that this was the ship's last voyage before going into drydocks for refurbishing. It was amazing that she made it back home to Italy. I must have fallen asleep eventually. When I finally woke up, the storm had subsided. Seeing Table Mountain again in the distance was a sight for sore eyes. But it would not be until the next day that we could actually approach the harbour for docking.

The next morning it seemed that everyone was on deck watching as we approached the harbour. I was standing behind two Brits and listened as they discussed the mountain, which is now one of the seven new wonders of the natural world. "It does not look like a table to me," the one said. They were both laughing and the other one piped up: "I wonder if the Impis are still running around half naked toting assegais?" To them it must have seemed very funny. Inside I was fuming. Like the Australians, they simply had no idea, could not tell one part of the country from another, but still felt entitled to criticise. It also reminded me of what I was returning to. I was coming back to my in-laws who had seemingly made it their mission in life to criticise people and find fault with everyone.

It was early in the morning when we docked. Within a couple of hours of our arrival we were booked to leave by train to our final destination. Early next morning we were approaching Johannesburg. I felt relieved to be back in familiar surroundings. Even with all the problems that the country faced, home was home.

We were greeted by Polly and Maurice at Johannesburg railway station. It felt good be home. I think Polly was happy, too. When we got to their house where we would stay until we could reorganise ourselves, I found that Lady was not there. Polly told me that she was in the kennels as they were away and she had not wanted to leave her at home. Later that day we went to fetch her and when she saw me and I her, we were overjoyed. I cried and I think that if a dog could cry she would have, too. It was a miracle that her tail remained attached to her body as she was wagging it so vigorously. In the car, she promptly sat herself on my lap although there was space enough for her on the seat next to me. She sat there and refused to budge. She was determined in her own way to make sure I was not going to disappear again. Finally and to my relief, she at least stopped licking me.

It was good to be back. After everything was sorted and it was decided that we would stay with them until we could find a place to stay, life continued and soon things fell into place. For the first time, Polly said nothing about the pregnancy and almost seemed happy. I insisted on going to my own doctor in Auckland Park and when this met with no resistance from Polly, I grew optimistic. Perhaps it was a good thing that we had gone to Australia.

I was fortunate as I was re-employed at Avalon Stationers where I had worked before leaving. The only drawback was that because I was pregnant on re-engagement, there would be no paid maternity leave. However, beggars cannot be choosers, as they say, and I was only too happy to accept the job on that basis. We fell into a routine and Ernie decided to try his hand again at running his own business. As an excellent upholsterer, he could bring old tired pieces of furniture and vintage car interiors back to life.

Bought home in Kensington

Ernie's stepfather Maurice also took it upon himself to assist us in buying a house instead of renting. We were fortunate enough to receive a loan from the United Building Society and bought a house in Kensington, a block away from the Kensington Golf Course, which was a blessing and a curse at the same time. A blessing, as it was one of the golf courses used for big tournaments. You found guys like Gary Player playing there once or twice a year together with the other big names. The result was that you sometimes met these celebrities. But on the other hand, if you forgot to lock your gates, you would find cars parked in your driveway, or even on your lawn. During the golfing season, one could come home from work and not find parking in front of one's own house. I even once received an apology from the great Gary Player himself. I could not park my car as somebody else was occupying the space in the yard. As his day of golf was over, he smiled and cordially offered me his parking space in front of my house. I smiled back and said nothing but, amused I thought: "The cheek of that man."

Another miracle that happened at that time was that Ernie bought me my first car. I was very happy as I would no longer have to rely on buses. Polly did not offer me secondhand furniture this time round. She allowed me to choose my own furniture. The kitchen was fully fitted, and I bought a teak dining-room suite from the previous owners and they also left me all the curtains in the house. How blessed can a person be? All I needed was a lounge suite and then beds for all of us.

Christmas arrived too soon as usual and we had a lovely time at Polly's home with all the family. The only exception was Eddie who was still in Australia. On Christmas day, Ernie even took me to West Park Cemetery to put flowers on the grave of my parents. I was somewhat shocked that this met with no opposition from Polly or Ernie. We also visited Anna and William who had moved to Kempton Park. They had sold our parental home. This was sad but they had needed more space and William worked in Kempton Park. Things were really looking up.

There were no problems with the pregnancy. Between my sister "Stomp" – so-called as she was very short in stature (her real name was Magrieta Louise), and Polly, they bought most of the clothes for the baby.

In January nineteen-seventy-two, Ernest started school at Leicester Road Primary. The Principal was Mr. Braun, who was Chairman on the National Olympic Committee. He believed that every child in the school had to take part in athletics. Come sports day, when the different houses (or groups) competed against each other, the parents behaved a bit strangely to say the least. Ernest took part in the relay, and believe me he was no runner. One of the fathers commented sarcastically at the way he ran. All one could see were arms and legs flying through the air. He came stone last, admittedly it was a bit comical, but he was my son and I certainly let that father know it. In the end he had to smile, too. Let us face facts: my Ernest was not a sprinter.

His teacher Mrs. Warburton, sent me a note informing me that she wanted a word with me. The following day I left work a bit early to meet with her. A summoning to school was rare, especially when you knew that your child was neither a poor student nor badly behaved. She wanted to know what time he went to bed, as he kept falling asleep during class. I was astounded to say the least. I told her the routine: bath time was at five, supper at six, some family time with the kids, reading stories to them and then off to bed at half past seven.

She could not find fault with that, so we left it till report time. When the end of term report was issued, the teacher was pleased to inform us that he had mostly A's and one or two B's. Today they are called "gifted children" and are catered for according to their level of intelligence.

Since we had arrived back from Australia, things had gone wonderfully. I could not believe the difference in his family's behaviour. Even Ernie had changed and he now showed real interest in his family and immediate surroundings. I was naturally over the moon. He helped in the garden, cut the lawn and started a vegetable patch. It seemed that going to Australia had paid dividends. Polly was really doing her best to help with everything; I was even included in their discussions and not treated as an unwelcome intruder. I felt part of the family. Ernie, having started his business restoring the interior of vintage motor cars even picked Ernest up from school each day as one of the streets the child had to cross *en route* home was a main road and very busy. Such interest he had not previously shown. I was in shock, but it was very pleasant.

On our new property there stood a building separate from the house that resembled a British conservatory. It overlooked a large section of the garden. It was a wonderful place for birthday parties. Older people could sit in comfort inside the room watching children playing outside, so it suited all ages. Lo and behold, mister decided that it would be perfect as an aviary. My heart started racing, my throat seemed to close. I thought I was going to have a nervous breakdown.

Oh well, so peace had not reigned long, after all. My hopes flew out the window. I told him in no uncertain terms that it was a no-go. He huffed and puffed, but I was not going to allow him to turn the place into a backstreet slum. Again he was not very happy, and so the ritual harangue started: I was the most selfish person on this planet. Entering the last stages of pregnancy, he began his endless moaning again. There I was, thinking that he had developed some sense of pride in his surroundings, but I was mistaken.

Polly did not interfere too much this time. I told him that he should first build an aviary, and then only bring birds onto the property. Mercifully he did just that. It was not long after the bird episode that I went into labour. I was rushed to a nursing home in Emmarentia as the doctor, given the difficulties with the homebirth of Derek, did not want to take any risks. Once again I was dumped there and Ernie did not stay for the birth. Seemingly, he could not get away fast enough. I arrived at eight o'clock and my little girl was born at twelve thirty on the second day of February 1972, weighing six pounds and two ounces. She was named after her granny and one of my sisters: Louise Margery.

After the birth, they transferred me to a ward, but I could not contain my excitement. I had actually given birth to a little girl. I was lying in bed, but I could not stay still as I had been instructed to do. Anyone who heedlessly stuck their nose into the ward had to listen to my babble: "It is over, and it is a little girl" I kept repeating. I moved around so much that in the end I was lying in a pool of blood. A sister was sent to me by the nurses as they could not get me to relax and sleep. I told them about the wetness in my bed and when the sister lifted the blankets she nearly had a heart attack.

They ran around, transferred me to another bed, and gave me a sedative. While I struggled to stay awake, the sister stood by, talking to me. She told me that if I did not rest now there would be serious complications. I just looked at her and shook my head, but fortunately the tablet took its toll and I fell asleep. I slept until late afternoon and when I was fully awake again, I received a shock. I nearly fainted: next to my bed sat his lordship, father Ernie. I was dumbstruck. Plus he had brought me some flowers. "Lord, what is going on with this man?" I could not believe it. I did show appreciation, but unfortunately my trust in him had vanished completely in the last couple of weeks. The enthusiasm that he had shown after we had returned from Australia had by now dwindled down to zero. Polly sent some flowers again, which I really appreciated.

I was allowed to go home after spending just three days in hospital. When we returned from Australia, Cynthia, the lady who had worked for the Quinns (the family friends who had put us up just before departing for Australia), asked me if I needed help. A friend of hers needed a job. The friend would be willing to look after Louise, the baby. Well, I needed all the help I could get, and the offer coming from a dependable source, I grabbed it with both hands as there was no question about it: I would have to go back to work.

My answer was yes. She introduced me to Mina, who turned out to be a gem among gems. She was definitely a bonus for me as, with her to help, I would not have to do any cooking when I came home from work. This would give me time to spend with the children. I really appreciated all these little miracles that God placed along my path to soften the journey somewhat.

Once home I still felt very weak, and Mina insisted that I stay in bed at least until the weekend. I really appreciated that. Curious, I asked Ernest what he did at school that day. He told me that the teacher had wanted to know where we worked and what our professions were. He had told her that his mother worked as a bookkeeper, but that daddy stayed at home. I sadly found out that he only worked in the morning and, after picking up Ernest from school, he did not go back.

It infuriated me when Ernie lied to me. I felt cheated and such a fool. Now his fuzziness about work made sense to me. The place he claimed to be working at was not far from the branch where I worked. Earlier I had suggested that I walk over to his place where he worked so that we could travel home together. This would save money spent on travelling. However, he had quickly made excuses. It would not be feasible since, at times, there was a late job, or at other times,

Sam might ask him to stay for a drink and so on. He thought it best for me to catch the bus home. Funnily enough, he was never home when I arrived, so where was he? Ernest was there, had been walked home by Mina from school. It seemed he would wait until it was time for me to arrive and then vanish for a while before coming back.

I felt a proper nincompoop. Unfortunately Ernie did not possess the discipline to run his own business. Without informing me, he had applied for a job at South African Airways on recommendation of a friend of his, and he was successful in getting the job. This was, indeed, very good news. My hopes were again soaring. There would be a steady income and together with mine we would really be comfortable. Fortunately, he had bought a car for me. This would come in very handy now as we would be travelling in opposite directions. Also, he would no longer able to pick up Ernest from school. However, the school was on the way to my work. Ernest was only six and not ready to walk home by himself, so I fetch him during my lunch break to take him home and then go back to work again.

But, I told myself, if it was going to improve our lives by bringing us some financial security, it was worth it. There was peace in my soul, a new hope. I told Ernie that I was so glad, and that we could move forward with the knowledge that we would work together for the sake of our family. There was a sort of unity between us. Ernie seemed to like this, as he had not enjoyed this in his own home. The little that I had managed to gather about his life told me of an irresponsible and wasteful father and a mother who had always had to struggle to put food on the table, and to provide a roof over their heads, particularly after the father had deserted them. Ernie glowed with confidence and pride.

We got talking, which rarely happens, and I told him about my childhood, about my parents' relationship. My father would not do anything without first discussing it with my mother, especially if it was going to affect the family as a whole, especially the children. Children need stability in a home; they need to know that their parents are there for them. Above all, I told him, we need to show the children that we respect each other, so that they can learn by example. Being a parent carries with it a huge burden of responsibility. It is not about you and it is not about me: it's the children that matter.

He actually surprised me when he uttered his agreement. He told me he would like our children to grow up in a stable home with caring parents and promised his support. Secretly I was rejoicing. I stressed again the importance of working together as parents to create a stable environment. I prayed fervently that he would keep the promises he made and that we would work together as a team.

I went back to work two weeks after giving birth with legs of jelly. The first month I worked half day only. I was very upset that I had had to return to work as quickly as I had not had time to really bond with my little girl. When the luxury of two weeks off and half day work was over, the routine changed. I dropped Ernest off at school in the morning and at lunchtime I fetched him and took him home. Then back to work again. After a while, rushing up and down transporting Ernest, Mina offered to fetch him every day until he was sufficiently streetwise to make his own way home. She was a real gem. I thank God again for all the small mercies that he bestowed on me to make things a little bit easier.

Things were going smoothly between Ernie and me. It really felt like we were bonding with each other and my hopes were kept alive as he came home from work each day and played with the children. Their favourite game was riding on his back. One heard squeals of laughter erupting every now and again. I felt really contented.

Uncle Dick and Aunt Hetty sold their house in Linden and moved to Walkerville. One thing about Uncle Dick was that he was very meticulous in everything that he did. Everything had to be perfect, which was good, but the problem was everyone else had to follow suit. Tea time was at ten, not a second before or after. Aunt Hetty was always so nervous. Even the cutlery had to be placed a certain way on the serving tray. After I got to know her better, I told her she must hit him with the tray over the head. At least she laughed. We started to visit them quite often and got to know them very well. There were times when I voiced my opinions and then Dick would glare at me, but he let me alone for some reason. If it had been someone else, he would have asked them to leave his house. At times we took Polly along with us. It was a nice drive and the children enjoyed the open land. They lived on a ten-acre plot. There was enough space for the children to run around with the result that they got rid of their surplus energy. Usually they were so tired when we arrived back home that it was a race to get them into the bath and bed before they fell asleep.

Working for the South African Airways also had its perks as we were allowed two free flights a year, one local and one overseas, any destination. So we travelled to Durban to be by the sea practically every year, but it was only later, after Gregory's birth, that we started to venture overseas. Life was good and Ernie had become more relaxed and was keeping his side of the commitment that he had made when he had started his new job. He was a fantastic upholsterer, but had no business sense. Being employed suited him best.

Ernest started playing soccer at school and father had him enrolled in a local soccer club for children. He even started to coach a team of youngsters, and I caught a snippet from his past: Ernie had played for a team at primary school. I was naturally glad for the family unit in the making. It was also time for the Rand Easter show and it was the "must go" event of the year.

While we were walking around the show grounds, Ernie spotted a caravan exhibition. We had a look at them and he decided to buy one. As a family we could go fishing when summer came around again. Only the best was good enough for him and he opted for the biggest in the range: a Gypsy 5. It was beautiful, I admit, and we could afford it, if he paid the instalments. I knew it was futile to try and stall the purchase, as we were just getting nicely back on our feet again. He wanted it and that was the end of the story. If I said no, he would still have gone and bought it. That was Ernie. He never thought of the consequences of any deed.

It was with great excitement that we waited for the delivery of the caravan. Ernie worked shifts and sometimes even on weekends. We took the first available weekend and set off to go camping as a family. We had a glorious time. The two boys thoroughly enjoyed themselves. As Louise was still an infant, I took care of her and we enjoyed the peace and quiet. I really embraced these moments. She just lay there looking at her surroundings with such wonder on her little face. If she could talk, she would have verbalized her utter amazement and delight. Except when she was either sleeping or drinking milk, she smiled and gurgled all the time. I felt so relaxed and full of the joys of life.

Ernie enjoyed the fishing. Even Ernest and Derek tried their hands at it. Ernie also appeared relaxed. Actually for the first time that I could recall I looked at him and felt warmth within me. I had never seen him like this. Alas all good things come to an end and soon it was time to pack up and return home again. The kids complained bitterly, but were placated with promises that we would go fishing soon. It was one happy and contented family that went home that evening. This trip is one of the most treasured memories I keep tucked in my heart. It gave me the conviction that all things are possible. My trust restored, I looked forward to a brighter future. At least once a month we tried to go fishing. Having the caravan meant we did not have to depend on the weather. It was a home away from home.

One tends to believe the adage that lighting does not strike the same place twice. With a vague sense of foreboding, however, I became concerned when I received the news that Ernie had joined a fishing club and would take part in competitions. I did not mind the fact of his joining. However, I had reservations about the impact of this new development on the closeness of the family that had been steadily building the last few months. I did not want to see it shattered. I did not share my fears with him as I would have been accused by the B family that I did not want him to have any fun. It sounds absurd, but that was how it worked in that family. They felt they could do what they wanted as it was their right to live their lives, but this rule did not extend to the spouses of Poppy's children. My fears were soon realised, unfortunately. On fishing trips we became a burden to have around. No longer dependent on his family for reassurance, he had once again established an external source of recognition to bolster his ego. It appeared that family unity was not that important to him. We went with him a couple of times, but it became very demoralizing for the boys as they were not allowed to sit with him at the water's edge. They made too much noise and disturbed the fish. It was heartbreaking to observe the disappointment on their faces. I tried to distract them. I bought little fishing rods for them. Away from the crowd we tried to fish, but they soon lost interest as I was not as good as their dad, and dad had no time for them now.

When the next fishing weekend came around again, I was told that this would be a big competition with other clubs involved, and he felt that we were too much of a disturbance and preferred to go alone. I cannot even begin to describe how wretched I felt. I told him that he had to tell the children as they were looking forward to these weekends, despite the fact that he did not take notice of them any longer. He refused, packed up the caravan and left. I had to deal with the children, tried to distract them as those little faces were a picture of misery. They were so heart sore. It was disconcerting to have something one looked forward to suddenly snatched away. I could not complain to Polly as I would be told that he worked so much and he needed time to relax.

We went together to the cinema. They seemed to enjoy the experience, but it was just not the same. Again the family was split as from then onwards we were no longer part of his fishing trips. I had to find ways to amuse the children and at times that was not easy. I visited my sister who was living in Kempton Park, not far from Kensington, and at least there the children had their cousins to play with. That became a treat for them. Unfortunately, visiting Polly without Ernie was actually terrible as she had reverted to her former self, and I was ignored when I went there alone. So there was no comfort there. If Eddie was there it was fine as we could talk for hours. This helped me to get rid of my frustration. I was desperately trying to hide my hurt feelings so as not to disturb the children.

I made it very clear to Ernie that if he wanted to stay in this marriage he would have to bring up his side financially, at least, or hit the road. He could move in with his mother again. He complied as he knew I would otherwise throw him out.

At times when it was convenient for him, he would play with the children. They enjoyed this very much and it was a treat for them to have father home over a weekend. For the children's sake, I had learned to be contented with the few crumbs that were offered to me. At least I had something he would never have and that was to enjoy the company of my Lord Jesus Christ and most of the times I took my burdens to Him. I found peace at the foot of the cross. Many times I wondered how long this road was going to be. But through His living presence I managed to cope in the day-to-day struggle.

Derek started school in 1975. He was the opposite of Ernest. Ernest was a quiet child. He liked to investigate anything that would take his fancy. He always liked to take his toys apart to try and see how they were made and most of the time he assembled them again. I had learned very quickly to buy toys that he had to build himself, like Meccano sets. But Derek was a boisterous child. He always got into scrapes. This adventurer would crawl around in the ceiling to see what he could find there, for instance. Louise was a quiet child, playing with her dolls and having tea parties like other little girls. I liked to dress her, she was so beautiful, and still is today. She is the artistic one of the family. I was told that granny Lancaster was an artist, I cannot recall anyone on my side who was art orientated.

Around this time I took up the piano again. I had the good fortune of buying a piano at a good price from the accountant at Avalon Stationers where I worked. It had belonged to his mother who had passed away and no one in his immediate family wanted the piano. He advertised it at work and I jumped at the opportunity. He was only asking two hundred rand. It was imported from Germany by his mother in 1914. As a small child, I had started piano lessons, but had had to abandon them as we had not had a piano. Taking it up again brought the benefit of keeping me busy during the many lonely hours when Ernie was occupied with his solitary pursuits.

Once again Christmas was approaching. As I was standing in front of the grocery cupboard, Mina walked in and with a laugh she asked: "Are we going to get lucky this month?"

"Oh, Mina," I groaned. "I do not know, let us see, perhaps a miracle will happen."

My words were hardly spoken when Evelyn walked in with a box of groceries.

"I thought I would bring you some groceries for Christmas as I know that my brother will not buy any, and if he does it would be a miracle."

I, with my pride, was taken aback, and I thought: "What a Christmas present". Unfortunately I saw it as an insult to my person. And I told her that I really appreciated it and would accept it, but felt it insulting for her to buy groceries knowing that her brother could well afford it, but failed to do so. She took offence and once again I was branded an ingrate.

Even if she meant well, I was not used to receiving groceries as a present. It was senseless for them to feel guilty for his shortcomings. Ernie failed miserably in fulfilling his responsibilities and all they were trying to do was to make up for the lack of interest their brother demonstrated towards his wife and children. They should have, especially Polly, with her experience of not having a supportive husband herself, spoken to him, but instead they defended him. If I brought it up then I was called ungrateful and told that I should appreciate what Ernie did for us. I could never understand their logic, and never would.

When Evelyn left, I turned to Mina and asked her if I was wrong in my thinking. She just shook her head and with tears in her eyes she left the house, I suppose to compose herself and to try to understand it all. I was truly grateful to her for this, but it did not solve the problem. Now he would think that he could shy away even more from his responsibilities. I felt angry and insulted. Why could Polly not go to the heart of the problem, Ernie being her son, and try to solve it at source. Why cover up for him, he would never learn anything by it. Try as I might, I just could not understand the logic of it.

Needless to say, the whole episode was reported at headquarters. I was treated as the most insensitive person on planet earth and it turned out to be one of the most miserable Christmases I had ever experienced. I was completely ignored and treated as a leper, but I was regarded as good enough to wash the dishes. There was not one Christmas lunch thus far in my married life that I had spent with my family. It always had to be at Polly's place. After lunch I thanked them for the lunch, gathered my children and left. Ernie stayed behind.

Once home, I let the children play with their presents and felt emotionally drained. I went to find solace in our bedroom. In the morning before leaving for Polly's, I had expressed to Ernie my deeply felt wish to go to the West Park Cemetery to place flowers on my parents' graves. His answer had been: "Yes, of course I will take you," but once we had arrived at his mother's the general consensus had been that visiting graves was a waste of time. At this time of the year, my longing for my parents was especially acute as their wedding anniversary coincided with Christmas – they were married on the 25th December 1923. I wanted to be near to them and, as stupid as it might sound, being at the gravesite normally brought me some peace and reassurance. But even this solace I was not afforded. I yielded myself unto God and prayed for this terrible ache within me to subside. God had been my refuge since childhood. He is my comforter. Jesus is an everlasting help in trouble. I knew that I could go to him any time, day or night, and He would be there, waiting. After a while, lying there on the bed, I felt the peace that surpasses all understanding fill my being. I was not alone, the road might be difficult, but help and comfort was close by. The B family did not know the pain that went with the loss of a loved one. Up to that point, they had only lost Granny Lancaster for whom they had not really seemed to care.

One Sunday I was alone as Ernie had taken the children for a drive, something he rarely did and most likely to go and visit their grandmother, which I did not mind as I wanted them to know her, when there was a knock on the door. Richard, his lifelong friend, stood there. I was surprised to see him and told him that Ernie was not at home. He said he did not want to speak to him but to me. I found it odd. Moreover, I was in the middle of washing the kitchen floor as Mina, as all other domestics, went home for Christmas and New Year.

He told me that he was on his way to the airport to meet his mother who was coming to visit for a week. She was a beautiful old lady and a mother-in-law to treasure. It was an awkward situation as I could feel he did not know how to ask his question and he really looked sad.

"What is it, Richard? What do you want to ask?" He looked at me with sadness in his eyes, and asked; "Why did you not tell me about Ernie and Martie?"

"I tried, I phoned the bank where you worked, but you were in a meeting at that time so I left it. Remember when I left him at your place and drove all the way home at 1 a.m. and you brought him home the next morning? Did you not find it strange then that I would have done such a thing, completely out of character? Richard, what would you have done anyhow, listen and believe their version, or would you have believed me? It was just a difficult situation, and I really did not want you to be hurt. Anyhow, it is water under the bridge and both of us are just in a horrible situation that we cannot escape. Marriage for you is as sacred as it is to me. And what about the children? Do you think they should be left to such irresponsible people?"

He looked at me after my little speech, and shook his head and said: "Yes it is not a nice situation to be in, but thank you, at least I am not alone in it, we are in the same boat."

"That is right, so let us just walk the road for the children's sake and see where it leads us," I replied.

We hugged each other and he looked a bit more relaxed.

"At least we are there for each other. If you feel like talking, I am here my friend. You had better go now, your mum is waiting," I said.

Years later when their children were grown up he divorced her and is now happily married. I am so glad for him.

Another change pending

Another kink in the cable, another change. We were at Polly's house one Sunday afternoon when Alan and his family walked in, the children very excited. They were looking for a place in the country, away from city life. They had found a ten-acre smallholding in Walker's Fruit Farms near de Deur, also near Uncle Dick and Aunt Hetty's farm. I was glad for them, as Rosettenville, where they lived, was not the safest place for small children. They were due to move soon. We were all invited to come for a visit the following weekend. It set Ernie off, he also now wanted a place in the country. He would be able to keep chickens and cattle, pigs and he kept on naming what he could do on a place like that.

I thought to myself: Oh yeah, and who is going to do all the work?

He was quick on the draw but very slow on the trigger.

With his uncle and brother staying on smallholdings, there was no stopping him. He launched himself into the search for a place to buy. I felt exasperated, as I knew what was in store for me, and I was actually powerless to do anything about it. Circumstances beyond my control had asserted themselves again. With Uncle Dick verbally supporting him plus Alan and the rest of the family, what chance did I have? To crown it all, when we visited them our children were beside themselves and also wanted to live on a "farm". Needless to say, Alan's house in Rosettenville looked much better than the one they had just moved into. Unfortunately for me, a ten-acre plot became available soon after and Ernie jumped at the opportunity. He immediately put in an offer to buy without discussing it with me. Ever so excited, he longed to take us there to see the masterpiece. I was in no mood for this and told him that I was not ready to move. I was expecting another child and the birth was due in March and it was almost December. I was just about to go on maternity leave and the move could wait until after the birth.

As usual, he went running to his mummy and told her the very sad story that I had refused to move. Of course, he did not bother to explain to her why I did not want to move at that particular time. Again I became the selfish, heartless person who does not care about her son's happiness. Being a woman who had delivered eight children, she had no compassion with my predicament whatsoever. I asked him about our house: "Are we going to sell it or rent it?

"Oh I had not thought about that," he told me. I could have ripped him apart, I was so angry.

When we had moved into our current house, there had been no wardrobe in the main bedroom. Ernie's Uncle Benjamin had taken pity on me and had fitted a steel frame the length of the wall at his own cost, as he knew Ernie's character. The arrangement was that Benjamin would provide the frame and Ernie would buy and fit the doors himself. It was the least he could do after Uncle Benjamin had gone to such lengths to help us. I was extremely grateful to him for this. Ernie had not shown the decency of helping him with the installation and nor did he thank him after it was done.

Needless to say, the doors were not fitted. As a makeshift, I had hung a sheet on the frame to protect the clothes. He did not seem to take any notice of this. It might bother others, but not him. Again I wondered under what circumstance his family had lived before Maurice Wright had come into their lives. All that was on his mind at that moment in time was the move to the plot. I had not even had the opportunity of seeing it yet. Also, I could not afford to hire someone to fit the doors as the money I earned was spent on the children. Moreover, as a point of principle, I refused to do so. Ernie had no pride in himself and neither did he worry about our dignity or comfort.

One thing was certain – before we could even think about renting the place out, some things had to be taken care of. I ignored the door situation and left it to see whether he would eventually take responsibility for it. As I expected, potential renters were put off by the doorless wardrobe. Under this pressure, he succumbed and fitted the doors. I felt exhausted and listless.

Ernie had learned something during the years of our marriage. Try as he might, he could no longer fool me. I had grown accustomed to his lying. He started to realise that I was no longer concerned with what Polly or her brood had to say. Thus he changed tack, working on me through our children. He knew I could not resist them. Although the property had already been purchased, the next step was for him to convince me to move there.

"I have not even seen the property yet," I told him.

He told me that we could go on Sunday as he was not working. But again I saw that he did not give a thought to the implications of the move: the costs that it would involve in travelling to work, the children's schooling and my pregnancy. How far was the nearest school? But he had an answer for everything.

He knew deep in his heart that without me he would be nothing. I brought security, a sense of belonging, and stability into his life. He knew that whatever happened, I would be there for him. Most of all, he knew that I would not divorce him. I was the anchor in his life that he had never had before. He liked this, but he missed something important and that was that one had to give in order to receive, a biblical truth. In addition, he knew that, because of my faith, the odds were in his favour.

Polly's life philosophy was simple: "Take out of life whatever makes you happy, that is all that matters." She did not care about the impact that decisions had on me or the children as long as her child was happy. This philosophy was not a nice legacy to leave your children. Unfortunately, it did not seem to work: none of her children were actually happy.

We had many talks about relationships. I told him how I grew up, the love we had as a family, the unity we enjoyed. All he ever said in reply was that he wished that his family had been like that. However, he never elaborated on how his family had actually functioned nor did he seem capable of developing a loving and caring attitude towards me or the children.

I would have preferred it if he went and stayed on the plot, leaving me and the children in the house in town. I suggested it to him, but he was not at all pleased.

"Let us go and look at the place first before you make a decision," he said.

"What is the good of that? You made the decision to buy the property without consulting me, so what difference does it make? Neither my opinion, nor my happiness means anything to you. It is only and always about you and you alone."

Given the pending birth, I was concerned about the distance from the plot to the hospital. It boiled down to pure selfishness on his side, and with the B family behind him it was horrendous. If I was at the first stages of pregnancy, I would not have felt so scared. I could have at least familiarized myself with the surroundings. What was going to happen when I was in hospital? What about Ernest, Derek and Louise? How were the boys going to get to school? To him it was all arranged in his mind. He would take leave and, if that was not possible, his sister-in-law Alice would look after them while I was in hospital.

"You do seem to have all the answers, but when it comes to implementation they disappear into thin air, don't they?" I stated.

"You only see the bad side of things. Think of the openness, think of the space the children will have to explore and play in. They can learn about animals. We can get some horses, which you like," he responded.

It might have possibilities, I thought. But at that moment I was just not in the mood to think about them. If only he would take some of the responsibility for raising a family. I think I would have loved the fact that we were moving to the country, as I like big open spaces. But knowing him, I had my misgivings. Once there, all the promises would vanish.

Sunday arrived and the children were over the moon as all of us were going for a drive. The chance of seeing Aunt Hetty again put my heart at rest a bit. The drive took the best part of an hour, which to me seemed very far and impractical if one considered driving to Johannesburg to work each day and Ernie himself had to go all the way to Kempton Park, which was even further. Another thing was the cost of transportation. These things had not been reckoned with.

When we arrived at the wonderful property my heart sank into my shoes. The people he bought it from had retired and their children had not wanted them to stay there any longer. They had therefore moved some time earlier, so the house – a cottage in fact, a round rondavel type structure – had been abandoned for some time.

With a great flourish, he produced the key to the house. In fact, this turned out to be the key for an ordinary padlock hanging at the end of a chain that had been pushed through two holes in the double door which was the entrance.

"Father God, this cannot be true, surely this is not part of the long and difficult road You told me about when I was ten years old, it cannot be it, can it?" I asked silently.

"If it looks this bad from the outside, what is awaiting me indoors?" I asked myself. Ernie could see that I was not impressed, so he opened the door with all the flair he could muster, as if it would soften the blow I had received outside.

There were two bedrooms, an open dining-room-cum-lounge, a bathroom and a kitchen, all the rooms in the most peculiar shapes. Seen from above, three circular rooms were connected with adjoining outside walls forming three oddly-shaped triangular rooms, making six rooms altogether under one thatched roof. Being round on the outside and with the curved walls on the inside, it was difficult to fit furniture with straight backs against these walls. There were no inbuilt cupboards. In the bathroom, one of the triangles, there was a sort of a platform built about a foot high with one of those old Victorian baths with four legs perched on the centre of it. What the purpose of this arrangement was, I could not fathom. At least there was a modern toilet and a shower hidden in one of the strange and weirdly shaped corners.

At places the plaster was coming off the walls. The kitchen was in one of the odd-shaped triangular rooms. It had an old-fashioned cement sink and on the one side, in a corner, there was one of these round little black combustion stoves. The kitchen door led out onto the backyard. It also had a padlock on. Going outside all I could see was the khaki bush and weeds the length and breadth of the property. There was a fenced off piece of land which I assumed had at some point been a vegetable garden. There also seemed to be a borehole that would be used to pump water into a big water tank that stood elevated on a large steel frame.

There was a big apricot tree and an old fig tree that stood next to a granite outdoor sink which I assumed was used to wash freshly harvested vegetables. There was a massive chicken run which I knew would not go unused, a milking shed and four pigsties. There was another borehole and a dam further up the farm and near the servants' quarters.

I was told that the plot was on the water grid since the property was zoned by the local municipality as peri-urban. The borehole water would be used to water the gardens and the municipal water would be for household use only. There was electricity, too.

Detached but close by the house stood two small buildings. One was christened "the church" due to its steeple-shaped roof and it became Ernest's bedroom. The other building adjoined the garage and became Derek's room when he grew older. Louise had her room in the house. Greg, not born yet, would be in our room for the meantime.

Ernie could see I was unimpressed. How could I fit my furniture into this malformed house? He waxed effusive with promises of fixing the place. I was skeptical to put it mildly. The children were ecstatic. They ran around exploring the new surroundings. An old couple were staying in the servants' quarters. They had worked for the previous owners. They approached us wanting to know their fate. As this was during the apartheid era, their options were very limited. My heart went out to them. William and Martie were their names. Ernie promised them that they could stay. William could work in the garden and Martie could help in the house.

"So what do you think?" he asked.

"What does it matter what I think, you do not really care, do you?" I retorted.

"You could stop working once we move in," he said, knowing full well that it was my heart's desire to stay at home with my children. I told him I would think about it.

But, I asked myself, was giving up work to be with my children worth all this? Would he ever fix the house as promised? Deep down I knew it was God's will. The question I had asked earlier was just a desperate plea. I felt that moving to this forsaken place held a deeper significance. I looked at the children and they were so happy. They came running to me and asked: "Are we going to stay here, Mum?" I looked at them and at Ernie who was standing nearby with a big grin on his face: he knew he had won the battle.

Afterwards we stopped at Uncle Dick and Aunt Hetty's place and they were so happy that we would soon be living close by. I looked at Aunt Hetty and she had tears in her eyes. I knew she was pleased that we would be near to each other. I had not given my approval, but it was useless as it would count for naught anyway.

My prayer: Let there be peace within me and give me the strength to keep positive and most of all let it be that I am exactly where You want me to be Father God.

Move to the plot

On the first of January 1976, the big move took place. During the week, Mina and I started to pack all the things that would not be of immediate use. It included the linen, photos, wall hangings and such like. I asked Ernie to put them in the caravan. This would be convenient as the truck organised by Alan, Ernie's brother, would then only be used to carry the furniture in one load instead of making two trips for these other items.

With much excitement, the big day arrived and Ernie hooked up the caravan and left with Eddie and Alan in tow. Mina, the children and I followed in my car. When we arrived at our new abode, the children could not wait to get out of the car to start exploring. Mina and I looked at the excitement on their faces as they could not decide which way they would go first. There was so much space. They were truly spoilt for choice. Towards the middle section of the land there was a dam which they spotted and off they went. At least it would keep them busy and would give us the much needed time to try and set things in order before nightfall.

As we entered the house, we found that there had been a break-in that had probably happened the previous night. I was a bit confused and in shock because there could be nothing of value there to attract thieves. Everything that we owned was standing outside either on the truck or packed in the caravan. I looked at Ernie, waiting for answers. We had previously discussed the move at length and decided that, for security reasons, we would only transport our belongings on the day of the move. The house stood far from the nearest neighbour and was badly in need of repair. The front door was locked by means of a chain and padlock and should have been replaced by the man of the house before the great move. In the house I saw a number of empty boxes. They had been haphazardly torn open and their contents had been removed.

"What is going on here? I specifically asked you to put all the boxes in the caravan, did I not?"

It dawned on me what had happened. He had transported some of the boxes the day before to have a head start and had done so in spite of the risks. He had not gotten round to fixing the front door as he had promised he would.

"The caravan was big enough to carry all the boxes at once, why did you move some of them yesterday? Please do not tell me you wanted to save time or money. This way you had to tow the caravan here twice."

As usual, his response was just another shrug of his shoulders. I was so angry that I could hardly speak.

"Explain yourself," I screamed at Ernie. "We discussed this. For security reasons we agreed it was not viable to store anything in this place before the actual date of our move. We agreed that all the boxes were to be packed the caravan. There was ample space. You promised that you would replace the front door that was hanging on its hinges like a bat. You promised to do so before we moved in. You did not do it. Why, why, why?"

As he had no answer to the obvious stupidity of his acts, he screamed back at me that he had not had time to fix the doors or the locks.

"No time?" I yelled at him. "No time? Tell me where you found the time to transport all these boxes here in the first place, instead of doing what you were supposed to do. Your first priority should have been to secure our safety. Now you want to tell me you could not find the time?"

It was with great sadness that I discovered that I had lost most of the souvenirs that I had brought from Australia and Singapore. A shawl that was a present from my sister to me when Ernest was born was also gone. I was devastated. I had used the shawl for all the children and I wanted to keep it to give to Louise when she would give birth to her first child. It would have been nice to keep as a family heirloom. Another dream shattered by his irresponsible actions.

Eddie went outside to further investigate and noticed that his car was also missing. He had helped Ernest move some of the boxes the day before and had left his car there on purpose to give the impression that someone was in the house. Not only had it not put the thieves off, they had even had the audacity to take the car and use it to cart their loot away. Very convenient, I thought. Now I understood what had happened. To save space and maximize the windfall, they had taken the contents out of the boxes and thrown them into the car and left. They had not taken everything and it appeared that the remainder had been set aside for a planned return trip the next night. A number of boxes had been opened but the contents remained there for later collection, I supposed. I was beside myself with anger at Ernie's stupidity and underhandedness.

I just could not take it in and asked him again: "How could you? I asked you specifically to put all the packed boxes in the caravan. There was enough space. Why is it that whatever we discuss and agree upon, you turn around and do just the opposite? All these things had great value to me. How will I ever replace the things we bought on our journey to Australia and Singapore?"

As usual, I was simply wasting my breath. I had not been at home during the day as I was still working, so it had not been possible for me to keep an eye on things. I mistakenly thought that he had packed all the boxes in the caravan. I had trusted him. Now he just stood there, pulling up his shoulders in a shrug and walked off without answering me. Mina's eyes were full of anger and tears seeing me so upset, but with reason. Eddie was very upset, but said nothing and Alan just shook his head and kept quiet.

After Ernie and Eddie left for the police station to report the theft, I noticed that an attempt had been made to paint the inside walls of the house. I had been too shocked to notice this when we had arrived. But between the three of them, that is Ernie, Eddie and William, the farm help, it had not dawned on even one of them to cover the floors. As a result, there was paint everywhere. Even the boxes left by the thieves were spattered with paint. The excuse given was that they had forgotten to bring old newspapers with them to spread around on the floors. Typical males, they were not the ones who had to clean the floors afterwards. Later, in Polly's presence, I mentioned my gratitude for the effort put in, but my disappointment, too, regarding the lack of foresight in not covering the floors. Polly shouted at me and called me an ingrate.

Eddie had warned me before that Boykie, as Polly called him, was her little pet and that she would always cover up for him regardless of what he did.

The possibility existed that the thieves were planning a return trip the following night to collect the remaining goods. As a result, a sense of unease settled upon us all. As Ernie and Eddie had left to report the theft, I thanked Alan for all his help after which he also left and I got on with preparing for the first night.

Being heavily pregnant, three months from giving birth, one would think the B family would have at least shown some courteousness in offering some help, but apart from the two brothers, there was no sign of the rest of them. I was devastated and so cross with Ernie for moving the boxes to the farm, I could hardly focus on the tasks at hand.

I regretted agreeing to move to the farm. Apart from the painting of the interior walls, nothing had been done to prepare the house. He had promised to replace the front door. Not done. As before, none of the promises he made were kept. I was very little concerned about Ernie and his wellbeing at this time. My heart shut completely to him. I could not be bothered to care about what he would do next. He did not really care for us as a family. He had achieved what he had set out to do and that was to move to the plot. Whatever happened as a consequence concerned him not at all. To him it was mission accomplished immaterial of whether I was happy or not. My happiness did not figure in his equation.

I asked myself why on earth God wanted me to be here in this place at this time. I wanted answers, but there were none forthcoming, just a quiet reassurance that He will be here with me. Just trust and obey. "How long still, Father?" I asked and silence followed.

I had agreed to the move. What choice did I have now but accept the fact that this was where I should be at this time in my life.

Things that held so many precious memories for me were lost forever. I was in total shock. I could not get over how selfish this man really was. He gave no regard to the needs of anyone but himself. Arrangements had been made at the municipality to reinstate the water and electricity connections. At least he had had time for that.

With the children well occupied, Mina and I busied ourselves unpacking what was left of our precious cargo. We moved the beds into the bedrooms, or at least Mina did as she refused my help. I made the beds. We were all in desperate need of a good night's rest. We had all had an exhausting day one way or the other. I felt mentally and physically bushed. It was getting dark so we were expecting the children to come running in from their adventures. I hoped that Ernie and Eddie would also arrive soon, hopefully with something to eat and with some milk at least. Soon the children burst through the door thoroughly exhausted and hungry. Mercifully Ernie and Eddie also arrived back from the police station where they had been told that there was little to no hope of recovering the stolen property, but that they would try their best. Luckily for Eddie, while waiting to be attended at the police station, he had looked out of the window and had seen his car. It had been abandoned in a nearby township and the police had towed it to the station. I was so glad for him.

Ernie and Eddie must have felt the hunger pangs, too, as they arrived home bearing food and milk. Ernie connected the exposed electric cables to the kettle and we were able to boil water for a decent cup of tea, something we were all in desperate need of. After the children had supper and something to drink, they each had a quick wash. They looked totally worn out. They were put to bed with a much appreciated sweetie bought by Eddie. Poor little Louise's eyes were drooping and she was the first to fall asleep. There were several giggles from the boys and then silence, a definite sign that they were also fast asleep. After tea, Eddie also decided to call it a day and returned to Alan's farm where he lived. He had a herd of cows to be milked early the next morning. Mina chased me to bed as she saw that I had reached my limit.

Mina voiced her opinion about the place which we now called home. She was very disappointed and not in the least happy with me wanting to stay here. She agreed to stay with us until the birth of the baby. She could not understand why I would give up the house in Kensington to move to such a rundown, derelict place. But when she saw the joy on the children's faces, and after I explained about the dream I had had when I was ten, being a very dedicated Christian herself, I think she understood.

As I lay in bed reminiscing about the day's proceedings, the tears started again. Ernie, without saying a word, climbed into bed and reminded me that he had to go to work the next day. Then he turned his back on me and in seconds he was fast asleep.

If he at least apologized it would have made the hurt more bearable. Instead he tried to justify his actions, and showed no remorse regarding the things that had been stolen. With time one tends to become more and more resentful towards people who just do not care about others. I must have fallen into a deep sleep as when I opened my eyes again it was already morning. Ernie had left. Mercifully he had not woken me. That, at least, was one kind deed he had done. I felt refreshed and decided to put yesterday behind me and focus on shaping this place into something that resembled a "home". God was still in control. With renewed energy, I showered and joined Mina in the kitchen where she was busy unpacking and trying to find a place for everything. There was no sign of any cupboards or any shelves. The only space was underneath the sink, which she had already given a thorough scrub. All the cooking utensils and some of the crockery that were used on a daily basis were placed underneath the sink. The dining-room table and the sideboard were used for the rest of the crockery and cutlery. One thing lacking was a grocery cupboard.

The children were fed and were busy exploring again. At least they would be occupied and we would only see them again when the hunger pangs drove them back home. As the men never considered putting any sort of cover on the floors while painting the house on the inside, paint was spattered everywhere. It was a laborious task to clean it up and it made me unhappy. But how dare I complain. I would be called an ingrate again. Though I had gotten quite used to Polly's sarcastic quips and had started to ignore them, they nevertheless affected me. Eddie was right. Even if his brother committed murder in front of her, she would still cover for him.

Unfortunately, because of the curved walls, the furniture did not fit properly. It quickly filled the space in the dining and lounge area. The kitchen was the worst as there was no cupboard space and my kitchen table covered just about the entire open floor space. My sister Anna and her husband William came through after I complained about the lack of space. Seeing the state of affairs, she felt prompted to ask me if I needed a psychiatrist. Who on this earth would want to stay in a place like this? she wondered aloud. To the B family there was cause for complaint. I was just spoilt and wanted everything my way. I must say for the first couple of months, I was ashamed to have people over. Only family visited.

As for the kitchen table, William found the solution. He cut a half-moon shape on the one side of it to fit the wall. This created space for a person to move around without squeezing past. I bought an electric stove as there was no way I was going to make a fire each day and cook on the little combustion stove which, again according to Ernie, was passable and good enough to be used for cooking. William also put some shelves up for me. Again he had to cut the wood to fit the awkward shape of the walls. The holes in the floor of the kitchen were not fixed as yet, one had to walk carefully and, with me being pregnant, I had to be extra careful. I would wait another two months for the miracle of Ernie fixing the floor, but that would not come to pass so eventually I bought some linoleum to cover the ghastly holes.

Mina and I spent nearly a week getting the paint off the floor. We washed and packed everything we could in the available areas. Groceries and crockery were stacked all over the place. There was no point in waiting for Ernie to do anything about it, so I went out and bought a cupboard for the crockery and one for groceries. I was to stop work at the end of January to go on maternity leave. Ernie promised that I could stay at home after the birth that was due the first week of March.

From time to time the children stuck their heads through the door, and the sheer joy that shone from those faces made everything seem worthwhile. It was only when the hunger pangs became unbearable that they would come in. It made me feel so happy to see them enjoying themselves compared with being stuck in the house in Kensington as father had always disappeared over weekends leaving them at home. Here was so much more to do and there was this neverending jubilance that poured out of them.

With the house looking as respectable as we could make it, I turned my attention to the outside area. There were about two acres of ground fenced off around the house. At the front there was a huge lawn. There were no flowers anywhere in sight. The place was overrun with weeds and a prickly-pear tree stood on one side, almost in front of the room dubbed the church. At the back part of the church there was an odd three-foot wide room built with one opening: a doorless archway. I could not figure out what it was used for, perhaps for the storage of animal feed?

At the back, there was a cattle shed and four pigsties. Standing at the kitchen door, to the right but fortunately at some distance, stood a large chicken run. It was on this that Ernie had focused his attention, entirely ignoring the house. It was a discovery I did not want to make as it reminded me again that his needs came first. I remonstrated with myself and resolved to remain positive. God is in control. At times, however, I despaired, all seemed so futile. "There is a reason why I am here," I kept reminding myself.

Keeping chickens or ornamental fowl was a family tradition that had started, I believe, with Granny Lancaster. It was carried on by Uncle Dick, and now we were subsumed into it. I did not mind him having a hobby, but I felt that the needs of the family should come first and said as much. As expected, once again I was denigrated by the B family as selfish and inconsiderate towards Ernie. The fact that none of Uncle Dick's children wanted anything to do with the family tradition left no impression. He took it upon himself. He was duty-bound to uphold the tradition.

We visited Uncle Dick and Aunt Hetty quite often. They did not receive many visitors and she always seemed so happy to see me. As time passed, I found that she was in the same boat as me: married to a womanizer. We became very close and I became an outlet for all the hurt that she accumulated over the years. Everything always had to be done his way, and if it was not she got screamed at.

There was something I wished Ernie would learn from Uncle Dick. Everything in and around their home was in immaculate condition. Uncle Dick was a stickler for order. He believed that each show chicken had to be kept separate from the normal egg laying brood. This quality in Uncle Dick I admired greatly. So it was with sadness that I discovered what an insensitive, selfish person he really was. Though he was elderly, he was unable to keep his hands off woman. He reminded me of the person I was married to. The main difference was that I was not Aunt Hetty that would "Yea" and "Amen" to everything he demanded.

The Rand Easter Agricultural show was the biggest of all the shows held in South Africa. Every poultry enthusiast would exhibit there in the hopes of winning the top prizes. Uncle Dick usually walked away with a fair number of them. The poor chickens that had not made the grade were destined for the pot.

He was also one of the judges. As show time neared, Aunty Hetty would became a nervous wreck as Uncle Dick examined and prejudged his feathered friends beforehand. The ones who passed his specifications had to be washed and groomed by Aunt Hetty according to the rules laid down by him. Suffering from arthritis, it had become increasingly difficult for her to perform the task. The bird had to be held a certain way so as not to damage the feathers, and as the bird did not want to sit still, she found it an extremely laborious task. Did he care? The answer was no. If Ernie thought for one moment that I was going to go through these motions, he had another thing coming.

It was not long before Ernie's first batch of chicks arrived: Uncle Dick's favourite white and black Leghorns. They were soon followed by Australorps and Silkies and, last but not least, several of the Indian game varieties. They were placed in the room next to the garage. There was hardly enough space for them to run around. There were only about two hundred of them to start with.

There was the chicken run that could accommodate even more. I had better count my blessings, I thought, it could have been worse. With the arrival of his feathered friends, the expenses increased. Keeping ornamental fowl is a hobby, not a business proposition: there was no money in it, only prestige. There was chicken feed to buy and it did not come cheap. But Mister could not understand that family needs must be placed at the top of the list. He did not understand what a budget was either.

One might have thought that because Polly had had such a hard time feeding and raising her eight-children family, she might have encouraged her sons to act more responsibly than their father, who had drank and gambled and eventually had abandoned them. But instead she supported Ernie in anything and everything he wanted to do. No one was to stand in his way. As she kept repeating: "He works hard for his money, so he should be left to spend it as he pleases."

Forgotten were the promises of renovating the house and replacing the fence around the property. The existing chicken run needed upgrading. It had to be divided into sections and had to be securely fenced off against thieves and stray dogs. A proper roof had to be fitted to protect the chickens from the elements. The welfare of the chickens came before his family. The chain at the front door still dangled there serving the dual functions of keeping the doors together and securing the place from outside intrusion.

Greg's birth and the Rand show

The Rand Easter Agricultural show in 1976 was scheduled to start on 18th March. Uncle Dick, one of the leading poultry exhibitionists who had travelled all over South Africa to participate in countless shows, would be helped by Ernie. He informed me that he would be very busy helping his uncle prepare with the administration of the show. He would be checking all the entries from participants from all over the country. He felt very important now. He got caught up in the euphoria of the whole process and even applied for leave to enable him to concentrate fully on this important task. Uncle Dick knew full well that I was on the verge of giving birth, but failed to advise Ernie to wait until after the birth of the baby before volunteering his assistance. I found this appalling.

With Greg's birth only days away, they were not in the least perturbed. Polly approved of him getting involved and helping Uncle Dick and continuing the family tradition, immaterial of the fact that he was about to become a father again. He spared no thought on how I was going to get to the hospital which was over an hour's drive from our new home. According to them, my complaints were nonsensical and I was merely seeking attention.

Due to the distance from the hospital, the doctor decided to induce labour and wanted me to be in hospital at six on the night of the tenth of March. Ernie nearly exploded when I told him.

"You have no choice unless you want to bear the wrath of my family. Your child's birth should be placed above what you want. You have a responsibility here and you will take me to the hospital. It is the doctor who has ordered it. This is not my personal preference. He decided to do it this way since we stay so far from the hospital. Tell me what is more important to you: your child, me or the chickens?"

The answer was just his standard shrug of the shoulders. He had no answer for his self-centeredness. This was the start of my intense resentment of his chicken hobby that would grow over the years to come. Little did I know what was still in store for me, what his new obsession would bring upon us.

He did take me to hospital and as usual I gave birth alone while he was enjoying himself elsewhere. He drank up the attention that he received in his administrative role, liaising with applicants. He was highly commended for his hard work and for generously giving up his time in helping with all the preparations for such a big event. He must have been very busy as there was no phone call to enquire about the birth that was in progress. Gregory Hugh Bezuidenhout was born on Thursday 11th of March 1976 at 6:25 am at the Park Lane Clinic, now a Netcare facility in Parktown, Johannesburg, after nearly twelve hours of labour.

Unfortunately both Greg and I ran a fever for which they could not establish the cause. And we would not be allowed to go home until it was brought under control. All I could do was give thanks to God for his goodness and grace. However, a call did come through from Polly during the day to the front desk to enquire about our wellbeing. That evening father arrived. He was in such a hurry to get back to the show, though. I told him not to hang around as both Greg and I were running a fever and I did not know when we would be discharged, but that I would let him know.

He commented that it was lucky he had not entered any of his own fowl. In that case, he would have had even more to do and he had enough on his plate already. I listened to him and thought: What does he want me to say? Perhaps: Oh, how sorry I am for him? He showed no regard for me or the children. He had actually abandoned us in order to prove himself to a bunch of strangers and Uncle Dick. If it had not been for Mina and the farm crew, I would have had a nervous breakdown. If he had had any thoughts of me praising him for the work that he was doing to help Uncle Dick, he had another thing coming. It was also insensitive and selfish on Uncle Dick's part. I asked him to leave as I was tired. On his way out, he did not bother to go to the nursery to take a first glance at his new born son. All his thoughts were on the Rand Show as he hastened to return there.

I had no phone and was therefore unable to inform my sister of the birth. Ernie certainly did not have time or inclination to phone any member of my side of the family. To my relief, my sister called the clinic and got the information. She left a message. She sent all her love and congratulated me. She promised to come over and see me soon. I was relieved. I was worried about the children at home, especially Louise. She was only four years old, and with mummy and daddy not at home, what could be going through her mind?

I was enormously relieved by the news that the fever was now under control and that we could go home that Sunday, an important day at the show, so father would be unhappy. I managed to get hold of him from the front desk and told him that we were now able to go home and he could come and fetch us at nine o'clock on Sunday morning. He mumbled something about making arrangements for us to be picked up. I butted in and told him that if that was the case, he could go directly home, pack his stuff and get out before I returned. I would ask my sister to come and pick me up. He quickly changed his tune. He told me that he would be there and that I should not ask my sister to pick us up. When Polly heard that I had threatened her little boy, she called me and went ballistic. She wanted to know who gave me the right to threaten her child. Shame on you, I retorted, and put the phone down.

Once we arrived home he was in a hurry to get back to the show. In addition, he wanted me to go with him.

"Are you mad?" I asked him: "Have you no interest in my welfare? I gave birth four days ago. My legs are still wonky and I feel weak".

"I cannot see anything wrong with you. You just don't want to support me in anything, just like my mother said," came his reply.

Unfortunately Mina lost her temper and told him exactly what she thought of him. In the midst of the apartheid era, and with the B family racists by nature, he was beside himself. Before he could lift his hand to strike her, I told him to get out of the house and back to his show. He also saw the rest of the farm help standing around us and quickly lowered his hand. He got into his car and left.

All I could do was give praise to my Father for His protection. With Mina's help, I was soon settled in bed with Greg in my arms. The children gathered round and stared in wonder at his little face. Louise, typical female, terrified of hurting him, touched his little hands very carefully. I told her to sit down on the bed and I put Gregory into her arms. Her little face just lit up, excited by the prospect of holding a real live baby. They were all thrilled and happy to have me home again. It had been a gruelling time for me, but also for the children and Mina. The farm folk were also over the moon to have me back with an addition to the family to boot.

I spent a couple of days in bed to get over the birth and build up my strength. Greg was flourishing. Ernest and Derek were settled in Meyerton Primary school and Louise was in her element as she had me all to herself. We had great fun and she loved helping. She fetched nappies, watched me bath Greg and even gave me a hand in doing so. The most precious time for her was getting to hold him. I let her do that until she was tired. Louise really enjoyed this experience each day and the two of them had time to bond. She really became very protective of him. She was his shadow all through infancy and in the toddler stage, too.

The boys had to take the school bus provided by the Department of Education for children living in rural areas. Ernest was a tall and lanky child, but Derek was a bit on the small side. As always there had to be a bus bully. He took great pleasure in slapping Derek around and all the children were scared of him. He was big and in standard five. As a result, Derek came home crying every day. I made an appointment with the school principal, and told him my grievances and he promised to attend to them. The principal was true to his word, but that afternoon Derek got a double dose. That was all that I could take. Father was not prepared to get involved. In his view, children had to learn to fight their own battles.

"Not if the child is in standard five and Derek is only in grade two. Surely you can go and speak to the principal," I retorted.

He refused and the following afternoon I waited for the bus that stopped at the end of the road not far from our property. While waiting, a car pulled up and a lady got out and came over to where I was standing with Louise by my side and Greg in my arms. To my surprise, she boldly introduced herself as Ethel Rylander. I had seen her before and I told her my name and that we had moved into the cottage at the beginning of the year. I invited her for coffee whenever she could manage. With a newborn baby, I was a bit housebound. She accepted. I cringed when I thought about the state of our house. It was not up to standard. It would stay this way despite promises made by Ernie. I could not see the envisaged repairs happening any time soon.

I told her what was happening on the bus, and she told me she guessed the culprit was a boy of Portuguese origin known only by his surname De Oliveira.

I also explained that I had gone to the principal and that he had called De Oliveira to his office and had given him a caning, but it had not stopped him as Derek had received a double dose from the boy as a consequence. Derek was really upset and did not want to go to school. He told me that De Oliveira kept on pushing his head against the window and called him a mummy's boy. I decided that I would take matters into my own hands and that was why I was here waiting for the bus. She told me that he was a real menace and that he always terrorized the small children.

Finally the bus arrived and the children got off. I could see that Derek was very upset, an indication that he had been tormented again. I asked the bus driver if I could have a word with the menace, and he called De Oliveira without waiting for me to tell him who I had meant. He came forward and the driver told him with a big grin on his face that he was in for it. I passed Gregory to Ethel and I yanked him out of the bus and I told him without hesitation:

"I want you to listen, and you had better listen very carefully. If you ever lift your hands to hit Derek (and I pointed to him) or push his head against the window, you will regret it for the rest of your life. Not only will I push your head against the window, I will push your head through the window, am I understood? You should be ashamed of yourself. Only cowards prey on the weak. You obviously do not have the courage to challenge someone your own size."

I pushed him away from me and he scrambled up the stairs of the bus. He was quite shaken. The children on the bus started clapping, which made it worse for him. The bus driver told him that it was a sweet, sweet day for him as he had been waiting for something like this to happen for a very long time. According to school rules, the driver of the bus had no authority to discipline the children in his charge.

As the bus pulled away, Ethel started laughing. I looked at her a bit bewildered. Her whole body shook as she stood there with Greg in her arms. "I agree with the bus driver, he had it coming for a long time. I thoroughly enjoyed seeing the terrified expression on his silly face. Hopefully he will stop his nonsense now. Wow, I really enjoyed that one. Well done."

She left with the promise that she would drop by sometime next morning for the cup of coffee. To say the least, I did not feel triumphant at all. In fact, I felt a bit stupid and dejected. I had had to resort to this kind of response to solve the problem. Still, I was not sorry that I had done it. Who knew, perhaps he would behave himself from now on and in doing so I might have saved other little children from the same kind of treatment.

The following day I went to the office of the principal to explain my actions in the event De Oliveira's parents should complain about what I had done. I told the principal what had happened. I told him about my warning to push the bully's face through the window if it should happen again. According to Ernest and Derek, De Oliveira kept to himself and was very quiet after that incident. My mind was put to rest. My child would no longer come home traumatised.

The morning after the incident I received the promised visit from Ethel. True to her word, she popped in for a quick cup of coffee. I was happy to see her as I needed some company, someone to talk to. When I told her that, she laughed, and told me that I was not the only one who found it difficult to make friends. We instantly clicked and were friends. At least we could share our hurts, our laughter, hopes and it was just good to communicate. She was originally from Southern Rhodesia, now Zimbabwe, had met her husband Bobby when they moved to South Africa after the war had broken out. He was born in the Walkers Fruit Farms area. She had a few acquaintances, but nobody she could call a true friend.

She also told me that she nursed both his parents. First she had taken care of his mum until her recent passing. Now she was looking after his ailing father who could not come to terms with the death of his wife.

She looked around the house and I said: "Yes, not an ideal place to stay, but it is at least a roof over our heads. It cannot be compared to the house we left behind in Kensington."

"Do not worry," she replied. "We are still staying in a garage, as we are busy building our house. We did not want to borrow money, so we are building it step by step as money comes in. This has been going on for a number of years. Your house has been standing empty for several years and only needs a few repairs." Little did she know that my dear husband was not inclined towards fixing anything in a hurry.

After a long chat I knew God had sent me a true friend. Being a loner and not one to share my feelings, I nevertheless – like everyone else – needed at least one special person that could be called a friend. I needed someone to trust, and I found that someone in Ethel. It felt like it was just meant to be. She invited me for coffee the next day and after giving me directions, I promised that I would be there.

In farming communities all over the country, one was almost certain to find a "farm" store, in these parts normally run by South Africans of Indian descent. I was introduced to Abdul by Ethel. During those awful apartheid years, businesses could only be owned by those classified as whites. I learned that the shop was registered in Ethel's name, but belonged to Abdul. Well, I thought, if he could trust her with all that he owned, so I could trust her as a friend.

The chicks in the room next to the garage were growing in leaps and bounds. There was only standing room left for all of them. When mister came home that night, I drew his attention to the problem. I told him that he would have to fix the chicken run properly to protect them from the elements, prowling dogs and thieves.

No problem for him, it seemed. In double-quick time, the roof of the run was erected and proper nests constructed for the hens to lay their eggs in and perches for them to roost on. Special rust-proof feeders were bought for their feed. Only the best was good enough for his fowls. At least the chickens would be taken care of and there would be more than enough space for them to move around in. At first they were totally disorientated. They all sat on their haunches, and it was actually quite comical. They looked around as if they could not figure out what had happened. They must have thought that they had landed in paradise. After a while they stood up and stretched their legs and started strutting up and down along the fences of their new abode. At least they had freedom to move and were no longer squashed into one little room, all two hundred of them. How they had survived the ordeal was anyone's guess.

I wondered where all the money had come from. I asked him if he had collected the rent for the house in Kensington. Hemming and hawing, he told me they had not paid.

"It is three months now that they have not paid. How did you manage to pay the bonds? We cannot afford to miss any instalments on the two bonds. I can tell you now that I feel it in my bones that you are lying to me. You do this each time you're in a corner. What happened to the money the people paid you?" No answer.

"I am warning you. We stand to lose our property if we don't keep up the payments. You have lost properties before and given your family to believe you forfeited them for my sake. But you well know that you lost them by not fulfilling your obligations. Let us take them one by one, shall we? The house in Greymont you sold to my brother. You claim now to have been swindled by him. You agreed to the price and we took the decision to sell together before leaving for Australia. We needed the money to tide us over until you found work there. The ten-acre plot at Four Ways, Sandton you lost because of a dispute with the town council on payment of

151

utilities and tax bills. You refused to pay giving the excuse that there was no house on the property and you were therefore not living there. But the law is the law and that property had to be sold to pay those bills and the bond. The one in Umtwalumi facing the Indian Ocean on the Natal south coast you exchanged for a car, the Holden Monaro, but you let it be known to others that you were swindled. You will remember that I told you not to do it, but you wanted that car. Last but not least, the one in Sandbaai in the Cape you lost to the courts. You again failed to pay the utilities and taxes. Monthly accounts were sent to you and yet you ignored them. The Sandbaai City Council applied to the court for permission to sell the property to cover the outstanding amounts owed to them by you. You were informed but you chose to ignore that, too. The court also advised you of the pending procedures, I personally gave you all the notices, but you threw them into the dustbin believing you were in the right. The result was that the court ruled in their favour and all the money paid for that property was lost. You bought that property while we were staying in Greymont years ago and you totally ignored the utility and tax bills the whole time. They sent you letters and a summons, but you ignored them, and yet you were outraged when the court ruled in the Council's favour. You had no right to be upset, you were in the wrong. Please do not come with the story that the renters have not paid. What I do want to know is what you have done with the money. You had better answer me or else I will get in the car and go through to Kensington right now and find out what is going on. I can sense the bond for that house is not paid. If that is the truth, I will take my belongings and move back there after giving the renters notice. You can stay on this plot by yourself and stay in this hut of a house."

He started to walk away as he had no answers, so I stopped him.

"What happened?" I demanded.

Then he started formulating some excuse, I told him I was not interested in excuses. I wanted to know what had been done with the money. Had the bond been paid or not?

"No," was the blunt answer.

"Now, humour me, what have you done with the money?"

"Spent it."

"On what did you spend it?" As usual he shrugged his shoulders and gave no answer.

"You had better listen now, and listen well. You have a choice to make. The children love it here. They are in their element and in a way I am, too. I have always liked open spaces, but I am not going to forfeit another property because of your inability to keep the promises that you have made. I have worked long hours together with Eddie and William to get rid of the khaki bush that had engulfed half of this property. I have put in a flower garden that I am proud of. Even passers-by stop their cars to look at my garden. I have named this place Rose Cottage and put a sign at the gate. I am proud of the fact that the garden does justice to the name. You have not lifted a finger to help me. You sat against the church wall watching me cutting the grass, front and back. Look at the vegetable garden. Oh yes, you take credit for that, too, but the credit is unjustly taken, is it not? Now and again you do weed the garden when you know your family are coming to visit so as to give the impression that you are working your fingers to the bone. Your mother always accuses me of being too demanding. According to her I do not appreciate anything. This vegetable garden is William's doing, not yours. How can you take credit for it? Also get it in your head: you are not a Lord of the Manor, it is not for you to strut around here and demand what must be done, when and how. You are not Uncle Dick either. Everyone is scared of him, but I am not. If you want to be a perfectionist like him, start to see to the needs of your family, meaning me and our children. Set aside your obsession with your chickens and start doing some work around this place you call home. We are just plain working-class people who are trying to make a living the best we can. These are your children, too, and you had better get your act together, you have responsibilities. But coming back to the present, you will give the renters at Kensington the option to buy and if they do not wish to do so, you will put it on the market. And Mister, I want to see paper work by Monday night. I want proof that the bond has been paid. Where you get the money from I do not care. If you do not do so, I will give the renters notice and move back to Kensington. The children will be disappointed, but that will have to be so."

Soon after my speech he drove off in his car. I went into the house to prepare food for the children. I could see them heading towards home from where they had been playing. After they were fed and the hunger pangs had been attended to they would be off again. I was sad about the instability of our marriage but I vowed to hide this sadness from the children.

Plot saga continues

There was one thing the Bezuidenhout family had learned over the years: my "yes" was my "yes" and my "no" was "no". Ernie knew I would pack my things, take the children and go if I was pushed too far. Unfortunately at times I did take long to reach the end of my tether. But in the end, when I had decided to do something, it was final. I felt emotionally drained after the heated discussion with Ernie. I went and lay on my bed to recover. I knew Ernie was on his way to his mama as there was nowhere else he could go for money to pay the bond. I only expected him home towards the evening. I started to speak to God as I had always done whenever I needed guidance.

"Father, if my prayer finds your favour, I would like to ask for reassurance that I am in the right place. I do not want to be rebellious. My earthly father warned me not to be. He told me at the time of the dream that I should be obedient to the voice within me. My mind tells me that I can do better, that I should take the children and go, that I am a trained Bookkeeper, that I should not accept all this uncertainty and unpredictability. The continual lying makes it so difficult, I am so tired, and I do admit that I am feeling sorry for myself at this moment, but I need to know that you are in control."

For a few seconds, perhaps minutes, I was not mindful of anything happening around me. While I lay there in this semiconscious state, words started to form in my mind. They became a whisper and grew into a voice saying: "Trust me and obey me, just like Abraham did."

"Abraham Lord?" I asked after I regained control of my senses.

An assurance filled my being and I said out loud that I would go and read the account of Abraham's life. I did not realise that the children were standing at the bedroom door giggling. They must have thought their mother had lost her mind, had really gone bonkers. I must admit that since returning from Australia, the initial stay with Polly and her crowd and then all that had taken place in Kensington followed by the move to this place, I had started to doubt myself. I rarely attended church or read the Bible any more. I had really needed this session with God and it did not matter to me how ridiculous it appeared. I felt good and rejuvenated. After they had had their fun, they were off again and I envied them all the energy that they had.

Just before I had taken leave to await Gregory's birth, Walton's bought a firm called Palladium Stationers that had come into financial difficulties. Due to the staff move to our building, I had the privilege of meeting a lady by the name of Jessie Sardini who later played a key role in my life. We became close friends, it was God directed. Jessie introduced me to the Walkerville Baptist Church and also lived in the Walkerville area. The church was not far from us. In fact, it was very close to Uncle Dick's place, and one could actually walk to the church from their house. This was the first time since Greymont days that I started attending church again. I truly felt drawn, as if this was the church God wanted me to join. I started to seek guidance from God again, not that He was ever far away, but my involvement with any church had been minimal since moving to the farm and due to in-law pressures. God was drawing me closer to him. Once more I experienced the quiet assurance that comes with staying open and close to Him.

It had been only twenty years since I had had that dream, but it felt more like ages. I had an odd sensation that my life was going to take a radical turn on the plot. The children were fed and as I looked at them I saw the happiness on their faces. My heart warmed. There was always something to do and at the time Ernest was building a tree house with the help of his siblings. They had tired of nagging their father to build it for them. He had promised them that he would, but it had never materialised. It had been yet another unfulfilled promise. I hated it when he made promises he could or simply did not keep. I felt that while he could do this to me, it was not permissible to do so to the children.

Everything seemed so peaceful and quiet and I return to the bedroom and read what was written about Abraham.

The Lord said to Abraham, "Leave your native country, your relatives and your father's family, and go to the land that I will show you, I will make you into a great nation," Genesis 12.

Abraham was seventy years old but without hesitation he took his wife Sarah, his nephew Lot and all their possessions and left as the Lord had told him to do. He trusted God in every situation as, though he had encountered many dangers, his faith never wavered.

In Hebrew eleven we are reminded of this faith:

*HEB 11:8 By **faith** Abraham, when called to go to a place he would later receive as his inheritance, obeyed and went, even though he did not know where he was going. ⁹ By **faith** he made his home in the Promised Land like a stranger in a foreign country; he lived in tents, as did Isaac and Jacob, who were heirs with him of the same promise. ¹⁰ For he was looking forward to the city with foundations, whose architect and builder is God.*

HEB 11:11 By faith Abraham, even though he was past age--and Sarah herself was barren--was enabled to become a father because he considered him faithful who had made the promise. ¹² And so from this one man, and he as good as dead, came descendants as numerous as the stars in the sky and as countless as the sand on the seashore.

It was as if the Lord wanted me to know that, even if I could not see the end of the tunnel, I was to take comfort through the faith that He would always be there for me. He would protect, comfort and guide me. Through faith in God, He would pick me up when I fell, give me strength when weak, and stay by my side till the very end, no matter what the outcome would be.

With renewed strength, I got up and went to investigate what the children had been up to. Quite high up in a tree, they had constructed a platform from pieces of wood they had collected. It was large enough for them to sit on and hide between the branches. Ernest showed a lot of initiative for his age, then only eleven. While we were admiring his handy work, father arrived from his trip. He was in a foul mood. The children were so excited to show him their work. Before he could start criticising, I gave him one of my looks. Instead of sending them off, as was his habit, perhaps feeling guilty, he became uncharacteristically generous and praised the treehouse they had built. Sometimes with just one look, I could stop him dead in his tracks. It was moments like these that made me realise that God was with me.

The kids were happy and I went to make tea. Once in the house, I asked him what had happened. He told me that the renters had absconded.

"You really want me to believe that? Before you left, you told me that you had spent the money. If they had paid you, why would they just take off?"

The story changed. He said that they had decided that they would rather move. To avoid further confrontation, I asked him about the bond payment. I was told that he gave the account details to his mother and that she would make the payment. The bank where the bond was held was not far from where she worked.

"Did you tell her why it had not been paid?"

I could see his brain ticking along at breakneck speed searching for a convincing answer. None came.

"Did you tell her I was to blame?" No answer, so I knew that I had been blamed for the fiasco.

From experience with Polly I knew there was nothing I could tell her to refute the story he had told, she simply never believed a word I said.

"What is going to happen now? Are we going to put the Kensington house on the market? I am not prepared to go through this trouble each month," I said.

The house was sold and the proceeds were enough to pay off the first bond and most of the bond on the plot. I insisted on using part of it to renovate the farm house. He agreed, but little did he know that I had transferred the money set aside for this purpose into my account. I wanted to make sure the work on the house would be completed. I also told him I would get a professional to do the job. He nearly had a heart attack.

"I will do it," he shouted. According to his family, he was a great handyman. However, having seen the outcome of his efforts thus far, I had my doubts.

"All right," I said. "But I will make sure that it is done to perfection."

He wanted to know what had happened to the money for the renovations. I told him that I had put in on my account and that I would make sure that it was spent wisely and in the interests of us all. He was not at all happy, but kept quiet. After a couple of weeks of renovating the house, he got tired of it. Apart from going to and from work, he could go nowhere. Every spare moment I made sure that he was working on the house. At last he finished the renovating and I cannot say who was more relieved, he or I.

The bathroom was no longer an eyesore. A new bath was installed and the one standing on a pedestal was removed. The toilet was also replaced and we had a wash basin. There were proper cupboards in the bedrooms plus carpet tiles were laid in the bedrooms and lounge.

The chickens were relocated. The outside rooms were renovated for the boys. It was still a bit early as the boys were still too young, but I kept them under lock and key to prevent Ernie from using them as locations for his next hare-brained adventures.

With that under my belt, I could relax as I would not have to worry about the rent not being paid, or Mister using the money for his pleasure. I felt a bit happier.

But it was not to last. Now that the renovations were done, the vegetable gardens flourishing, Ernie started to work night shift on a permanent basis so that he could have his days free. He was hardly ever at home. What he got up to only he knew as I was at home. We rarely went anywhere with him unless we were visiting family. When I asked him where he was I was told to mind my own business.

One summer day he came home with a horse, a beautiful chestnut. I loved horses. My grandparents had had a farm, and as kids we loved going there just to ride the horses. When I asked where he had bought it, he told me from across the road and that he had paid something like three hundred rand for it.

"But it is lame in the one back foot," I said.

He looked at me and replied condescendingly: "That is why it was so cheap."

I looked at him and just shook my head. Derek and Louise were thrilled, but he would not let anyone touch it. On the Saturday of that week he disappeared together with the children. He returned a few hours later with a pony, Tiekie, that he had bought for the children as it was also cheap. It had belonged to the Boswell Willkie Circus. Their base of operation was in Henley on Klip, not far from the plot.

Derek, Louise and Greg took turns riding on Tiekie's back. As she was trained for the circus, all she knew was to walk in circles. About a month later, I saw him coming through the gate with a horse trailer in tow. "And what is this now, what has he been up to?" I asked myself.

There in all their glory were two speckled grey horses, one for Derek and one for Louise.

Exasperated, I looked aghast and asked him: "What is this now?"

"Oh, stop moaning, you do not want the children to enjoy themselves."

"That is not the point, where do you get the money from, and what about the cost involved in feeding and caring for them?"

At least Derek and Louise took care of their horses, but his horse, well she was looked after by William.

Yes, it did seem as if I was always moaning, but for goodness' sake, there was just no end to this man's spending. A real worrywart, I was.

Again, I asked him where he got the money from, and how he planned to cover the maintenance costs. They would need special horse feed which was expensive.

"We will manage. The vegetable garden is coming on nicely, you will save on that and it is nearly time to slaughter one of the bullocks. Then you will have meat for a long time."

"There are other expenses you know: water and lights, paying for the horse feed and petrol to get to work. There is still part of the bond to pay and we still need to buy groceries. We cannot plant coffee, tea, flour, soap, toothpaste and the detergents one needs for the house. And don't forget the school fees and books. And where are you going to put the horses and the pony?"

"Oh, for the moment, they will stay in the pigsties until I can build proper stables."

"And the pigs?" I asked.

"Oh, they will just have to double up in the meantime."

There were only two, a male and a female, but the female was pregnant.

"Are you aware that the female is pregnant and cannot double up with the male?"

I was tempted to ask him how many brain cells he had as I just could not believe that one could be so short-sighted. There were four pigsties, two were occupied. I left him standing there and walked away.

Once back in the house, I prayed for strength and insight: "Father God, please help me here before I have a heart attack. Teach me how to cope without stressing."

"Do you trust me, Maria?"

"Yes Lord."

"Do you really trust me?"

I felt ashamed and again said yes. That stopped me in my tracks.

"Learn to take one day at a time. I will give you peace and do not fret. You will survive, trust me."

I got the picture, and from that day onwards I left Ernie to his foolishness, as he had a total lack of common sense. As long as it did not interfere with me or the children, he could do what pleased him.

Another batch of chickens arrived and he wanted to use the outside room reserved for Derek. I told him over my dead body would he put the chickens in that room. The room had been painted and carpeted and now he wanted to put chickens inside.

"I do not think so," I said.

After much howling and moaning he settled for the room without a door at the back of the church.

"You had better put a door there for protection," I told him. "The dogs might get in or perhaps a cat."

Instead he improvised. He got a piece of hardboard and placed it in the doorway. I just looked at him and shook my head. I had decided to be obedient and I was not going to worry about his lack of foresight any longer.

It was not long when a cat discovered the free food ready for the taking and caused considerable mischief. Ernie heard the noise and came running. He screamed at me and demanded to know whether I was deaf.

"Why?" I asked him. I had heard the noise, but had left it as it was his business.

"Can you not see or hear the commotion. A cat is killing my chickens."

I shrugged my shoulders and went back to the house. What happened next was shocking. It is unbelievable that a man can be so cruel. First thing I heard were the screams of the children. Ernie had gotten hold of the cat by the tail and was hitting it against the wall. The cat was screeching and the children were crying. He ignored them. He was completely out of control.

I calmly took the children into the house and tried to distract them by switching on the television. I asked them to sit there with me. They were visibly very upset, but slowly they became enthralled by a show and started to relaxed.

William came running from his room where he'd been taking lunch. He just looked at the chaos, and shook his head. He started to clean up the mess and removed the dead cat.

That day I got a wee insight into the way Ernie and his siblings had likely grown up, most of the time exposed to violence in various forms. I kept my thoughts to myself, and went outside to assess the damage. I did not know how many chickens there had been. They normally came in batches of one to two hundred. There were quite a few dead ones.

He looked at me, but my face must have said: "I told you so." This was not a time to lecture him but I think he got the idea. The old pair of front doors was lying in the garage. It had been replaced by a proper front door during the renovations. William went to fetch it and soon a reasonably safe barricade had been erected. It took them all of twenty minutes.

"Now why, I ask, did you not do this in the first place?" He just shook his head. I went into the house to prepare the evening meal and after he ate he left for work without saying a word. Not even goodbye. Because of the commotion, I allowed the children to watch an extra show and they were thrilled.

The following morning when he arrived home I asked him to sit down. First he wanted to avoid the situation and started to make excuses, but I firmly insisted. I wanted to ask him something.

"Taking everything into consideration, what do you want from life?"

He looked at me as if I was speaking Chinese, and told me he was happy with things as they were.

"You might be happy, but have you considered me, do you really care how I feel?"

Looking at me he said: "You have to make your own life, whatever makes you happy."

"With what? I have the garden, but there is no money for my hobbies. To be married is to share, to care for each other, especially one's feelings. Happiness means working and doing things together, enjoying and cherishing the moments we spend together as a family. Taking pride in what each one of us achieves. It is not a one-sided affair. We've had this conversation a number of times already, and every time you promise me that you will bring up your side by treating me as a human being and not someone that happens to be here to look after you. You work at night, and during the day you are all over the place. We seldom see you. Yes, you bought the horses for Derek and Louise and a pony for Greg, but what about Ernest, what about me? Why? Marriage brings responsibilities, and any man should see that his family is well cared for. We should be there for each other, but you are never here, always helping other people and we have to wait as there is never time for us? What do you want from life? What have you given? You promised so many things, some have come to pass only because of me fighting for them, and the rest were dumped along the wayside. There is no money for me to go and buy anything to keep me busy. It is just about you and you alone. When are you going to build the stables for the horses? I am getting very tired of hoping you will spend more time with us. Also after all the years I still feel like an outsider in your family. Everything I do is wrong, I am always accused by your mother of being selfish, and I always just want things my way. I do not want things my way, what I want is a family. I want to discuss our future, our children's future, and things that concern us. I want a family that does things together, I want someone to talk to, and I want to be loved."

I paused awhile and then continued.

"What I am trying to do is to create unity in our family. I want us to feel secure. I want to know that I can trust you to care for us. I want our children to feel safe and that they can come to us for anything and not feel scared to approach us. In essence, I want us to be happy as a family. The children are happy to be staying here and so am I, but you are never here. Why? Do you not want to spend time with me and the children? If you do not want to spend time with me, we might as well get divorced. I would not like to spend my life in this manner, and I do not want my children to grow up without their natural father. What do you want? I am not fighting with you, I just want to know where to go from here, and what is it that you want? There are limits to what one can spend, and you are just spending as if there is a bottomless pit of money. I am tired of promises. The horses for instance, were they necessary? Why only for Derek and Louise? What have you bought for Ernest? I suppose Ticky is for Greg. What about me? You do not even discuss anything with me or ask my opinion. It is just insane. You want a wife and children, and I suppose they make you feel secure, but you are not willing to spend time with us. You must remember there is also a limit to what one can endure," I concluded.

"You must find something to keep you busy. Stop expecting me to be at your beck and call all day. You have wasted enough of my time. Now stop hoping as it is not going to happen. I need to go now as I promised someone that I would be there by ten," he said, and with that, he left.

The wind was completely taken out of me. I felt like a proper idiot. I would really have to reassess my life, I thought. As usual I asked for guidance, and again I felt comforted. Not knowing what to do, I was sure I would find an answer soon. Still, it was a cruel blow. Except for himself, Ernie was not interested in anything or anybody.

I found it odd that he had not mentioned the friend's name. I started to wonder what he was up to this time. My thoughts went to his love for women. I had noticed a lady about four plots from ours who rode passed the property on horseback each day around noon, and I also noticed that Ernie had developed a habit of busying himself in the vegetable garden at around the same time. I knew him and I hated these thoughts coming into my mind.

Since Gregory's birth there was had been no intimacy between us and it did not bother me. Before he could get to the car to go meet his friend, he was interrupted by the arrival of this lady. She did not ride past but ventured onto our property. He was quick to help her dismount. I smiled at this. I wondered about his friend who, only a few minutes before, he had been so anxious to meet.

She explained that she had seen him there ever busy in the vegetable garden and she was curious to know how he did it. Had he green fingers? She had been trying to create a vegetable garden and thus far all her efforts had been in vain as the seeds just refused to sprout.

"Could you please come and have a look at my garden and give me some advice?" she asked him, then turned to me: "You do not mind, do you?"

"No I really do not mind but for the record, the vegetable garden is not his doing, and neither is the front garden, but you are welcome to his advice. I do hope he will help you to plant the seed and that his knowledge might inspire them to grow," I answered with a big smile.

"Oh, and do not forget your friend that is waiting for you," I reminded him.

I got such a dirty look from Ernie at that moment. If looks could kill, I would have been ten feet under. I was so tired of him taking credit for things he had not done.

Everything was taken care of at home. The animals were fed, cages were cleaned, gardens were in fine shape, but the fences needed attention. Now, however, he was on his way to show someone how to plant seeds. What about the other friend who was waiting for him? Where was the logic?

When he came back after about two hours, he avoided me, but I felt nasty, and asked him if the seeds had been planted.

"Yes," he answered, but could not face me.

Relentlessly I persisted: "Was it nice, I mean, sharing your expert knowledge with her?" I emphasised *expert*. "I would like to go and have a look at the garden at a later stage. Will you take me?" I asked.

One could see that he was not enjoying the conversation, but he did not know how to get out of it. Feeling cornered, he just turned around and marched out of the door.

"Don't forget your other friend is still waiting for you," I yelled as he got into his car and left.

Again I asked myself: "What am I doing here?"

My mind told me to go, but for some reason I was not sure of, I just felt I had to stay. Trust like Abraham, was the injunction. I would trust, I resolved, even if it took my last bit of strength. All of us, the children and I, were now used by him. We were his safety net. The safety net had grown in strength. It was no longer only an unrelenting wife who refused to divorce him, but also four children that he would have to pay maintenance for if she did leave. We were bound to him. What more could he ask for?

I told Eddie, and he was absolutely appalled. But what could one do? I was up against Polly all the time. He asked me if I didn't think it better to move my children from Meyerton Primary to Broadlands Private Boarding School. He had a low opinion of Meyerton Primary, and thought that their standards were not up to scratch.

"Where do you think I would get the money from? Do you really think that your brother will pay for that?"

"I did not ask for money. I will pay for all of them, that is, Ernest, Derek and Melanie. Next year, when they start school, I'll pay for Louise and Judy as well."

I just looked at him in disbelief and muttered: "Yes, thank you".

Broadlands was a Private Boarding school that accommodated day scholars, and they also provided after school care. This would mean that, if I enrolled the children there, I could go back to work. As things stood anyway, it was becoming increasingly difficult to rely on or trust Ernie to provide for daily needs, never mind making provision for his children's education. His interest in his wife and children were minimal in this regard.

Once during a visit at Polly's we had discussed the children's education. I declared boldly that I wanted my children to go to university. Polly had almost fainted.

"Under no circumstances will they go to university. Standard eight is good enough for them. They should go and learn a trade like their father and earn money. What is university good for?"

"Well, I have news for you. My children will go to university, whether you like it or not."

After what I had been through with this family, I vowed that they would not intimidate or overrule me as far as my children were concerned. Polly had more to say but one glance from me shut her up. She got up, pushed her chair back, and stormed out of the room.

I gathered my children, and told Ernie I wanted to go home. He made a show of asserting his authority, so I interrupted him and demanded the keys to the car. I resolved to go home with the children and leave him there. Seeing he had no choice – I was on the brink of "losing it" as he now saw – we left together.

That night I lay in bed thinking about the day's events. All at once, I received the assurance that I was under the protection of angels. Seeing as to the fact that most of the time Ernie and I were alone on the plot – the children were either playing somewhere out of sight or at school – he had ample opportunity to hit me like his father had apparently hit his mother. However, after the incident in Greymont, he had not once lifted his hands to me or the children. Since I understood well his propensity for violence, I praised God for taking care of me and the children.

School holidays and going back to church

It was school holidays and Anna allowed her children to come and spend a week with us on the plot. It was good to have them all there, Sharmaine, Shaun, Warren and Wayne. I was busy in the house doing the normal chores, and on that particular day I had done some washing. Once it was done, I decided to finish the jersey I was knitting for Ethel's husband as his birthday was due in a few days. The next minute I heard screams and I recognised the voice of Greg who was almost three years old. He had the habit of shedding his clothes in the hot summer days, and as I ran to look what was happening, he came stumbling into the house through the front door with his head and part of his shoulders covered with bees. I grabbed him and luckily for me or call it providence, I had not let the water out of the bath where I had rinsed the clothes. I submerged him in the water to try and get rid of the bees. I thanked God that the bath was full as otherwise I would not have been able to react so quickly. There was no time to open taps. The bees were going crazy. I pulled them out of his nose, ears and washed them out of his mouth. I just plucked them off with my bare hands. When I was done, the whole bath, and it was one of those big old-fashioned baths, was filled with bees. I pulled him out of the water every now and then for some air. It was horrific. I tried to start the car as I needed to take him to hospital, but it would not start. The reason was that Ernie had drained the tank no doubt to fill his car.

I ran to phone Ethel and asked her to come urgently. I had to get Greg to hospital and, as Mister had taken all the petrol, I had no way to get there. She said she would come but she would contact Abdul as her petrol gauge was also in the red. Mercifully, Abdul came and we rushed through to Vereeniging hospital, which was the closest, and Ethel told Abdul to go through the whites only gate as every second counted. The guard refused entry. It seemed at that moment that Ethel would do him an injury. She screamed at him that this was an emergency and we had no time for apartheid rubbish. He responded promptly and opened the gate. I received instructions from both of them to keep Greg awake. I may not let him fall asleep, they said. Upon arrival at casualties, we were rushed through to the emergency section. The doctors ignored all the other patients who were waiting. The doctor who attended to Greg gave him a histamine injection and said that he would need to be kept overnight for observation. I did not want to leave him there by himself, but I also needed to go home to find out what had happened and whether all the children were okay. I was torn in two, and was cursing Ernie in my mind for bringing the bees to the plot and for the petrol. I was very upset about having to leave Greg in hospital all by himself, but the doctor assured me that he would be sleeping right through the night and he was in the emergency ward next to the nurses' station. It was with mixed feelings that I left the hospital. With Greg attended to, I looked at Ethel and saw she had a black ring around her face. I asked her what had happened. She looked into the rear-view mirror and exclaimed:

"Oh my word, I was busy putting colour rinse in my hair. I just wiped it off with a towel as I was running to the car. I never looked in the mirror."

With everything that had happened, it was exactly the antidote we all needed. She looked funny with this ring around her face, and we all burst out laughing. Once we reached his shop again, I thanked Abdul for all his help and Ethel took me home to assess the damage created by the boys' adventure and for a nice cup of tea.

The bees were still in a state of extreme agitation and were swarming and attacking anything that moved. Martie, Williams's wife, chased the children into the house, closed all the doors and windows and kept the children inside with the exception of Ernest Junior. He was busy studying the bees. I nearly had a heart attack. Luckily Sharmaine, my sisters' daughter, and Louise were playing in her bedroom. They had not seen the ordeal, and thankfully they had not been stung.

The bees formed a column hanging in mid-air. Ernest wanted to know why. I supposed that they were protecting their queen. It was weird to watch their reaction to the disturbance of their hive. It was with great relief that we witnessed their sudden decision to move off. I had never experienced anything like that before. Amazingly, though Ernest had been so close to the bees, he had not been stung once.

The doors and windows were opened again. It was a sweltering hot day. The kids were anxious to know how Gregory was doing. I told them what had happened at the hospital. From their guilt-ridden faces I could tell that it had been the boys who had prompted the swarming. They were sorry for their part in causing the horrendous experience and promised they would never, ever interfere with bees again.

They all started to talk at once so I lifted my hands to quiet them all and asked Ernest what had happened. He told me that they had wanted to take some honey from the hive, so to get rid of the bees, they had stuck a broomstick into the hive. The next thing they knew, all the bees came swarming out and started attacking them. Gregory, the smallest of them all, had been left behind after they had run to get away from the bees. As he had been in the habit of taking his clothes off on hot days, he was the easiest target for the bees, and they took revenge upon him.

Shaun had a sting or two, but the rest of them were lucky and had escaped the onslaught. Apart from Greg, the bees attacked the poultry and livestock. William opened the intermediate gates and chased the calves to the far end of the property, but fourteen chickens were stung to death and also four ducks.

I was angry at the children, but on the other hand, I thought that they had not known the implications of their actions. They had received an enormous fright and a lesson had been learned that day that they would never forget: one does not mess with bees as it can be life threatening. After tea, Ethel took her leave and the children settled down in front of the television. I supposed that the outdoor adventures of the day had exhausted them. They preferred to stay indoors. They all sat still in the lounge area in front of the television.

I phoned my sister and told her about the episode and assured her that apart from Greg, the rest had come off lightly. Ernest had been the luckiest one as he had escaped without being stung. She told me that our father had been like that. In his younger days he was the one who had been called upon to either remove a swarm of bees or to extract honey from them. The bees never attacked him and it was the same with Ernest, he stood there and not a bee bothered to touch him.

Shaun had a bit of a swollen lip, but Anna told me not to worry about it. They would be there on Sunday to visit and fetch the children as school would be starting the following week. I asked Ernest why he had stared at the column of bees. He just shrugged his shoulders and said he wanted to see why they formed such a peculiar formation, but failed to form an opinion. This event occurred in the days before the marvel called the computer had come into existence; if it existed then, he would certainly have been searching the web for answers. The curiosity to find out *why* and *how* stemmed from my father's inborn thirst for knowledge. Ernest and I had the same trait. I wondered at times what my father's reaction would have been if he had lived long enough to share in the experience of seeing a man walking on the moon, never mind the rest of the space programs.

The bees that Ernie kept were called African bees. They were documented to be extremely aggressive when disturbed, and had been known to kill as I can today read in an article drawn from the internet.

"Honey Bees, especially African Killer Bees, have always fascinated me. Most people do not realise that "Killer Bees" are really Africanized Honey Bees. They are basically a hybridisation of the aggressive African Honey Bee with the European Honey Bee. These "African Bees" are highly aggressive and defensive compared to the mellow European variety, which have been used primarily by Bee Keepers for honey production and for agricultural pollination. Killer Bees are known to viciously swarm, attack, and in some cases sting to death, an animal or person that inadvertently wanders into their territory. These bees are so aggressive that they do not have to be provoked to attack. In fact, in many cases the mere sight of an animal or person is enough to provoke them to attack. Even noise or a vibration can provoke a Killer Bee attack."

After reading the above, and taking into account what had happened thirty odd years ago, I can only thank God that Greg survived. All the glory belongs to Him.

When Ernie arrived home, his concern was not directed at Greg's welfare but on the consequences of the event on his ability to exhibit honey at the Rand Easter Show. This he had been planning to do, but now his honey crop would be poor, particularly if the hive had been lost. The bees might leave the hive entirely as they were clearly very temperamental.

Even though I had grown accustomed to his self-centeredness, I was still shocked by his lack of concern for Greg. I told him off for draining my tank of the little bit of petrol I had had, and his answer was that he had to get to the station. He was now sacrificing the luxury of travelling by car and was commuting by train to save money. He had bought a train ticket and he was left with no money to buy petrol.

"I am just lost for words, do you know that? This is your child versus the bees, and you are more interested in the state of your bees than in your own child. You do not deserve to be called father. I hate myself more each day for marrying you."

There was no response. He simply turned round and walked out. Polly was up in arms again, as he related the story to her in his way. She blindly defended him as usual.

"None is as blind as those who do not want to see, or recognise where the problem really lies." Upon that remark, she slammed down the phone in my ear.

I was disgusted to the core of my very being. I could not bear the callousness of Ernie and could not understand Polly who mollycoddled him all the time.

The following day Ethel arrived to take me to hospital. Thankfully Greg had recovered outwardly from his ordeal. Once home, however, it was one big battle as he would not go out and play. If a fly came near him, he went hysterical. I carried him everywhere and Martie helped by strapping him onto her back, as the custom is amongst the African population. I was so relieved to have him back home. He soon tired of being carried. He wanted to play with his toys, but he still did not want to go outside. The ordeal seemed to have been a bit too much for him. He would not leave my side for a couple of days. I took him around the farm. I made him walk by my side until he was satisfied that there were no flying things around.

Anna and William arrived on the Sunday to fetch their children. I showed her all the little white spots where the bees had stung Gregory. It is still there after all these years and he is now nearly thirty-eight years of age. She wanted to scold her children and I told her not to do so as they were also suffering in their own way. All but Greg had taken part in the attempt to harvest some honey. It was over. She offered to have my children stay over at her place for a week the next school holiday. I agreed, but did not dwell on it. It was in the future, and anything could happen in this place, I felt. Ernie and I were sitting on a time bomb.

Abdul dubbed Greg the Bee man and allowed him to do whatever he liked in his shop. As children would, he quickly grasped the fact that Abdul had a soft spot for him. He was allowed to go behind the counter to the sweet section and help himself. I complained bitterly to his wife since it was useless speaking to Abdul, but she just shrugged her shoulders and laughed, saying that she could do nothing to prevent this.

I had joined the Walkerville Baptist church, but had not attended regularly. With Ernie one never knew what would come next. In order to avoid confrontation and for the children's sake, I stayed at home. However, after what had happened the previous week, something within me snapped and I had a longing to go to church to fill the void that I knew only God could fill. I felt drawn to go as if by some magnetic force. I recognised the signs from years of experience: God was indicating a new beginning.

I woke the children early and told them to dress as we were going to church. They seemed happy about the outing. It was time to return to my roots, and fulfil my promise to my father that I would bring up my children to know God. Perhaps, also, if we went on a regular basis, they could make new friends other than their school chums.

As I was getting into the car, Ernie emerged from the stables. I supposed he had gone horse riding as I had not been able to find him anywhere earlier on to inform him of my decision to go to church. He wanted to know where we were going, and I told him and asked him if he wanted to go, too. He declined and said:

"I thought we could go to my mother for lunch just to get out of the house, you know, spend some time as a family."

For a moment I was speechless as this was the first time he had ever mentioned family time together. Perhaps he was thinking about the conversation we had had a couple of days before. But I was no longer interested in any grand gestures. They were as vapours in the wind, they meant nothing, and it seemed only a ploy in the given circumstances, something to put us off going to church.

"You do not look very happy about my suggestion. It is what you wanted, isn't it? The family spending time together, isn't it?" he said. I told the children to get into the car and that I would join them shortly.

Facing him I said: "First of all, you and your lady friend left here the other day for a seed planting demonstration. After you two left, I decided to go to the shop just to get away from the house, clear my head and think things through. On my arrival at the shop, I found a group of ladies and Abdul talking and laughing, but as I entered they all stopped and stared at me. I told them they must carry on as they do not have to stop on my behalf. 'What is the big joke anyway?' I asked. And do you know what Abdul said to me?"

He shook his head and clearly had no idea of what I was about to tell him.

"Abdul had the courage to tell me that they were laughing at your love for women. Apparently there are quite a few that you visit on a regular basis. Now I understand why you are never at home. I have never, ever felt so humiliated in my life. You are the stud of the community, and I am the dumb idiot that has to endure the embarrassment of it all plus the humiliation. I am the laughingstock of the community. The one thing that hurt me most was that Ethel, who is supposed to be my friend, was also there taking part in the conversation. I felt so hurt, so humiliated; there are just no words to describe how I felt. At that moment, I would have appreciated it if the earth had opened and swallowed me whole," I said.

"I made a decision and it is long overdue. I decided to start living my life with my children and I am going back to my roots and the calling I received in my childhood. I am going back to church which I have not attended in years, and there I will follow His commands, wherever they may lead. I will no longer please Polly and continue to live her Godless ways. We have now been married for fifteen years and there is no sign of commitment from you towards me, or our children. Financially you will support us even if I go back to work, but it will only be a marriage in name. The children need a father. As a family we will visit your family only on special occasions, like birthdays and Christmas, but you are free to go and visit Polly any time you like, I will never stand between you. But to carry on hoping that you might discover the importance of being the head of the family and to provide for us in a responsible manner is a pointless and fruitless dream. You were never taught to take responsibility for your actions. You will never change and not because you cannot, but only because you do not want to. Everyone else always receives the blame if something goes wrong, so nothing is ever your fault," I continued.

"I am living like a recluse, doing everything I possibly can to make things easier for you, with no appreciation, but with a lot of criticism. And you have the audacity to take credit for what William and I have accomplished on this plot. Sorry this is the end of it. As Polly told me the other day, you have your life to live, now live it. I give you permission. Not that you have bothered about my feelings in any way but you are free to do as you please. But don't you ever bring them home, is that clear enough? Again I am telling you that our marriage will be in name only from now on," I concluded.

He stood there looking visibly shaken. He never thought his actions over the years would lead to this. I could feel the tears forming in my eyes and did not want him or the children to see them. I abruptly turned round, got in my car and we left with him standing there watching us. I do not think he fully understood what had been said and, if he did, he was too stunned to argue. He had not anticipated my outburst. One thing was certain, he knew me well enough to recognise when I meant something seriously. And he knew it was now over.

For the children's sake, I tried to stay calm. But my mind was in turmoil and inside I was shaking. While driving I silently asked God:

"What is the use of my life here, Lord? It has been one uphill battle and I still have the feeling that I have not reached the end. You said that the road would be long, but how long is it going to be?"

If I had been alone, I would have burst into tears, not because I saw it as the end of our relationship − there never had been a relationship to speak of anyway − but because I felt lonely and abandoned. Physically there was no one I could count on. If it was not for the presence of God in my life, I would honestly say that I would not have been strong enough to withstand the emotional pain that he and his mother had and still were inflicting upon me. A bit melodramatic, I thought, but nevertheless true.

What he did, I do not know and for the first time I really did not care. I would find out on our return from church. It was the first time that I had told him exactly how I felt. It must have been the right moment in God's calendar as I felt no remorse for what I had said and I felt blissfully free. The tension I had built up over a period of time left my body. I could feel that I had reached the turning point in my relationship with Ernie and his family. I could not foresee an easy way out, but I knew that I had received the assurance within me that God would be with me in a way more powerful than ever since I had had my dream at the age of ten.

I was just tired of waiting for Ernie to fulfil his responsibilities. Whatever I wanted, I had to fight for. I was done with that. He had never offered assistance in the upkeep of the property. Promises were used as bait. Once he got his way, they were all forgotten. I was also tired of Polly's interference. If Ernie did not get what he wanted, he would run to mommy. Then the story was that I was to blame as I was asking too much of him. She wanted to know how I dared to expect him to be there for me or for the children all the time. And to think, this rebuke came from a lady who had had to endure a very unhappy marriage. I could not understand her.

All he ever did was act Lord of the Manor. It was a full-time job to keep the plot in the shape it was in. It kept us pretty busy all year round. I was beginning to lack confidence in myself as I felt that there was just absolutely nothing I could do that would ever meet with Polly's approval. I told Eddie how I really felt.

"I told you that long ago. I cannot think why my mother is protecting him so much, but the best thing for you to do is to start living your life as you deem appropriate. Deep down he is well aware of the fact that he would be lost without you and, as you said, the children need their father, too, whether he is worthy of their admiration or not."

Unfortunately, because of his selfishness or perhaps due to the violence that was present in their childhood years, he had destroyed our marriage completely. He even asked me once to treat him as one of our children. If he should get into trouble, I should bail him out. It sounds bizarre but it is true. I told him he must be completely mad if he thought I would do a thing like that.

In some ways I felt sorry for him, but I also knew that I needed more from life than to sit and hope that things might change for the better. Perhaps going to church would provide a new perspective in my life and I would not feel so useless and without purpose. Nevertheless, this was the end of our relationship. Strangely enough I felt no anger, disappointed perhaps, but even this was fruitless. There is a saying that goes: "If you cannot beat them, join them." But I could and would not disgrace myself by living a life of debauchery.

Over the years people have come and gone. Some have entered my life a little while, some for a season, the timing and length always entirely God's will. I have stayed in contact with some, lost contact with others. One person I can single out is Jessie. She is the only one who understood my "calling" and I loved and respected her for it. I took to her instantly. It had been the same with my marriage to Ernie. I had seen him at the age of eleven and I had immediately known I was to marry him. I had not known what his name was or where he stayed. All this time, I had Jesus with me, and therefore I was never alone. The signature tune of the Student Prince came to mind many a time through my journey: "I walk with God." I walked more on the water than spent time in the boat as it was never stable. However, it did not matter: Jesus was there all the time.

We arrived at church and the children were a little apprehensive. They kept close to me. Jessie was already there and she introduced me to the Pastor, Jim Robinson, and his wife Pat. I found the people very friendly and open and it was not long before the children were marched off to Sunday school. They seemed willing to go and went without a backward glance. That was a good sign, I thought.

There were a few churches in the area but for some reason, I felt drawn to Walkerville Baptist Church. It was difficult to understand but one thing was certain: I was not to resist the nudge in my spirit as it would delay the outcome. This was the place the Father wanted me to be, about that I was certain.

After the church service, tea was served. Jessie and I had a long talk. I told her what was happening in my life, and also mentioned that I had thoughts of going back to work as I could no longer live this way. The uncertainty was getting to me. I never knew what to expect. She said to me that they were looking for someone to head the creditors' department at Walton's.

"You developed the structure of that department. I don't foresee any problems if you continue with your work there. It would be less trouble than training someone new." She would speak to the accountant, Rob, and let me know.

"You have done that job before, so why could you not be head of department? I don't expect anyone to object."

I told her that I would be grateful if she could put in a word for me. She also told me that Jim the Pastor was very mission-oriented, and that he was in contact with people from America in connection with teaching illiterate adults to read and write. This was during the apartheid era of our country, and education programs for the non-white population were barely in evidence. The Catholic schools were opening their doors to all races, which at least was a beginning. But there were a lot of adults who were totally illiterate. That little bit of news caught my attention and set my heart racing. If my heart was racing it was an indication to me that this was the road God was leading me to. I felt so excited, but time would tell.

The children came running to me. They were out of breath, but you could see the pleasure on their faces. It made me feel happy and relieved. Frank, Jessie's husband, arrived and after saying goodbye, they left. The children were more relaxed now and were singing the choruses which they had learned in Sunday school. It was in a really happy mood that we arrived home. Ernie was not at all happy about having been left out and looked very disgruntled. The children wanted to go and swim in the dam as William had cleaned it and filled it with water. There was a quick change of clothing and off they went leaving the two of us.

"What took you so long?" he demanded.

"What do you mean 'what took me so long'? How long do you think a church service lasts? And then there was tea afterwards. I met Jessie there and we had a talk, and there might be a possibility that I get my job back. You are not interested in us or what I do. You have never shown interest before as you told me I must make a life for myself and that is exactly what I am going to do. I am no longer going to run around bottlefeeding you. I am not a nursemaid that is going to run to wipe your nose any longer. Unfortunately for you, the part I played up till now has ceased. I have tried for years to make this marriage work, but it is just a one-sided affair. It is what you wanted, so why worry what we do? You never worried before," I said.

"You, Mister, are on your own now as far as this plot is concerned. You never helped, but yet you claimed credit for it. The only time you are in the vegetable garden is when you know your family is coming and you want to give them the impression that you are working so hard. And it is the only time, too, when you are at home for a whole day. You are on permanent nightshift, and during the day you are all over the place, 'helping' people as you say, again I am left on my own, but you forget I am also in need of company. Why help other people, when your own place is in need of attention. Please do not go down that road, after what happened on Friday when my suspicions became reality," I concluded.

He got angry and started yelling: "They are all lying, the lot of them."

"Stop right there. This is not the first time you have been messing around with women. You have never stopped. I have been living with it for our entire marriage. You cannot fool me. What really is wrong with you is that you are the most egocentric, perpetual liar, and irresponsible person that I have ever had the misfortune to meet. You do not care about me, or for your children. I would even go so far as to say that you do not even care for Polly. It was and is always just about you. I am well-acquainted with your lifestyle and it makes me sick to the very core of my being, and as I told you this morning, it is over. You can do as you please but remember: you will support this family even when I am working. I hope to start working very soon. I have tried and I have failed to make you see the importance of caring and being part of a family, your own family, you, me and the children," I responded.

"I am telling you now we will go to church on a weekly basis, whether you like it or not. The children had a chance to meet other children and they had a jolly good time. You could have gone out, as you have done before, there is nobody stopping you."

"Who do you think will look after the place if both of us are out?"

I could not believe my ears. I was speechless for a second.

"Now tell me what would have happened if we had all gone out to your mother's place? Who would have stayed behind to look after the place? There is no logic in your argument, so drop it." He stormed out of the house, got in his car and left.

I went into the room as I felt angry, angry because of the situation I found myself in. I felt trapped and it was suffocating me. I had sincerely tried to show him what a true family life consists in. No one system or rule was a hundred percent fool-proof. There would be ups and downs, but as long as we supported each other, somehow it would work. I opened my heart and I told God how tired I was, and how dispirited I felt after Ernie's outburst. I felt that it was so unfair. Why did I constantly have to bear such showdowns? I had had such a wonderful time at church and my spirit was soaring until I came home and everything was spoilt by his attitude.

I received a clear message to read Psalm forty-six – the year I was born in. I was quite shocked. I knew God had guided me before, but never so directly.

PS 46:1 God is our refuge and strength, an ever-present help in trouble. PS 46:2 Therefore we will not fear, though the earth gives way and the mountains fall into the heart of the sea. PS 46:3 though its waters roar and foam and the mountains quake with their surging. *Selah.* PS 46:4 There is a river whose streams make glad the city of God, the holy place where the Most High dwells. PS 46:5 God is within her, she will not fall; God will help her at break of day. PS 46:6 Nations are in uproar, kingdoms fall; he lifts his voice, the earth melts. PS 46:7 The LORD Almighty is with us; the God of Jacob is our fortress. *Selah.* PS 46:8 Come and see the works of the LORD, the desolations he has brought on the earth. PS 46:9 He makes wars cease to the ends of the earth; he breaks the bow and shatters the spear, he burns the shields with fire. I continued to read until I was abruptly stopped at verse forty-six. I was completely stunned. PS 46:10 **"Be still, and know that I am God;** I will be exalted among the nations; I will be exalted in the earth." PS 46:11 The LORD Almighty is with us; the God of Jacob is our fortress. *Selah.*

The very first verse upset me even more. If God was my refuge and strength, my ever-present help in trouble, then why were these things happening in my life? It was life-draining. I felt weak and defenseless. I did not want to fight any longer. I just wanted to give my children a reasonably comfortable life which would be possible if only he got his priorities right. I was not asking for a mansion, I just wanted to live free of stress and worry. But it seemed as if he just could not conceptualise such a life. "I am so tired, Father, and this saga of mine seems never-ending, I am just human and I feel so drained and so very tired," I wailed.

I went down on my knees and asked for forgiveness. I received a word from the Lord and He gave me the assurance again that He would be with me and would continue to be there to give me the peace that would surpass all understanding. He would be with me and give me direction, strength and patience, and I should stop trying to "fix" it by myself. The door was open now: "Live your life as I will direct you." It came down to the cliché: "Let go and let God." I thanked God for his unfailing love and strength, and with renewed energy I got up to prepare supper. There was no sign of Ernie yet.

The telephone rang and it was Polly. Taking on the same attitude as her son, she demanded to know what I had been doing in church that morning. Ernie was very upset because he had been left at home alone. She added that I should also take into consideration that he worked all week long and still had to take care of things on the plot. She stated that there was no appreciation from my side for all that he did.

I listened to what she had to say and then I told her to ask her son to tell her the truth, if he was capable of it, which I doubted. I added that I had never in my life met people that could lie like her children, without blinking an eyelid.

"Yes," I said, "I admit that he does a lot of work, but not on our plot. He is forever helping everyone else and, according to him, giving them advice on how to achieve success. He sees people stopping in front of our house to admire the flower garden that nicely frames the thatched roof of the cottage in the background, like an old English cottage garden. That is my doing. The vegetable garden is ninety-nine percent the work of William. And it is he who looks after all the animals and mows the lawn and keeps these acres of grass around the house looking like a lush green carpet. Your son sits with his back against the wall, basking in the sun watching us, and takes the credit for it all," I continued.

"And If Ernie spends time in the gardens it is just to walk around and find fault. And when he knows that you are coming, he flutters around the vegetable garden pretending to be busy. I am sorry to say that he is a master of deception, a liar and cheat. The stables and pigsties are washed and cleaned out each day. The horses and cattle are let out for the day to graze. The hundreds of chickens, and I mean literally hundreds as he has developed an obsession with them, are fed and the water containers are washed and cleaned on a daily basis by William. When passersby stop to admire the place, he not only takes credit for it, he even has the audacity to come and tell me what they said. When I asked your hardworking son why he did not tell them that it was William and me who kept the gardens in such a beautiful condition, he chose not to answer," I fumed.

"But as always you believe everything he says. It is Sunday and therefore he has nowhere to go and he is bored as there is nothing for him to do. William even comes in on a Sunday to milk the cows, and feed the animals. Please convey the following message to your hardworking son. If he ever gives anything that is produced on this plot to any of his lady friends to curry their favour, he can pack his bags and move back to you," I continued.

"As it is, he contributes very little to the household expenses in spite of his promises. A promise means nothing to him. But luckily we have food to eat. We have vegetables from the garden and slaughter our own cattle for meat. As a result, I can sleep well knowing that there will be food on the table for our children. The only regret I really have is that he participates in the eating. I still have to fight to get the water and lights paid. Are you listening to what I am saying?" I said.

Polly acknowledged that she had heard, and with that I put the phone down. I was terribly upset with Ernie as I had not been raised to speak to older people in such a nasty and horrible manner. I would have to apologise to her in person the next time I saw her.

I knew that as a mother she had had to battle to put food on the table for her children. I could not, therefore, understand why she would not insist that her son do the same. But she could not find fault with him, and I got the blame. If there was no food in the house, it was me that had spent the money on unnecessary things. It was furthermore impossible to plan. He was so unpredictable. One never knew what would be on his agenda next. I was becoming a nervous wreck, and I would not allow him to do that to our children. It was after dark when he arrived home, I supposed he had been hoping I would be in bed.

The children were asleep already, but I was watching the television when he walked in. He could not face me, and walked right past me. He bathed and went to bed. I ignored him completely as there was nothing one could say to a person who could not recognise the problems he caused through his lies. One could not discuss it openly with him. I put it down to his troubled upbringing.

The following morning he got up when the alarm went off, but I stayed in bed. Since we had gotten married, I had made him breakfast in bed. I also packed a lunch for him each working day. However, after the events of the day before, I had decided to give both rituals up. I felt no inclination to get up and serve the master of the house. He pushed things around in the kitchen but he did not approach me or make any appeal for help. I heard him slam the backdoor with such a force that the frame rattled. I heard him start the car and he left.

At first I felt guilty but not for long. I felt a peace fill my mind. I stayed in bed and had my first quiet time with my Lord in ages. After that I really felt a new energy pulsating through my veins. I felt alive, and well, I got out of bed, prepared the children's breakfast and school lunches, and sent them off to catch the school bus.

I was busy in the house when the phone rang. It was my sister Anna. She had some disturbing news: our youngest brother Chris had had a stroke. It was a shock as he was only thirty-six years old. He had been airlifted from Standerton to the Pretoria Hospital. He recovered some time later though, regretfully, he lost the use of his left arm. Anna was the caregiver in the family. She had nursed Mum and Dad until their deaths and had also taken care of her sister-in-law who had suffered from cancer and had died, too. Now she was looking after our brother Chris. When I offered to help, she started laughing. I was taken aback, but she explained that it would not be viable with a husband such as Ernie, not to mention his family. She would advise against it. She assured me that she would cope.

A few days later Eddie's car drew into the yard. He came to tell me that he had arranged for the children to be moved to Broadlands Private School as day scholars in January of the next year. He looked very pleased.

I was very grateful, and I told him about the possibility of getting my job back at Walton's Stationers. Once that happened, I could pay him back. He told me not to worry. He was childless and just wanted the children of his brothers to have the best education available. Both his brothers, Alan and Ernie, as we both knew, only cared for their own welfare.

New school uniforms would have to be bought, I said to Eddie. I told him his brother would not be happy about these additional expenses. He told me to leave it to him. He would sort it all out with Ernie. He would make Ernie pay for the uniforms.

I told him about the church episode and Ernie's running off to tell mummy. He just laughed and shrugged his shoulders. He said to me: "I told you so. If I can give you any advice, do not divorce him – that would start world war three – just turn your back on him and make a life for yourself and the children, take what you can from him and move on. Things will work out."

"You are echoing the message I received from God. Maybe he is using you to audibly convey it to me," I told him. He smiled, and urged me to do as I was told.

Polly and Maurice came to visit the following Sunday. I waited for an opportunity to apologise to her for my rudeness the previous week. Ernie was showing them around the farm, what he was saying I could not hear. I supposed that Polly particularly wanted to see whether I had been exaggerating about the chickens. From the expression on her face, she did not seem pleased with what she saw. She gave a sidelong glance at Maurice and indicated with a nod the chicken cages.

What was said I do not know, but they did not look too pleased with the chickens. I was buoyed by a vague hope that she might even concede that I was right about them.

They were laughing and talking and Ernie looked very pleased with himself. I then decided not to apologise to her. I was not going to apologise for the truth. If she wanted to believe him, it was her choice as long as she did not discuss it with me.

Christmas was at hand once again and I was not looking forward to going to Polly for lunch. I wanted to visit my family for a change, as Anna could not go anywhere because of Chris and his illness. The B family was a large one and a nightmare to buy presents for. Ernie only gave me only a small sum for presents, and I was not willing to dig into my meagre household allowance, with the result that the presents were not of a high enough standard for the family. I was criticised and was told by Marge, the eldest sister, to stop buying her son and her such rubbish. I had bought him a long playing record but not by the original artist, and it had offended her to no end.

"I am sorry if I insulted you, but I can only spend as much as your brother gives me. But rest assured I will not buy anything in the future," I had responded.

She had looked at me as if bitten by a snake, but had said nothing further. There had been no word from Ernie. He had just stood there with a huge grin on his face, relishing his sister's verbal abuse of me, giving the impression that he agreed with her. I could not and would never understand how his brain worked. I wondered what on earth I had done in my life to deserve this, but I swore to myself that I would make Ernie do the Christmas shopping the next year.

Usually after these Christmas lunches at Polly's, I did the dishes with the occasional help of Eddie or Alice. There was more work in it for me than fun. Moreover, this year I wanted Ernie to take me, instead, to my sister's place to see her and also to catch up with my brother's recovery. His family wanted to know what was wrong with him and I told them, with immediate regret. This revelation was followed by a barrage of words from Polly telling me that only the rubbish of society suffered strokes.

"How dare you say that, do you know him?" I asked.

"No, but it's always the same: too much booze."

This was one thing that I hated most about the B family, that is, their hunger at the slightest provocation to rip people apart. They had never met my brother and yet felt justified in judging him. They did not give a thought to the hurt caused by such condemnation. The bible teaches us to take the beam out of one's own eye before attempting to take the splinter out of somebody else's. My eyes fell upon Maurice for some reason, and he looked at me, shaking his head, but said nothing.

I was happy to see my sister and her family and spent some happy moments with them. Chris was on the mend, but it would take time and I apologised to Anna for not being able to help her as much as I would have liked to. William, her husband, told me not to worry, they understood. Anna even came through to our place once carrying a box of groceries. I was very embarrassed. She told me that she could not explain it, but had felt a sudden compulsion to do this. I was all the more surprised as Anna had always been the cautious one. We lived far from her. For Anna to drive by herself all the way from Kempton Park, near the Johannesburg International Airport, to our place, took a lot of courage. She had had to use the freeway, to which she was not accustomed. But the groceries were most welcome.

The new school year started and the children were all excited, as they were going to a new school. For Louise and Judy it was the start of their school careers. The girls looked so smart in their new uniforms. There were two sets of clothing, formal and informal. Daily wear was informal and consisted in a white and blue checked dress. The formal wear consisted in a grey dress with a white collar, a grey cape and a white panama hat with a band displaying the school colours. The boys wore grey pants and socks with white shirts for daily wear. To make it formal, a school blazer was added.

Soon enough it was Easter again and preparations were in full swing. There was no time for anything else but preparing the precious feathered friends for the big show. Ernie even took two weeks leave for the great event. He had managed to pass the written exam required to become a judge of Leghorn breeds, and the show was an opportunity to take the practical exam. Apart from exhibiting chickens, he had entered honey and rabbits, too. One wondered where all the money had come from. It was a permanent battle for me to keep the wolf from the door, but he had spare change for luxuries.

The children and I went with him when it was judging day, more to assist Aunt Hetty than anything else. She would receive Uncle Dick's results of the chickens he had judged and she had to write out the final result cards. If she was not quick enough, she would be bawled out in front of everyone. So I helped her, and she was extremely grateful, but I swore to myself not to do it again. Later on in life Derek also became interested and became a Judge of his favourite breed, Silkies.

Thankfully, and with all my gratitude to God the Father, I would start work again at the beginning of May. Unfortunately it was after the show. I would have been happy not to be part of it at all and if I was working, would have had a convenient excuse to give it a skip. But this Easter I was not working and I had seen Aunt Hetty earlier in the week, and had taken pity on her. The poor woman was a nervous wreck. Count your blessings, Marie, I had thought.

It would be my last show. Earning a salary, I would be able to take care of my children in the manner they ought to be taken care of. Due to his self-centeredness, most of his salary went towards his hobbies, and according to Polly, he had every right to spend his money as he wished. Through the year there were local club shows, the East Rand, West Rand, Pretoria and the Southern Suburb shows and Ernie exhibited at all of them. Then there were the separate Rabbit shows, too.

During show times, at least, he stayed home most of the time and seldom disappeared. His hobbies were time consuming and claimed much of his time and energy. I refused to have anything to do with them at all unless he placed his family above them. Not that he really cared about involving me and never talked about it: he did not have time for idle chatter.

Going to church on a regular basis became normal for the children and I became a Sunday school teacher. The children enjoyed going to Sunday school. I also attended bible classes once a week on Wednesday nights. This helped me a lot spiritually and I found I was regaining my self-confidence again in leaps and bounds.

To Ernie's dismay, I refused to go through to Polly when she phoned to invite us for Sunday lunch. I told Polly that there would be no Sunday lunches as I was going to church and the children would be going with me.

"You have played your cards and now you have lost. I am not going to allow you to carry on relying on my sympathy due to your sad background. That avenue has closed. But how sad was it really? None of you speaks about it. All I am ever told is that your father was an alcoholic, but that does not clarify anything. If you care to remember, I told you, when your deeds were exposed, that this marriage was over because of your lack of interest in your family plus all your 'extra-marital' adventures," I said.

"When I complained, I was told that 'a man has to do what a man has to do,' well now, you can continue with your way of life, and I will do the same with mine. This will entail going back to my roots. I have sadly neglected my spiritual needs, trying to please you, but that has come to an end. Unfortunately, I learned over the years that you are untrustworthy. All your promises were broken as soon as you had reached your objectives, plus your love for women has and will never cease. I told you before that we, the children and I, will only go to your mother's place on special celebrations like birthdays and Christmas. I never get a chance to go see my own family," I concluded.

I had noticed that Polly did not interfere with her other children's marriages as she did with ours. I asked Eddie about it, and he just shrugged his shoulders, as there was just no answer.

Another highlight was that I would teach Aunt Hetty how to drive. We applied for a learner's license and she passed the test, to Uncle Dick's dismay. I went to their place twice a week, and she was coming on fine until Dick started complaining that she was neglecting her duties at home. His lunch was not ready on time and so he went on. Ernie was equally self-centred. Everything just had to revolve around them, but there was one difference, I was not Aunt Hetty. Ernie would not speak to me the way Uncle Dick spoke or screamed at his wife. He had tried, but had failed miserably. Needless to say, Aunt Hetty always went into a flap when Dick complained, and the lessons were eventually stopped. He told me that if she needed to go anywhere he would take her. I told him "Yea, when it suits you or when you are going to the chicken shows." He gave me a look that would have killed a thousand soldiers, but said nothing.

The children were not very happy about me going back to work, but there was nothing I could do. At least I had the assurance that they were safe as at the new school they would be there until five. I stood amazed as I saw God's hand in it all. I had to go back to work, and with the children at Broadlands, they would have to be picked up. At work, I had arranged it so that I would start an hour earlier in order to leave at four. This would give me enough time to reach the school before five, and the traffic at that time of the day was still quiet. Peak hour only began at five. I was the only one of my family to go out and work. None of my brothers' wives or my married sisters had to work to help support their families.

Back at work I soon fell into my old routine. I was given the job of head of department. The staff members were still the same and they told me that they were glad to have me back. "Back to normal," they said. There were a few changes, and one of them was Martin, the son of the founder of the group, Abe Chimes, owners of the business. He had graduated as an accountant from the University of the Witwatersrand and, much to the "delight" of the present accountant, was to be groomed for the job. Most of us knew Martin. He used to come and visit his dad every so often while he was still at school. He called me to his office and proudly showed me his framed university degrees. I looked at them and told him they were very impressive.

I said to him: "Your University degrees are going to be of little help to you when you want to apply them in the workplace, but that you will find that out as you go along." A couple of months past, and he once more called me into his office. He had the courage to tell me that I had been right. His education had only given him the outline. Real work was indeed another kettle of fish. It was difficult to make it work for you as one had to learn how to put theory into practice. He also said to me that he was told by his colleagues, including his father, that he did not have to worry about the Creditors' Department as everything there was run like clockwork. The system in use could not be improved and that I should keep up the good work. That was, indeed, a feather in my cap.

Back at the ranch everything was peaceful for a while. Now that I was working, even Polly left me alone. Her sixtieth birthday was looming and I had never seen any of her children ever do something special for her. It was always cake and tea at a gathering at her home. I was not looking forward to going, but I had said that I would visit on special occasions so I did not have a choice. Eddie, Alice and the children came for a visit as Ernie, Alan were seldom at home. The children went off to play and I asked Eddie if there was something special that we could do for Polly's birthday. He looked at me suspiciously, and I said:

"I know she is driving me to drink because of Ernie, but I have noticed that none of your sisters have ever done something special for her. After all, it is her sixtieth birthday. How about arranging so that the family comes here and each one brings something and makes something different for her, what do you think?

"You are a glutton for punishment, you know that, but I think it is great idea." Alice said. We discussed it and decided that Eddie and Alice would speak to the family and between them they would get the ball rolling.

"But we must try and keep it quiet, she must not know," I said. It would be good for her, too, I thought, after all; she has had a hard life. The Rand show would be over so there would be no excuse for Ernie not to pull his weight, too, as her birthday was in May.

Sunday came, and we were off to church again. I saw him walking towards the car as I was about to leave. He asked whether this was going to be on ongoing thing, this going to church each Sunday.

"I told you that I was going to go to church each and every Sunday, the children are having a great time. I am enjoying talking and interacting with the crowd. Yes it is great, you should make an effort to come. It is uplifting and it gives one a purpose."

He just snorted, and went into the house.

Getting to study the bible again was fun. The Baptist Union arranged a yearly scripture exam and even the children participated. Uncle Dick even gave Aunt Hetty permission to go, and I picked her up on my way to church. She enjoyed herself very much. A break from old grumble socks renewed her energy. It was an opportunity for her to relax and be fussed over a bit.

Lo and behold, I nearly fainted from surprise. The following Sunday Ernie came to church. Afterwards he said that he had enjoyed it. Being an outgoing person, he quickly chatted to a whole lot of men folk. It was not his usual crowd but he seemed relaxed. The following Sunday he again came with us to church and the pattern continued for a period and he even taught at Sunday school. He was the first Bezuidenhout that I knew of who had ever done that. I was surprised, but alas it only lasted a few months. I do not know if Polly found out and prohibited him from going, or if he got bored, he never told me.

There was also a period when the children went to scout meetings in Henley on Klip. Ernest soon started earning merit badges and managed to obtain all of them in a very short period of time. Unfortunately, my children had to forfeit going to scout meetings when I went back to work as then there was no one to take them each Friday. When I think back, my kids missed out on so much.

Alice phoned to say that the party for Polly was on and Eddie had arranged with each one what to bring. Maurice would bring Polly through on Sunday on the pretext of visiting her brother Dick, and perhaps drop in at Ernie's place. Polly had no idea, as her actual birthday was only on the Thursday. It sounded good and the excitement mounted. I told Jessie at work what was happening and that I would not be at church on Sunday.

Early Sunday morning, Eddie and Alice arrived with the children who disappeared with ours to go and play. One thing about staying in the country was that there was never a lack of something to do for the children. Their favourite was the dam. They splashed around there for hours.

There was a huge pine tree in the backyard that provided ample shade. Eddie and Ernie put everything in place for the barbeque later on. The tables and chairs were arranged. The horses received an extra brushing as the children would go for rides. Louise had become a very capable horse rider. She was very diligent, too, as she would get up at five in the morning before going to school to brush and feed her horse Vicky.

When the family arrived everything was neatly set out and all they had to do was to place their contributions on the tables. Ernie showed them around the gardens. He had started a new project: growing tomatoes to sell at the Johannesburg Produce Market. Margery had a couple of things to say about the house. She commented on how awful it was that her brother had to stay in such a place. I just looked at her, surprised myself when I turned and walked away. Eddie had a word with her, and she promptly went and sat down, ignoring me for the rest of the day.

All Ernie's siblings and their spouses and children were there. The only exception was Gladys' husband who had not attended family gatherings for years. He refused point-blank.

Uncle Dick and Aunt Hetty arrived, too, and soon afterwards Maurice and Polly.

Polly seemed pleasantly surprised as she had not suspected a thing. The afternoon was a great success, and when it was speech time, Ernie took the lead. He welcomed everyone to the great occasion of their mother's birthday, and thanked his brothers and sisters for their contributions as it all helped to make this occasion a momentous one. I looked to where Eddie was standing, and I saw he was red in the face. He looked at me and walked into the house.

Obviously Ernie got the biggest pat on the back, and Eddie was at least one of the children, but Alice and I? Our contributions were ignored, and we felt terrible. Ernie was praised, and was taking great pleasure in it, too. I expected it but I think Eddie and Alice were skeptical about my warnings. Now, however, seeing it firsthand so to speak, they were shocked. It was not nice to be ignored. It is only human to want a pat on the back for a job well done. I decided not to protest and just busied myself with clearing the dishes. I must say they did themselves proud. Polly was very happy, and Ernie strutted around like a prize cockerel.

Eddie made sure his sisters all helped with the washing up and everything was neat and tidy by the time they left. Uncle Dick and Aunt Hetty at least came to thank me and I told them that Eddie and Alice helped me. Uncle Dick just shook his head in acknowledgement and they left. After the family departed, Eddie and Alice let Ernie know how disgusted they were with his monopolising all the credit. He just turned and walked out.

At least they could now see how frustrating it was. Ernie could swing anything into his favour, time and time again. I advised them not to complain to Polly as she would only defend Ernie. But they were not used to it. I had developed some level of immunity to it. It was not easy to please someone incapable of showing gratitude. I had cried myself to sleep many a night, but had resigned myself to it. I just let him do as he pleased. I would just continue doing what I felt the Lord wanted me to do.

Plot Continues, Waltons' Mbathu Seminar

This morning I listened to a sermon by Dr. Charles Stanley talking about GOD'S TIMING on television. He is senior Pastor of the First Baptist Church Atlanta, Georgia in the United States of America. It was entitled: "Waiting upon the Lord," which, throughout my life, I have found very difficult to do as this book has revealed thus far. Life on that plot had been tough. There had just been no letting up, so to speak. It had been one calamity after the other, accompanied by buckets of tears. It is a wonder I have any tears left. God has picked me up time and time again, dusted me off, and sent me on my way once more with renewed strength.

After all the divine training I have received, I have learned, slowly and painstakingly, to recognise God's voice and to follow His instructions, instead of crying out "when will this thorn-paved pathway ever end?" At intervals I became rebellious, but it was soon quelled. It was exciting to wait for the guidance to become reality, but waiting was still a pain to me as I wanted everything done pronto.

Talk about timing. I had another restless feeling troubling me. I prayed that this time it would mean something good. I could just imagine how the Lord smiled down upon me saying to Jesus: "Son, she is in for a big surprise."

Each year Walton's rewarded the sales reps by hosting a weekend seminar for them. That particular year the venue would be Mmbathu Sun Hotel in Mafeking, now known as the North West Province. To the astonishment of the clerical staff members, we were also included which was a first in the history of the firm. Jessie and I accepted the offer which was not well received at our homes, but we felt it might be a once-in-a-life-time opportunity.

We were all excited as we boarded the bus for the five-hour journey to the hotel. Once we arrived and settled in our rooms, there was a short meeting explaining what was to take place the following day. After breakfast there would be a seminar in one of the lecture halls that would last until lunch. After that we were free to do as we pleased. The bus would leave on Sunday morning at eleven.

Jessie and I explored the grounds around the hotel as they had the most beautiful gardens and before we knew it, it was supper time. Afterwards everyone dispersed. Some went to the disco, but most of us went to the gambling section. I had never seen a one arm bandit in my life, and Jessie and I laughed and we tried our hand at one for a short while. It was fruitless – it just kept taking our money and not giving anything back in return. We did not enjoy parting with our hard-earned money. We spent some time watching people's reactions as they won or parted with their money. Either the machine got a slap, kick or a few profanities were uttered, depending on how much was taken by these bandits. No wonder they call them that.

We were standing behind some of the staff members. Most of them were winning and enjoying themselves, but Jessie decided it was time for bed. I joined her, but then they called us back and asked us to stay. Their fancy was that if we stayed, they would win, if we moved away, they would lose.

Jessie declined as it had been a long day. We had left the plot at five, and it was now nearly midnight. I stood awhile, but got bored and left without them realising. It was on the

12/13th of June 1981 just around midnight. As one leaves the casino, one enters the lobby. Between the main entrance and reception there was a flight of stairs leading to the guests rooms.

I started to climb the stairs with a feeling of anticipation. I thought it was strange, but hoped it would be good. It was an intense but not a scary feeling. I felt strange. As I reached the landing I was stopped by an invisible force. I was physically turned around, and from the landing one could see everything at one glance, one could see what was going on in each hall. There was a disco, a dance hall for the not-so-young, a bar with people drinking, the casino and a lounge where the older people were gathering, enjoying each other's company.

I heard the same voice I had heard when I was ten years old asking me:

"Is this what you want, Maria?"

My immediate answer was: "No, my Lord"

At that moment I felt the most extraordinary feeling going through my body. I cried and laughed and my whole outlook changed so drastically, I found it hard to take it all in. I managed to get to our room in a state of shock and amazement. I could not believe it as it was the second time Father God had spoken to me. I was shaking and bubbling with laughter. Twice in a lifetime! I could not take it in.

Jessie was still awake, reading her bible. She wanted to know what was going on. She thought I was drunk and did not look very pleased. I told her what had happened, and assured her that I was not drunk, but that I had this feeling within me and it was good. It felt like I was on cloud nine.

"You are experiencing what the twelve apostles experienced on the day of Pentecost, you have been baptised with the Holy Spirit," she explained. "All the people in Jerusalem said that they were drunk."

I sat for a while, still feeling as if I was floating. I started slowly to take in how gently, loving and caring Jesus really was. God knows what he wants for us. Every step of our existence on earth has been written in a book by the Father. All would come to pass only when we were ready and prepared for it.

"That is why my life has been split in two sections. First the dream where I met with Jesus and he told me that it was going to be a long and difficult road and that He would be with me all of the way. That part is true, as my life has been difficult and He has faithfully been with me at all the time. And now this. Jessie, does this mean that the difficult part is now over and things will improve?" I said.

She told me that it might not necessary be like that. One has to take each day at a time. I felt a bit deflated, but it was true. I knew that I would not be alone no matter what lay ahead. I did ask God to help me to be a true Christian and steadfast in my calling. I did not want to be a half-baked Christian. I really wanted to follow Jesus for the rest of my life.

When I look back it really makes sense. I had to walk like Abraham did, by faith, to learn how to be obedient and to believe and trust God in everything. I had been filled with the Holy Spirit and I would still be doing the same thing, walking with God but with more understanding. Closer than before, with Jesus by my side, and following the instructions given in:

Psalm 27:14: Wait patiently for the Lord. Be brave and courageous; yes wait patiently for the Lord.

The next step it seemed was that I had to learn to be patient and WAIT – something I found very difficult. Nevertheless, I found solace in the promise he gave in Jeremiah 29:1-12 as it is so true: "For I know the plans I have for you, plans to prosper you and not harm you, plans to give you hope and a future. Then you will call upon me and come and pray to me, and I will listen to you."

When the bus finally left I thought we would never get home. It was the longest journey I had ever undertaken. When

I reached home just after five that afternoon, I found Ernie in not a good mood at all.

Is he going to spoil my whole weekend? I thought.

The toilet was blocked, and he had had no tools, he complained. He was sick and tired of borrowing things so he had gone and bought all the tools and equipment he thought he needed. It had cost a fortune and the money had been spent on equipment that was unlikely ever to be used twice. I just kept quiet. All he really had had to do was to dig a new drain as the old one was full.

He did not even ask me how my weekend had been and whether I had enjoyed it. At least the children were happy to see me and we went into the house. I unpacked, and went into the kitchen to see what I could find to prepare for supper. With their appetites satisfied, they bathed and watched a bit of television.

When I started work Eddie suggested that I drop the children off at Alan's place. He would take them all together as he left later for work than I. I was glad for the children's sake, as they would not have to wait an hour before school started.

The following night Ernie complained bitterly as he had no petrol in his car. He saw no reason why we could not travel together it would save a lot.

"Do you mean 'we' must leave here at five in the morning so that you can get to work on time as you start at seven o'clock? Does 'we' include the children? How are the children going to get to school?" I asked.

"Eddie can come and pick them up on his way to work."

"That will be the day," I told him. "Eddie is doing far too much already for our and Alan's children. I cannot possibly ask him to do more. And since I am working, you have fewer expenses. Surely you can pay for your petrol? I am sorry but your plan is not going to happen."

"There you go again, it is all about you. You never want to help me. How am I going to get to work?" he said.

"Listen, I have done everything plus much more than any woman in my position would have done for you. I have pleaded with you, but to no avail. Look around you, everything here is what you want. You can cut down on the fowls, get rid of a lot of things that are just 'wants' but not 'needs'. Let me remind you, I was not keen on moving this far away from town, it was to please you that I brought all this misfortune upon myself and our children. Go and ask Polly for money or have you bled her dry, too? What are you doing with the extra money that you have now? I am sorry but you are on your own. I have asked you on numerous occasions: let us budget. You refused. For all I know, you could be spending all your money on your harem. Catch the train again, as in that case you only need petrol to get to the train station," I said.

He stormed out of the house, but returned soon after as he had not had his supper and must have been hungry. I saw to the children's homework. This was followed by an hour's play before bath and bedtime. When the children were out of the way, he came to me with another ploy.

"I thought we could try again to make the marriage work," he said.

"Look, there is one thing you can get out of your head and that is to try that ploy again. And, by the way, do you know what I accidentally found?"

He looked at me quizzically. I waited but no answer was forthcoming. I went to the bedroom and came back and threw a pile of playboys at him. I asked him what had possessed him to bring this smut into the house.

"You want us to start over again? Forget it. There is no way. You will never change and I am sorry I will never lower myself to your level just to please you. You have made too many promises and none of them were ever kept. Therefore, as I told you, it is over."

I do not know where he got money from, but he went to work the next morning. That evening I received a phone call from Polly inviting us to their home the next Saturday for Maurice's birthday, the first I could remember that had ever been arranged for him. I was amazed that it was a Saturday and not a Sunday. Perhaps she understood now that I would not go on a Sunday because I was attending church on a regular basis. I just shrugged my shoulders and told Ernie we were invited to his mother's house on Saturday.

"Are we going?" he asked. I told him that I had said yes to Polly. It was Maurice's birthday. I wanted our children to know their grandmother, as she was the only one. My parents had passed on before their births.

It turned out to be an enjoyable afternoon, and Maurice was happy that we were all there. We spoke in general, and I was spoken to for a change which I found a bit strange but yet encouraging. I wanted our visits to be on a friendlier basis as it would sooth the weight of the unbearable atmosphere that my presence caused them. Perhaps the reason was that I seldom visited any more unless we were invited.

On our way home, I noticed that Ernie was not in a very good mood for some reason. I decided not to probe as I did not want any angry words spoken in front of the children. When we arrived home, he disappeared to the milking shed and the next minute I heard a huge racket outside and William screaming. I rushed outside and shouted at Ernie as I could see he was hitting William. He dropped the steel pipe he was hitting him with and disappeared. William came crawling towards me, and all I could see was blood streaming down his face. "Ma, help me," he pleaded. Not knowing what to do I rushed inside to get the first aid kit and started to clean his face and tried to stop the bleeding.

I looked at him and I knew he was in need of stitches. The hospital was far away. It would take at least an hour to get there. I looked up to the heavens and prayed to God to please help me as I did not have money and I could not get him to the hospital. I stretched my hands out towards his face and cried out to God:

"Please, Father God help me, at least stop the bleeding." Everything was quiet, and I looked down as I thought William had passed out, and wondered what on earth I would do next. But to my great relief, I saw that the bleeding had actually stopped, and I could see a two-inch gaping cut on his head.

I kneeled down next to him and asked whether he felt any pain. He answered: "No, Ma," as he usually called me. He wanted to get up, but I urged him rather to sit so that I could clean the wound and dress it to prevent infection.

Where Ernie had disappeared to I could not tell, but he came back about an hour later. I asked him the cause of his anger. Why had he hit William with a steel pipe? He answered: "He was drunk as usual." I looked at him in astonishment and said:

"You mean to tell me you attacked and hit him with a steel pipe because he was drunk?" I could not believe what I was hearing.

"You came back from your mother's house and I saw that you were angry. Why?" He replied that he did not know. "The farm workers always get drunk on a Saturday night, and you know that. I should do that to you the next time you come home drunk."

He wanted to know whether William was all right. I told him that I had prayed for him as there was nothing else I could do. The wound needed stitches and he had lost a lot of blood. There was no way I could get him to a hospital. The bleeding had stopped, fortunately, and I had cleaned and dressed the wound as best I could.

There was no logic in his actions. I was not in the mood to continue with the conversation. I thanked God for his help as I truly did not know what I would have done if He had not stopped the bleeding that fateful evening. I went into the house, had a nice long bath, totally exhausted from all the unnecessary stress caused by his lordship. As soon as my head touched the pillow I feel asleep, mercifully preventing me from thinking over the day's events.

When I arrived at work after I had dropped the children at school, I received a telephone call from my sister informing me that Chris had attempted suicide. The police had discovered him in time. He was in hospital. My poor sister was in such a state. I urged her to calm down, and told her I was on my way to her. I spoke to Martin, my boss and he told me not to hesitate, I should go.

Once at her home, I was able to console her. She was so grateful for the moral support. I think because of the trauma I had gone through with the B family, I had formed the habit of taking everything in my stride. The result was that I was able to stay calm under most circumstances. I went through the motions automatically. She had been nursing him for months after his stroke. He had recovered to such a degree that he was almost able to start living a normal life, only his left arm was semi paralysed. He had a friend staying in Greymont and had gone there to visit him. Anna had been worried about letting him go out. But on the other hand he was an adult and had to take control of his life again. Somehow he needed his freedom to build up his self-esteem again, she had figured.

After leaving the friend he had gone to an open field in Greymont, a suburb on the West Rand near to where we used to live. There were a few trees there, but not enough to obscure the car from sight. On their regular rounds, the police had seen the car. Approaching it, they heard the engine running. Chris was inside, unconscious. They broke a window and took him to hospital. Sharmaine, Anna's daughter, was married to a policeman and he told us that, unfortunately, a suicide survivor often shows a tendency to repeat the attempt. This was a disturbing thought. We would all live in suspense now, thinking he would try it again.

After his discharge from hospital, Anna took him home again. It was a huge strain on her and their marriage and she asked me if he could come and spend some time on the plot so that they could have a break from all the strain. I said yes. We had the caravan which was standing there unused. Chris could stay in it.

Regrettably the B family heard about it, and they were up in arms. Poor Boykie, Polly said, has enough on his plate and now he has to babysit my family, too. I nearly had a stroke. Only cowards wants to end their lives, they said. If the circumstances under which he had come to stay with us were not sufficiently unpleasant already, a bout of rejection to top it all would certainly not help.

A panel-beater by trade, he could not find work as his left hand could not hold the "dolly" they used to knock out the dents in cars.

Ernie had two scrap cars he had brought from Polly's place. They actually belonged to Maurice. She did not want them there any longer as there was not enough place for her children's cars. The result was that the plot became their dumping ground. I was of course not consulted. Polly told me that Ernie was going to fix them for Maurice. I bit my tongue to prevent a barrage of unpleasant words from coming out of my mouth.

Chris really enjoyed it on the farm, and he got on well with the children. It all went well until Ernie got it in his head that Chris must do the panel beating on the cars. I tried to reason with him but he was adamant.

"He has to learn to earn his keep," he said.

"Isn't that is a bit rich coming from you?" I shot back.

He called Chris and he showed him the dents, and Chris said he would try.

The following day when he arrived home he went to inspect what had been done by Chris and the next thing I knew, Ernie was screaming at him. I ran out to see what was happening.

"Look what a mess he has made. There are more dents now than before. He is useless."

"He told you he could not do it, but you did not want to listen."

I asked Chris to demonstrate, and he did. As he had said before, when he held the dolly in his hand and tried to lift it to hold it against the inside of the back fender of the car, it was too heavy and kept falling out of his hand. William had tried to help by holding the dolly for him, but that did not work either. Out of frustration, according to William, Chris hit another dent into the car.

I felt so annoyed. Upon seeing Chris so crestfallen, tears streamed down my face. I looked at Ernie and told him: "Your day will come, what you sow you shall reap."

He turned on me and shouted: "I do not need your bible rubbish."

"Wait and see, shall we? This is the last straw. You will leave Chris alone. You have been niggling him now for quite some time, I noticed."

The following day when I arrived home from work, Chris was all smiles. It was harvest time and with Martie, William's wife, he had been pulling up carrots. He was happy, and that made me feel a bit more at ease. I was worried about the state of his mind and this job, regardless of how menial it was, seemed to boost him.

They worked for about two weeks. He would get paid for it and was clearly happy. There was a hint of pride showing on his face. I felt so happy for him. However, not long after, I saw tears running down his face. "What happened," I asked. Martie told me that according to the farmer, he had failed to fill the minimum quota, so therefore he was not paid.

Ernie had to put in his penny's worth and said: "I told you he's useless." That was like rubbing coarse salt into an open wound. I began shaking with anger. Chris disappeared into the caravan and we did not see him again until the next morning. He did not even eat his supper.

"I hope you are happy," I said to Ernie, "but as I said, your day will come."

The following day Sarel, Chris's friend, phoned and told him that he had found a job on the mines in Theunisen in the Orange Free State province. There was a possibility that he might find work for Chris, too, as he knew someone that might help him. He accepted. When I arrived home, he was waiting at the gate for me and very excitedly told me about Sarel's offer.

"What about your car, who is going to drive it all the way there?" I asked him.

Everything had been sorted out. The two brothers and their families were all moving to the Orange Free State and one of the brothers would drive his car. It seemed as if all details had been discussed and all arrangement made. It was quite sudden, the move was to take place that very weekend, and that was in three days' time.

I was still not happy, but with the circumstances being what they were in our wonderful marriage, it might be a blessing. I phoned Anna and told her about it. She asked me to wait as she wanted to speak to her husband first.

She phoned back, and told me that in William's opinion, there was very little that one could do. She asked to speak to Chris. I called him to the phone, and she had quite a long conversation with him. He was so excited telling her all about it, one could not help feeling for him. It had to be dreadful to be in his situation and feel that you were a burden on others. He handed the phone back to me. After hearing his excitement and his eagerness to join Sarel and his family, she consented and told him he was free to go if he really wanted to. Who could blame him? Staying here with Ernie was not an attractive prospect. Ernie had this thing about controlling people, he tried to dominate Chris, why, I don't know.

Anna also said that Sarel was a good person and fond of Chris. No harm could come to him. The main thing was to see him happy again. I did not tell Ernie, but he picked up on the activity in the caravan as Chris was cleaning out and packing his belongings. He looked like a man with a purpose. All of us need a goal, a reason to live. He came into the house and asked me what Chris was doing and I told him what had happened. He just grinned and left.

Saturday came and he was waiting at his car. Everything had been packed and was ready. They had phoned earlier to say that they were on their way. It seemed Chris might have another stroke if they did not arrive soon. I had never seen him in such a state of excitement. Finally, he spotted their car coming. He threw his arms around the children and lastly me. He gave each of us a hug. He thanked me for what I had done for him. The children and I waved him off and I prayed silently to God that He would have mercy on him.

The children were sad, but as kids, they seemed to get over situations far easier than grownups. Ernie was nowhere in sight. When he did arrive home, he told me that he had been called in the day before by his boss and asked if he could work permanent nightshift again. The new arrangement would be from the next week.

I told him that it was better that way as we would not have to see each other that often. With that he was not at all pleased. He would be home on Sundays though, he said.

I told him that Sunday mornings I would be in church and I was not changing that for anyone. He just kept quiet which was unusual for him.

We were moving from winter into spring, and I was longing for the warm days to arrive again. I had heard from Anna that Chris seemed very happy where he was and that she felt it might turn out to be the best thing that had ever happened to him, given the circumstances.

During the school holidays, Gladys asked whether the children could come and spend a week with them. So off they went, but alas it ended up with Louise breaking her arm jumping over the front veranda wall into the garden. She was such a fragile little girl. Whatever had possessed her to do that, I do not know. She ended up with a plaster cast that she would have to wear for six weeks. After the six weeks were over, we were well into hotter weather and the boys made a slide from a piece of plastic they found. They put some soap and water on it to make it slippery. Where they had gotten the idea from, I did not know. They were enjoying themselves and Louise had to sit and watch which made her one unhappy girl.

When it was time for the cast to come off, I wanted to take her to the local doctor, but Ernie refused as mother said she should go to the children's hospital in Johannesburg, which was free, but it was far away. I, of all people, ended up taking the cast off. She was so happy and before I could caution her to be careful, she had joined in her brothers' sliding game. All three slid across the canvas with squeals of laughter. Greg was too young at that stage and his brothers too rough for him.

To my horror, on her first attempt on the slide, she broke it again. I chastised myself to no end as we had to rush her back to hospital where she had to spend the night as they had to reset the arm under anaesthetic. The staff would not let me spend the night with her, and I was ordered home. Ernie had a field day. He told me that I should think before I leap.

"How could you even think of removing the cast by yourself?" he said. I felt rotten. I reminded him that, though it had been my idea, he had agreed to it. I knew the mistake was mine.

"I take full responsibility for it, of course, and that's more than you are ever prepared to do when you make any mistakes," I said.

The barrage of verbal abuse that came from Polly and company was indescribable. For the first time she had something against me and she, too, was having a field day. I kept quiet, and the following day I went through to the hospital to fetch her.

When we got home I told her how sorry I was. She was only five, and in the habit of sucking her first two fingers for comfort. Now, again, the favoured fingers were barred to her by the cast. This time I waited eight weeks and took her to the local hospital to have the cast removed. One good thing that came from the whole episode was that she finally stopped sucking her fingers.

My fortieth birthday was coming up soon and I wondered whether there would be a surprise birthday party for me. Ernie had never remembered my birthday, so surprises from him I could rule out in advance. I admit that it was a vain hope, but there were times when one yearned for something good to spring from the ashes. It fell on a Sunday. The children and I set out for church where I received a leather bookmark with the words of, believe it or not, psalm forty-six verse one: "God is our refuge and strength, our ever-present help in trouble."

I thanked God for these little assurances handed down from heaven to help me along this path paved with thorns. He had given me this verse before. But to rebuke me once when I was in deep distress and questioning him he had pointed to verse ten that reads: "Be still and know that I am God."

I was in a real pensive mood when we arrived home. I parked the car and walked around the house as I could see that Ernie was standing there with Martie and William. I noticed William had his hat in his hands. I felt something was very wrong as in African culture, that gesture was only performed when a person wanted to show deep respect. My heart was pounding in my throat. The thought crossed my mind in a fleeting second that it had something to do with Chris. As I joined them Ernie blurted out: "Your brother kicked the bucket."

The way that he said it sent shock waves through my body. I was in a state of complete confusion. My brain would not function and I felt terribly confused and asked him what he meant.

He laughed and demonstrated by kicking a bucket that happened to be in his reach. "You get it?" he asked me.

"I still do not know what you are trying to tell me," I said.

He stood there shaking his head and told me how dumb I was.

"A police officer came around to tell us that your brother Chris is dead, he kicked the bucket, do you get it now?"

I looked at him in disgust.

"How dare you tell me in such a barbaric way that my brother died? Can you show no consideration, no respect for my feelings?" I asked. I could feel my whole body shaking vigorously.

Ernie stood there with a sneer on his face and told me that he had no compassion for cowards like Chris. He had obviously been a weak man. He had been unable to take the blows life had thrown at him and had taken the easy way out.

I just stood there, and looked at him in a daze. The shock of hearing of his death was bad enough. But to deliver the news in such a callous manner was inexcusable.

"He had the bible open next to him. What good was that to him? It just goes to show how hypocritical you all are," he added.

I stared at him, shocked out of my wits. It took me a while to take it all in. I saw Martie and William standing there. I looked at them, and they were both crying, for Chris, for me, or for Ernie's wicked performance, I did not know which. I just squeezed their hands in a gesture of thank you, and turned around and walked into the house. The telephone rang. I knew it was Anna. By then I had regained my composure.

I picked up the phone and it was her. She was crying so much, you could hear the raw sobs coming down the line. After my mother and father had passed on, she had been the one who had looked after him as he was still at school at the time. I kept quiet, as I knew from the many losses we had endured, that one had to let it out, to cry. She continued to cry for about five minutes.

"Have you heard what happened?" she asked through her sobs. I told her yes, that I had received a detailed account of the event, but I did not elaborate on how it had been presented to me.

"What is going to happen now? How are we going to get the body back home?"

"Roelf and William have gone through with a kombi. It would cost too much to pay for transport from the Free State," she answered.

I was shocked, not for the way it was being done, but just the idea that one had to drive all those miles with one's relative's body in the back of the car. Chris had been ill for a long time and had no money. The family would all have to contribute to ensure that he was buried with dignity.

I said I would come round immediately to her place. She told me not to come as it was too far and would serve no purpose. She had just wanted to hear my voice. I asked her if they had determined the time of death, and she said it had been at midnight on Saturday. I asked: "Last night?"

"Yes," she answered. "He is actually better off now."

I told her how good God was and I mentioned the book mark with the verse taken from psalm forty-six verse one that reads as follows: "God is our refuge and strength, our everlasting help in trouble."

"Now tell me, is God not good? He knew he had taken Chris home, and this verse was chosen knowing that I would need to be comforted, and now I give it to you. It is in the book of Psalms, chapter forty-six verse one, make a note. He will give us the strength to make it through this trying time. God has always been there for us. Just keep the faith, sis," I said.

I did not tell her that she had forgotten my birthday as that would only have upset her more. She would remember in due time.

Her reply was: "That is why I love speaking to you in times like these. God has given you the ability to make a person feel better and to give hope. You are always able to encourage whoever is in need."

"Oh come on. To hear you speak, one would think I was the Archangel Gabriel."

She gave a little laugh, and replied: "Yes, you see, there you go, and I do feel better. Thank you."

It was late that afternoon when she phoned again to tell me that they had arrived with Chris at the Johannesburg morgue. They would let me know once all the arrangements had been made for the funeral.

The snide remarks that came from Polly were almost as bad as Ernie's performance. I decided not to pay any attention to them. It was not worth getting upset over. Then Eddie arrived and offered me his condolences. I thanked him and told him that Chris was better off now as he was with our mum and dad. Clive and Lucille also phoned, as for the rest of the B family, there was silence.

The morning of the funeral I told Ernie not to worry about taking me. I was going to work and would take time off and go by myself. He was not very pleased with that and had the audacity to ask me why. I looked at him with great incredulity.

"I just do not understand you. Clive and Eddie were the only ones who had the decency to convey their condolences, but you and the rest of the family showed no decency whatsoever. None of you even expressed any sympathy. Why should you want to go? You did not care for him. Please do not waste your precious time. Just one more thing, you are talking about our hypocrisy, believing in God. Go and look in the mirror and you will see the most hypocritical person I have ever had the misfortune to meet," I stated.

I could not believe it. I actually felt sick just looking at him. He showed no remorse for the way he had conveyed the message to me and, after all the cruel words he had spoken about Chris, he still wanted to go to the funeral. It did not make sense.

"But of course I want to go to his funeral," he said. "Chris was my brother-in-law."

"Oh? He was your brother-in-law and you treated him worse than a dog? If you want to go, you will have to do so by yourself. The funeral will be held at the Methodist Church, Newlands, as he will be buried in West Park Cemetery where all other members of our family have found their resting places." With that I started the car and left without him.

Arriving at church, I joined my family and sat in the front pew as usual. After the service was over, the pallbearers' names were called out and Ernie was one of them. We left for Chris's final journey in this natural world of ours. Arriving at the burial site, Ernie suddenly appeared at my side. He stayed close beside me giving the impression of a caring husband and even wanted to hold my hand, something he had not done since our courting days. But I refused.

The lowering of a coffin into a grave has always had a profound effect on me. The finality of it, knowing my brother was lying in that wooden box and I would never be able to see him again. The thought crushed me.

After the funeral we were invited to my brothers' house for refreshments. I could not face the ordeal with Ernie looking so sad. I explained to my brother that I had travelled alone and that I would prefer to go home, if he did not mind. He shook his head in agreement, and made no comment. I told Anna I would explain everything when we saw each other again. We hugged and I left.

William and Martie were relieved to see me and the children pleased to have mummy home early for a change. Ernie arrived home an hour after me, and wanted to know what my idea was, going home without him. It had so embarrassed him. I was very tired and not in the mood for his nonsense and said:

"You should have thought about repercussions when you told me last Sunday and demonstrated how my 'weak brother' had kicked the bucket and as usual, you forgot that it was my birthday, too. None of your family bothered to remember either, but that's nothing new. The only ones that showed any interest were your brothers Eddie and Clive and his wife. Just think for a moment. It is not a very nice memory I will carry in my mind for the rest of my life," I said sarcastically. "My brother died on my fortieth birthday. How do you think that makes me feel? Perhaps the memory of how you treated him might fade in time to come, but I doubt it."

"I was only trying to make the blow easier for you to bear," he tried to explain.

"Yes," I said. "Like you tried to make his life bearable while he was staying with us, just the same. You know, you are in serious need of help," I told him. "What was your objective at my brother's place? Did you want me to stand there watching how you were faking your sorrow, a false tribute to Chris? Chris loved staying on the plot. He enjoyed the children, and the openness, but you could not allow him his little bit of happiness. You were forever harassing him over one thing or the other. As I have told you countless times, your day will come and I hope I am around to see it. I am sorry but these last couple of months you have showed me that there is not a grain of humanity hidden anywhere in that body of yours, and that you really are only a hideous two-faced monster," I said wearily. "You might still fool a few people, but you will not come close in trying to convince me that you have cared for him. So drop the charade, I am extremely tired of it."

Luckily I did not have to prepare supper as we had hired additional help. Martie now cooked and there was Hendrik to help William, who was now well-advanced in years. After supper I made sure the children were bathed and ready for bed. I was mentally and physically so tired that I just changed into my bed clothes and went to sleep.

The following Saturday Ernie took to the streets again, going to the farmers' auction held each Saturday in de Deur not far from us. He took the children with him. I had the house to myself. I phoned my sister to find out how she was coping. She wanted to know why I had acted so strangely on the day of the funeral. I told her how Ernie had treated Chris, and the way he had told me of his death. She was shocked to the core of her being. She told me that they had witnessed how he had disregarded my feelings during our parents' failing health and finally their passing on, but they would never have guessed him capable of such behaviour. She was furious.

"I did not want to tell you at the time of the funeral, as I could see that you and William were under great strain, let alone the rest of our family. But, now you know and I feel much better for having shared it with you, as it was gnawing away at my insides. But do not upset yourself, as God is good, and Ernie will receive his just reward. It is just a matter of time, His time, not ours."

No answer from her. I asked whether she was still there. She answered yes, she was only trying to calm down, and Ernie might be glad that she was not there at this moment.

"It does not matter anymore, his day will come," I said.

"Yes, I know," she said, "but I am not you."

"You know him," I said. "He will cling to us for dear life. He knows that he would be lost without his family, and I know he is not bringing up his side, but the time to pack up and go is not yet on the cards. It will come."

"When will that miracle take place?" she asked me.

"When God opens the door, and it is not yet time. He will give me the strength and courage to carry on, and I am quite happy as I am very busy both at work and at home, and by home I do not mean running around looking after the animal kingdom. I told Ernie that it was his domain now, entirely, and if he does not take care of them, it is none of my business. I am only focused on my children, church and work. Believe me. Everything will work out in the end as God has promised," I said.

She had no answer for that apart from: "You are just like Derry," meaning our father who we called by that nickname for reasons no one could recall. I assumed it had started with my eldest brother and had simply continued down the line.

As time passed I got more and more involved with my church work. The Pastor started a program on adult literacy. We would learn how to teach adults to read and write. I joined the team who met on Saturdays. In the morning, we learned the theory. In the afternoon, we practiced. Farm help from the area who had never received a proper education were welcomed to learn how to read and write. I felt privileged to be involved in such a wonderful program. It was also good for the children. There was a facility for them where they could be kept busy and could interact with other children.

I was assigned to teach an elderly African gentleman by the name of Jackson. He was very shy at first, perhaps embarrassed that he could not read at his age. Each one of us has our pride, but with a bit of chit chat he was soon laughing and I could see the joy in his eyes. With a bit of coaching he felt more at ease and started to open up. He told me about his background. He belonged to the Zulu nation, one of the many ethnic groups in South Africa, and their tribal lands were situated in the Kwa Zulu Natal area.

We first started with pictures, which was easy enough. As I showed him the pictures that were illustrated in the book, I asked him if he recognised any of them.

221

He was quick to point to one after the other and told me 'tree', next one 'dog'.

"Now," I said. "We can move on to actually writing the words, do you think you can copy the words written at the bottom of each picture?" Eagerly he was shaking his head in a definite yes. I liked his confidence. I handed him the exercise book. He took it and when he opened it, I could see the surprise on his face − all the pages were blank. I told him that he was to write his words into that book and finally he understood and gave me a broad smile.

"Do you want to try writing your first words?" He nodded, but one could see he was very emotional. He opened the exercise book, placed it on the table and with his pencil in hand, as I had shown him how to hold it, he placed the reader above the empty book and started to copy his first words: "the man, the man has a hat." It was painstakingly slow, and the words were written a bit askew, but who cared, he had written his first words. With classes only on Saturday afternoons, one could not expect quick success. Progress differed from student to student, depending on how much practice they put in once they had grasped the concepts.

The excitement displayed as he wrote his first words was enough reward for me. It was a great feeling knowing that he was now well on the road to gaining some dignity. Over a period of six months he understood the principals of reading and writing and the day came when he wrote his own name 'Jackson' from memory. It was one of the greatest moments in his life, let alone in mine. He was so excited. I was so happy. I had not thought it possible to achieve the results that I was now witnessing. With tears running down his face he did a merry jig. Even Pastor Jim came to see what was going on, and he cried out: "Look, boss, look, I can write my name."

It was really sad to see what apartheid had done to our beautiful country. This man could have stood tall in any profession if he had been given the chance. His dream as a child was to become a teacher. He had been robbed of that opportunity. I am grateful today that De Klerk took the initiative to release Mandela. It was a joyful day when he was released from prison. Mandela is the most loved and respected leader South Africa has ever had. In his time spent as President of our country, and after his retirement, he showed great compassion for the people of this land, immaterial of the colour of one's skin. One famous Mandela quote rings so true, and provides us with a life lesson:

"What counts in life is not the mere fact that we have lived.

It is the difference we have made to the lives of others that will determine the significance of the life we lead."

Another positive outcome of the adult literacy program was that the students could do their own shopping once they had learned enough to read the labels. The labels on the tins were changed from time to time for advertising purposes. They would get used to a particular label design and were unable to recognise it once it had been changed. One could see their confidence growing as they depended less and less upon others for such basic needs.

I was approached by Jim Robinson and asked whether I would like to participate in teacher training so that members of communities could pass on their skills to other members. I accepted and we covered most of the churches in the Johannesburg area, even going as far as Pretoria. I was still working at Walton's on week days and seeing to my children at night. Physically it was difficult, but spiritually it was very rewarding.

Needless to say, Ernie was not impressed. I was busy all the time and did not get involved in any of his activities. In addition, I did not participate in his show activities any longer. He complained bitterly that he hardly saw me anymore. He was working night shift all the time and on weekends I was busy at church. I felt good, as it was rewarding to help others.

He told me that charity begins at home. I retaliated that he should lead by example.

The chicken shows continued without me. He had to do all the work himself and that was why he was complaining. The only child that showed real interest in showing and judging chickens was Derek. The only show I attended was the annual Rand show that took place over the Easter period, as it was always a great treat for the children.

I was kept busy, what with caring for the children, working and church related activities. This gave me a lift and I regained my self-confidence. It was therefore possible for me to identify with my first student and his joy at learning to read and write.

Polly was also not at all impressed. Ernie told her I was never home. He made it sound horrible, but I had to work and was busy at church over the weekends, and when I was there, most of the time the children were with me. Ernie was at home alone and it was this that he did not like.

All too soon it was Christmas again and we were off to take part in the annual ritual at Polly's place. After the gifts were handed out, which was Maurice's job, and one he thoroughly enjoyed, the children settled down to rip off all the wrapping to find out what they had received. Once all the excitement had died down, the women again made their way to the kitchen. I waited a while before I stuck my nose through the door and asked if there was anything I could help with. I was frowned at and so I closed the door and went to the bathroom in order to regain my composure. I was upset, but I did not want them to see it.

They must have checked to see where I was and could not find me. I suppose they thought I had gone outside, but on my return I stopped in the lounge as I could hear them talking and laughing in the kitchen and making fun of me. Maurice was sitting at the dining room table reading the newspaper and I saw him trying to draw their attention but to no avail. They were in full swing, each one taking a turn at making fun of my conversion. I heard Heather saying: "Now that she is a reborn," with the emphasis on reborn, "I wonder if she'll have champagne with her lunch?" This was followed by peals of laughter.

Marge gave a snort and said: "Are you daft?" Poor Maurice was stretching his head in all directions to indicate that I was standing where I could hear every word they said. I shook my head at him, and he settled down and continued to read his paper. I regained my composure and calmly walked into the kitchen and told them:

"Yes, I will definitely have a glass of champagne with you because, just for the record, I can tell you, if you do not know, the first miracle Jesus performed was to change water into wine at a wedding ceremony where they had run out of wine."

There were blurts and splatters of repressed giggling. Each one was trying to grab something to look busy and so as to hide the embarrassment. I glanced back at Maurice and he was sitting with his head bowed, giving sideway glances. He was smiling.

"It looks like I am not 'needed' here, so I will not bother you," I said.

With that I walked out and sat on the settee. There were some magazines lying there which I started to page through. Guess who then walked through the door? He went to the kitchen where Polly and his sisters were all busy and turned towards me as if to say something. Maurice cleared his throat, and looked at him instead. Maurice shook his head indicating to let it be. He closed his mouth and walked out.

The Christmas lunch was very nice, with all the trimmings but there was a strained atmosphere. The men at least enjoyed themselves, but the women were all subdued. After lunch was finished, I gathered the children, thanked Polly for the presents and lunch as it was excellent, and told Ernie he had a choice. You can come with me, or go home with Eddie as I am going to my sister first as I last saw her at the funeral when Chris died. He opted out to come with us. Polly was not very pleased as that meant they would have to wash the dishes, which was always assigned to me each year.

Plot continues; Word to Africa Literacy mission; Ernie & Abdul; Derek & Move

After the fiasco at Polly's house at the Christmas lunch, we left to go to my sister Anna. She was very glad to see me as we had last met at Chris' funeral. The children were ecstatic, and they could not wait to get into the pool as it was a swelteringly hot day. William and Ernie went to join them. Anna, remembering our telephone conversation, wanted to know more about Chris and Ernie.

It had been four months since his death. I told her the whole story, about the way Ernie had treated Chris. He had tried to make him panel beat his scrap cars. With his lame arm, it had been impossible for him, but upon Ernie's insistence, he had given in. He had really tried his best, getting the farm help to lend him a hand, too, but unfortunately he had made a mess of it. Ernie had screamed so much that I had run out to see what was going on.

Ernie had told him how stupid and useless he was, and he had felt rotten. I repeated what I had told her on the telephone, about the manner in which Ernie had told me of Chris's death, and of the B family's reaction. Anna looked at me, shocked.

"And to crown it all, it was my fortieth birthday," I said. "Some birthday I had."

It had been too much for me to absorb. I told her I could not tell her on the day of the funeral. She nodded, understanding. I also reminded her about the verse God had sent me that morning at church in the form of a bookmark with Psalm 46v10 inscribed on it that read: "God is our refuge and our strength, our ever-present help in trouble."

She threw her arms around me and said: "I wish I had your faith and strength."

"It is not my strength, Anna. It is only by the grace of God that I get through each day."

I smiled at her and told her about the message God had given me after I had come back from Mbhathu Sun about faith and wisdom. I had been lying in bed one Sunday morning when a suggestion entered my mind to read 2 Chronicles Chapter 1. I lay there thinking: But there is no such book in the bible. Surely You must mean Corinthians? But I was mistaken. I had mainly concentrated on the New Testament during my Bible readings and studied the exemplary life of Jesus, so my knowledge of the Old Testament was imperfect, to say the least. The book's name was confirmed in my mind, and so I opened my bible and started reading.

Solomon had taken control of the Kingdom after David, his father, had died and he prayed to God for guidance. That night God appeared to Solomon and said: "What do you want, ask for anything and I will give it to you."

At this point in my reading I felt compelled by some force to stop, I could not seem to read on. I felt prompted again: "I ask You my Lord, for wisdom and faith."

After I had asked, I read that Solomon had asked for wisdom and knowledge to govern the people of God. I had felt truly blessed and at peace after this.

"So do not worry about Ernie," I told Anna, "Chris is safe and enjoying his time with the rest of the family. Ernie will be repaid handsomely."

The afternoon sped by too quickly. The children had a good time swimming and playing and they were getting tired. We packed up and left and only arrived home after six in the evening.

During the night I received a vision from God showing me a map of Africa. It did not make sense. There were no directions, just the map. I whispered "Africa". I had become accustomed to waiting, and so I pushed the memory of it to the back of my mind. Its significance would be revealed to me at the appropriate time.

The following Sunday after the church service, Jim called me aside and told me he wanted to propose something to me. He suggested tea at his home that afternoon to discuss it, and requested that Ernie come as his consent would be needed. I was about to ask for more information, but I managed to prevent the question from leaving my lips. Ernie had met Jim, and had been impressed by his preaching during the brief interlude when he had attended the church.

Ernie had come to accept the fact that we attended church on Sundays and no longer offered any resistance. At tea, Jim and Ken, the associate pastor, discussed the situation with Ernie. Jim explained to him that they wanted me to join the Word to Africa Mission on a permanent basis. The remuneration would be the same as what I then earned at Walton's Stationers. One could see he was impressed that they had come to discuss it with him. His answer was that, if it was what I wanted, he had no objection.

With everything in place, I handed in my notice. Martin was not very happy, but he agreed that the new opportunity offered more scope for development than my present job, and that it would definitely be personally more fulfilling.

Jim wanted me to start as soon as possible as there were books to be printed. I looked at him and asked him who was going to do the printing. Then he told me that it would be my main duty.

"I don't know anything about printing," I retorted.

"We will cross that bridge when we get there," he replied.

At the church's last general meeting, everyone had voted in favour of Jim's idea to launch the Word to Africa Mission and to use the church as a base. The consensus held that it was too expensive to import the books from the United States. Moreover, the use of the English text had its limits. Bob was responsible for the translation of the English versions of the texts into each of the nine South African indigenous languages. It was agreed that he would translate them, and once each prototype was ready, he'd let us have them to print and subsequently to work with in teaching adult literacy in each language.

It was soon clear that a professional printing job would be too expensive. It was decided to buy a printer and to produce the books ourselves.

"I told you I do not know anything about printing," I repeated.

"We will teach you," I was informed.

Half of the garage was allocated to be used for the printing of these books. Why I had been singled out for this task, only the Lord knows. It could be that it had to do with the map of Africa vision that I had had.

The printing machine was brought and brief verbal instructions were given together with written notes. It was a small contraption fitted with a cylinder drum, and a place where I thought the ink must go. The ink had to be mixed to the right consistency, not too thick and not too thin. For a novice, it was a nightmare.

I cried so much and asked the Lord for help as I did not have a clue where to start. The written instructions did not make any sense. I had never laid eyes upon anything like it before. I did not know anyone in the printing business that could actually show me the ropes. I had been literally thrown into the deep end and I could not swim this time, I was drowning.

Unbelievably, after having my little crying fit, I calmed down and set to work. I started to do things I had not thought possible. It was as if I was standing next to my body and watching myself. I was guided by an unseen force preparing the mixture of ink, placing the prototype in place on the drum, and then pressing the button to set the machine in motion. After a few trial attempts, I got the hang of it. I started churning out books by the hundreds. It was weird yet exhilarating. My vision of the map of Africa now made sense. I was printing books in the African languages, to teach older illiterate people the basics of how to read and write.

The books were in the same format as the one used at church to teach the local people how to read and to write in English. This was the first translated copy printed in one of South Africa's indigenous languages. How I had managed to pull it off, I could not tell. I still had to see to the smooth running of the household, looking after the children, seeing to it that they did their homework and putting them to bed, at which point I would return to the garage to do more printing. Collating the eighty pages of lessons and instructions on how to teach adults was challenging, too. In the beginning, Ernie helped out. But it was a lot of work and he soon grew bored. He had returned to his hobbies.

The first batch of books was destined for a Mission Station on top of the Lebombo Mountains, Hluluwe, and Natal. The lady who was managing the station was so excited when she held the first copy of the books in her hands. She cried so much, and was so pleased. She had been waiting for such books for a very long time. We were also asked to present the module on how to teach illiterate adults. The workshop took place in a small church in Mtubathuba. We spent the weekend with them and saw some incredible views from the top of the mountain. The missionary showed us where Mozambique, Swaziland and South Africa were situated. It was breathtaking and an experience that I would treasure for life. Just to be part of a team helping people who had never had the opportunity to learn how to read and write, even in such a limited way, was indeed a blessing from God.

Back at church Jim could not stop telling people how successful the launch had been. A room was converted and Word to Africa took up office at the church. Soon there was another member of the team. His name was Hamilton and he had just finished Bible College. He was now a pastor and had recently married.

It did not take long until computers made their way into our office. It was brilliant to work at the church as it was only ten minutes away from home and I made a big saving on fuel. This was just wonderful. I still continued printing the books at home. These were kept in storage. Another blessing was that Jim had secured World Vision backing which was a blessing as the strain that our work had placed on the church's meagre funds had been too heavy.

On the home front, I had sadly stopped trying to show Ernie the importance of a united family. Everything I had done to impress this upon him had been in vain. I know it is biblical for wives to submit to their husbands, but in the circumstances of our relationship, it was not viable. That is, not viable unless one was prepared to lower one's standards or understanding of union, which I was not prepared to do.

Ernie had another brainwave. As he had grown tired and restless, he sought something that would impress the local community. He had decided to try his hand at producing tomatoes. He would make a fortune by taking his harvests to the Johannesburg produce market. As a result, a large part of the plot was dedicated to this new idea. The tomatoes were planted and he produced a bumper crop, too many to handle, actually. Needless to say, William had planted all the seedlings and nursed them to maturity and I must say it had been a success.

Made-to-measure tomato planks were bought to make boxes to pack them in. No one was allowed to touch these precious items as he was sure all others would make a mess of assembling them. But halfway through, he summoned our help as it was a mammoth task. Not having made any plans before hand, he did not know how many boxes would be needed. While he accepted our help with putting the boxes together, he was jealous of the sorting and packing job: he would do this himself. Picking the tomatoes, on the other hand, he was happy to leave that laborious job to us while he made his round of visits to the neighbouring farms, boasting no doubt about new venture and his bumper crop.

As the children grew older, they began to seek recognition from their father. However, all they received was his scorn. It was heartbreaking to watch. Still, Derek saw that his father was battling to keep abreast with all the washing and packing of the tomatoes and decided he would give him a hand without his permission. He spent a whole Saturday packing tomatoes. This he did without my knowledge. I had thought that all the children were swimming in the dam as it was a very hot day. He washed and packed the tomatoes in the boxes, ready for market. He was excited, and could not wait for his father to come home to praise his handiwork. When father finally arrived, he dragged him to the packing room and showed him what he had done and awaited the praise which he thoroughly deserved. Sad to say that, instead of a pat on the back, Ernie became angry and started bawling at him and one by one he tipped the boxes over and the tomatoes were sent rolling all over the floor. Derek witnessed all his hard work destroyed by this monster called his father.

He was devastated and ran into the kitchen. He was only nine going on ten and told me, through his sobs, that I must never, ever expect him to help his father again. I was puzzled as I did not know what he was on about. I asked him to explain why he was saying this.

With tears running down his cheeks, he told me that he had spent the whole day packing tomatoes for his father. Even William had been impressed and had told him it was just as good as when his father packed them. But he had just shouted at Derek and had thrown all of the tomatoes out of the boxes. My heart went out to this little boy who had put his heart and soul into trying to impress his father.

Trying to comfort him, I said that he must respect his father. He stormed out and returned with his bible and asked me to read the passages that he had marked.

COL 3:20 Children, obey your parents in everything, for this pleases the Lord.

COL 3:21 Fathers, do not embitter your children, or they will become discouraged.

"Well, Derek, do what is written. You have tried, and you have failed to impress your father, now impress your heavenly Father by putting this nasty experience behind you and concentrate on whatever pleases you. You have your Silkies and it is nearly time for the Rand Easter show. Go and put your energy into cleaning them and getting them ready, perhaps you will win a prize, who knows. I know it hurts, son, but what can one do? Life is not a bed of roses. It is difficult at times and sometimes we do not understand it fully," I said.

He looked at me with those big sad brown eyes, and I ached inside because I felt so helpless and heartbroken myself. I gave him a hug and he went outside.

Later I checked to see how he was coping. He seemed calm and relaxed. He was happily busy with his chickens, talking to them as if they could understand each word, warning them that they had to look especially good as he wanted them to win the cup for the best Silkie on show.

It was hopeless to try and understand what triggered such nastiness in Ernie. Where did it actually stem from? It no doubt had something to do with his childhood. Derek only wanted to help, but instead he got hurt by the reaction of his father whom he had desperately wanted to please. William assured me that the boxes were packed so perfectly, not even Ernie could have done it better. Everything we tried to do to impress him was in vain.

When Ernie came into the house he could not face me. I let him be. He went outside to where the tomatoes were scattered in every direction. I stood in Louise's room watching him through the window. His hand went through his hair; an expression of despair crossed his face. The devastation he had caused was appalling. I went back to the kitchen and saw Derek in the distance, running towards the dam.

A little while later Ernie passed the back door. I stopped him and asked who was going to clean the mess he had made. I was fuming.

He looked at me and must have decided it would be better to gather up the tomatoes himself, just to keep the peace. I wondered sometimes what kept him from unleashing his wrath upon me. I must have enjoyed some sort of "divine protection". I thanked my Heavenly Father for it.

"The wheelbarrow is over there under the fig tree with the spade," I said, and handed him some bags to put the spoiled tomatoes in.

"When you are done, I hope you can find the courage to apologise to Derek for what you have done," I said. "And don't forget to wash that floor."

I took a bucket of water and a mop and put it at the door. He cleaned the room and the experience marked an end to yet another financial disaster. He was unable to get the whole crop to market at the right time, and the venture overall had cost more than it had brought in. He had bitten off more than he could chew. Once more, he had not planned properly, and facing failure, he could not bring himself to admit as to the reasons, and learn from them. Too proud to admit failure, some other reason was always found to explain it away. It had become the B-clan's motto: "It is always someone else's fault.

He never apologised to Derek. This was very sad as it would have meant a lot to the child.

Ernest graduated from primary school and Athlone Boys' High school was recommended by Broadlands Primary school. Athlone Boys' High was two blocks away from Polly's house and it was suggested that he live with her during the school week. Once Ernest started high school, he lived with his grandmother. Each Saturday, father picked him up and brought him to the farm. Ernest did not like the arrangement, but did not complain. It went well until Ernie's sister Eve complained that it was a disgrace that her mother had to feed my child without remuneration.

"First of all," I said, "He is your brother's child, too, and Polly's grandchild. Secondly, why don't you reproach your brother for not paying your mother for looking after his child?"

She ignored what I had said and simply repeated herself.

"Look inside your mother's freezer, where do you think the vegetables and the meat come from? Answer me that."

There was no answer.

"From the farm, but it was not your brother who brought it. No, it was I. I brought it through to her. I will take Ernest out of Athlone and send him to Jan Smuts in Vereeniging so he can move back to the farm. At least I will not be compelled to visit this place any longer. Just one further question, as you don't deign to answer my first. Why doesn't your mother urge your brother to take care of his family? Your husband would not dare to do what Ernie does as the whole lot of you would come down on him like a ton of bricks. Why forever pick on me? Can you answer me that? I am afraid there is no logic in what you all do or say," I concluded.

Ernest was overjoyed as he hated staying with his granny. Later, when he graduated from General Jan Smuts High school, he was accepted at Wits University and studied

Astronomy, Psychology Mathematics and Physics. In his first year he averaged ninety-six percent in his exams.

Polly found out that I was working for the church on a full-time basis and went off the deep end again. So did the whole family, as they thought that I worked *pro bono* and poor Ernie had now to carry the full financial burden again. Little did they understand that I received the same salary as when I worked at Walton's, but they only heard what they wanted to hear, so I left their cries unanswered. The one thing that sent them into a frenzy was the fact that the outreach was mainly directed towards helping the black population. When not printing, I was kept busy with general office work and a multitude of whatever tasks popped up. I soon became a jack of all trades, but loved it as it gave me a sense of purpose and the joy of knowing that I was helping people.

One afternoon on my way home I stopped at Abdul's shop to pick up some things needed at home. He summoned me aside. I smiled and teased him by asking whether Ernie had been up to his old mischief again.

"Yes, but not that kind of mischief. I am so sorry to burden you with this. Unfortunately, Ernie has run up a bill for animal feed to a princely sum of ten thousand rand. He promises each month to pay something, but he never does, and the sum just keeps growing. I absolutely hate to turn to you, but I do not know what else to do," he said.

I just shook my head and said to him: "How many times have I told you not to give him anything on credit. I cannot afford to pay for that, you know that."

"Every month he has another story to tell me," he said.

"And every month you believe him? He does the same to his mother. He tells her there is no food in the house and then she gives him food which goes to his girlfriends. And it is I that gets the blame for wasting money. You know how underhanded he is, and yet you fall for his stories every month." I just shook my head as I could not believe what I was hearing at that moment.

"He lies like a rug, Abdul. He is such a swindler, manipulator, liar, cheat, and at the top of the list, a philanderer, you name it, but knowing all that, you still believed him. That hurts, you know? Yes, he was born with the ability to make people believe every word that comes from his mouth, but you of all people should know that by now. I am sure his excuses involved either me or the children. He knows that you and your wife have a particularly soft spot for us, especially Greg because of the bee story."

I waited for a reply, but he just gave a confirming nod.

"How do you think I feel when you believe the stories he tells you? I am so tired of being used in this manner. He always does whatever he wants no matter at whose cost. Have you seen how many feathered friends he has, apart from the rabbits, pigs and cattle?"

"His brother Eddie pays the school fees and I look after my children. He does not give me a cent of his money. You will have to draw the line somewhere, Abdul. There are about five hundred chickens on that plot. All show birds. It is totally absurd," I said.

"Perhaps I can make the following suggestion. Seeing as to the fact that my brother is no longer with us and there is no use for that caravan any longer, you can take it and have it valued. Sell it at the best price you can get. If there is a shortfall, he will have to pay you. At times you have to be cruel to be kind. At least you will get something back. But I ask you nicely now, no more credit. I am tired you know, I just wish at times that he would move in with one of his lady friends, but it does not look likely, I'm afraid," I said in conclusion.

"You should know that, after all that we have seen, my wife and I both have a lot of respect for you. We are ready to help you at any time; all you need do is ask. But if I saw that man lying in the street somewhere, I would not help him," he replied.

I thanked him for the kind remarks and asked him to consider taking the caravan and finding a buyer as I would not like him to lose money. After all, he had a business to run.

"I will speak to him tonight, and make sure he comes to see you to clear this up. Next time, Abdul, you will be on your own and your wife is my witness. By the way, is he still busy with his harem?" Both confirmed yes with nodding heads.

"He will not stop unless the husbands descend upon him I think," I said.

I left, feeling a bit deflated, but I pushed the negative feelings aside. I did not want the children to see or know what was going on. We were civil to each other. There were seldom big scenes unless he flared up.

That evening after the children had gone to bed, I told him I wanted to show him something. In fact, I wanted to speak to him about his bill, but not in the house lest he start throwing a tantrum. When we were far enough away from the house, I asked him about his bill at Abdul's. I asked him how much he owed him.

"Not much," he replied.

I asked again how much, and he became a bit agitated.

"Ernie, you are speaking to me now. I know how much you owe him as Abdul told me today, so you cannot lie. What I want to know is when you will stop using the children and me as your 'security' to gain whatever it is you want, and how you are going to pay him."

"I do not know," he said.

"I suggested to Abdul today that he should come and see you tomorrow to try sort out how you are going to settle the bill. The only way I know is for you to sell your caravan. It is just standing there, a large white elephant, not being used. Use it to repay the man what you owe him. If there is a shortfall, you will have to pay it."

"You cannot do that, it is my caravan, not yours, you cannot tell him that, I will not allow it," he said, visibly shaken.

"I do not think you have a choice. You don't have that kind of money. Who do you think is going to pay your bill of nearly ten thousand rand? It is very high, but not at all surprising given the number of animals you have here, especially the chickens. There must be in the region of four to five hundred chickens. Not to speak of the cattle, pigs, horses and rabbits. It costs money to keep them, which you have not got, unless you want to face a lawsuit."

"Yes, but you get money from me to pay the bond and the water and lights. What is there left for me?" he asked.

"That is part of your responsibility, putting a roof over your family's heads. Who pays for the food you eat each day? Who buys the clothes for this family? Who pays the staff on this plot so you can walk around doing nothing? You earn twice as much as I do, yet you have no money. Where does your money go? The bond, plus water and lights does not even add up to twenty percent of your earnings. What do you do with the rest?" He could not or would not answer me.

"You owe Polly a lot of money, too. I have never seen this money or whatever you have bought with it, yet it is I who gets the blame for it as I am the one who she says wastes your money. When are you going to pay her back?"

I reminded him that Abdul would be coming the next day to look at the caravan. I warned him not to go running off to his mother telling her that I had sold his caravan.

"And do not disappear either. He will be here between ten and eleven," I said.

With no sign that there would be a response, I turned and went back to the house. For the life of me, I would never understand him.

The following afternoon I stopped at the shop, wanting to know what had transpired.

"Did you manage to speak to him?" I asked as I walked into the shop.

"Yes," Abdul answered. "I will make arrangements to come and collect it." I could see that he was upset about the whole episode.

"How much do you think you will get for it?" I asked.

"I am not too sure. It is a very nice caravan and still in good condition, only time will tell."

"Were there any problems?" I asked.

"Not much," he replied.

"It is so sad that one has to revert to such measures because of his obsessions. Please, Abdul, no more credit, as you are going to be left short. Promise me that. And make sure that if there are insufficient funds that he pays the shortfall. I do not want you to lose out."

"Yes," he said, "I promise. I told him no cash, no animal feed. I had a good look at all the animals. This man is totally obsessed. I do not understand him."

"Abdul, please do not even try. It might drive you to the edge of insanity. I have learned the hard way," I said. "I ignore most of the things he does for the children's sake, as it would only lead to horrific arguments."

"I must ask, why did you marry this guy?"

"It is a long and complicated story, but it is a spiritual walk. I know it must sound very strange, but at the age of ten, I had a dream where God blessed me and told me that the road ahead was going to be long and difficult, but that towards the end, He would restore everything. I first saw Ernie at the age of eleven, but only fleetingly. He had been best man at my brother's wedding. I married him at the age of seventeen. I was never in love with him and he also only married me for his own selfish reasons. But as God foresaw, it has been a difficult road. But I believe that in the end, everything lost to me will be restored. The two of us are like chalk and cheese. So you see, I am only walking in obedience to God. I trust

Him. I know that all will be well with me and my children. I am not quite sure how long the difficult road will still last, but I am not worried, He has protected me thus far and He will carry me through. Does my foolishness make more sense now?" The two them just looked at me.

"In a way, I suppose. Anyway, I respect and accept it. At least I know you will come out the winner," Abdul answered.

How much he sold the caravan for, if he ever did, I was never told. He just left it at that. After that episode, on Eddie's advice, Ernie bought his feed from a supplier in Vereeniging. It was further away, but cheaper. This took the pressure off me. For a while, at least.

With World Vision support, the work expanded at such a rate that it was a full day's job to run the office alone, and the weekends were taken up by seminars, or teaching students at church.

I thought Hamilton's joining us would improve matters. However, instead of helping me in the office, he became Jim's shadow. I spoke to Jim and told him the workload was getting too much. Either Hamilton helped in the office or took over the weekend duties. I could no longer cope alone. I also had a family to take care of.

"By weekend duties I mean he has to prepare the materials needed for the workshops. Enough books have been printed. They should cover another two months of classes."

Jim looked at me as if I was crazy. I told him I was sorry, but I could not continue like this. He was not happy, but promised to do something about the situation. The following morning Hamilton marched into the office in a huff and asked me what I wanted him to do.

I suggested he could take over the printing and collating of the books.

"No," he said. "That will take far too much of my time. I must prepare for the weekend seminars."

"Okay, then you can take over responsibility for the weekend seminars. You can handle it." He exploded and said that he could not do that either. He did not know how.

"Then it is about time that you learn, don't you think? I had to learn. Which task do you prefer?" I asked.

"I was employed to do seminars," he said.

"Well then, you take over responsibility for the weekend seminars then. Think about it and speak to Jim. I cannot work day and night any longer, and I am not going to prepare notes for you anymore, either."

He stormed out of the office. Not long after that, Jim came in and asked me not to be so harsh.

"No, Jim," I said. "He walks around each day doing nothing. When we come back from a seminar, the books get thrown into a corner of the room. Books I have spent nights to print, with no regard for the efforts I have put in to prepare the materials. He expects me to pick them up and pack them in the cupboards. Do you think that is fair? I am tired, I also need a break and he was employed to make the burden lighter, not unbearable. If you want to, I will leave and he can take over. I am sure I can get my job back at Walton's," I said.

"That is not an option. No one can do what you are doing, I will speak to him and tell him to show more respect for the materials that are in use."

The sweet talk did not impress me and I asked: "What about the workload, running the office, printing and collating the books? Is he still going to sit with his arms folded?"

"I will make a plan. There is not enough space in the church to accommodate all of us. We are growing too fast." With that he got up and left.

I had my first vision from God regarding the church. I was nervous and decided to ignore it and went to the Apostolic Faith Mission Church instead. This carried on for three weeks until I felt so guilty, I could not find peace. I was agitated. The following week I went back to the Baptist church. That Sunday that associate pastor was leading the congregation. Ken asked whether there was anyone in the congregation who had received a word from the Lord for the church. I was amazed, and my heart was pounding. I put my hand up and he called me to the front.

I told them where I had been for the last three weeks.

"Now I am back here to give you the message. God told me to tell you that if the church does not start worshipping Him in Spirit and in Truth, He will remove the candlestick from this church."

An uneasy feeling fell upon the church. There were a few amens and some people nodded in agreement, but some, mainly the pastors, were a bit taken aback.

I was reprimanded by Jim and Ken because I had the nerve to bring such a negative message to the congregation.

"That is what God said to me, and I cannot change it." They were not impressed and asked me who I thought I was? Did I think that God would speak to me and not to them? I looked at them in disbelief.

"Over the years, many people have stood up and brought messages and these were always received amicably, what have I done wrong? I only did what I was told. Perhaps it means that it is time for the church to take stock of what it is doing. However, be that as it may. What I received from God, I conveyed to you. I will not retract it."

Both of them were not happy and left without saying another word.

At the next church meeting, Jim presented the problem of space that we were encountering. Also, he had to fly to the US to finalise the details regarding the Word to Africa Missions. He asked the church to approve financing for the additional space and the trip abroad.

He was told by the deacons that the church, being a rural one with a small congregation, was not in a position to cover the costs. There was not enough money available. Jim was not happy in the least and decided to move the offices. Confirmation was received from World Vision that part of the support needed for the move would be provided.

He found a house at a reasonable rent and, facing much hostility, vacated the church premises and moved to the house. I told them in no uncertain terms that I was not going to move with them. Jim nearly exploded, and demanded a reason. I tried to explain to him that the foundation of the mission had been laid at Walkerville Baptist Church where God had intended it to operate.

"If you move it will come to naught," I said.

"What do you mean?" he shouted.

"It is plain and simple, Jim. I am not moving. It is not in God's plan that we move. Word to Africa Mission belongs in this church."

"You will move with us. I do not believe what you are saying," Jim said in a softer voice, and walked out of the office.

Ken was sent to ask me what my plans were, and I confirmed that I was not moving. They would have to find someone else to do the work.

"Then you will sit here all by yourself?" Ken asked me.

I did not answer him and as I was about to leave a call came through from Abdul to tell me that Derek had had an accident with his motorbike. I had to go to Vereeniging hospital immediately as my signature was needed to carry out an emergency operation.

At first I was frantic. Once in the car, an unbelievable calmness came over me as I set out. I made the distance in record time to find that, for once, Ernie had managed to get there before me. I arrived just in time to encourage Derek as they were pushing him through to the operating theatre. It was a long operation. They were trying to save his leg. It had been mangled from the knee to the ankle.

Needless to say, Ernie was unpleasant. He screamed at me in the waiting room. He was frustrated by all the forms he had been given to fill. He actually knew very little about his children as he was never around.

He liked to be in control and show off but not knowing his own son's personal information embarrassed him. "Do you want to wait here with me until the operation is over? If so, kindly refrain from accusing me of things over which I have no control. He was in an accident. Let us deal with that first, shall we?"

But he persisted. "You should have been at home," he accused.

"Look, I really do not have time for any of your theatrics now. You are never with your family when we need you. So get in your car and just go home."

A nurse called me to a phone. It was Polly ranting and raving. Her son was under enormous strain. Where had I been? She screamed and why was I in the streets all day? They could not get hold of me and he had had to sit there in the waiting room all by himself.

"My son would not have been in the operating theatre if it was not for yours. The accident happened because of your son. He is always so very busy helping the neighbours. So he sent Derek to the post office to fetch his entry forms for the Rand Easter Show instead of going himself. So, please, just get off my back and mind your own business. You as a grandmother should be here," I told her.

Ernie was very upset because of the way I had spoken his mother. But before he got his breath back, I told him: "Do you want to wait here with me until the operation is over? If so, stop accusing me of things over which I had no control. He was in an accident. Look around you. People are not impressed by your performance."

It was humiliating. All the people sitting there in the waiting room, listening to him repeating himself over and over again: "You should have been at home."

"I was at work and on the point of leaving the office when I received the call from Abdul. I came straight to the hospital from work, do you hear me?"

One of the men sitting there asked him where he had been at the time of the accident. Ernie spluttered and stood there gaping at the guy. He stormed out and I did not see him again that night. I thanked the man. I had had enough drama at church without having to sit and listen to one of Ernie's outbursts. I was certain it would continue for weeks if not months, and Polly would add her bit, too.

He asked me what had happened and I told him that I did not really know. I had been at work when I received an urgent message from the shop owner, Abdul. My son had been in an accident and was rushed through to hospital. I was just about ready to leave the office when the call came through.

He looked at me and said: "But from what your husband was saying, it sounded as if you were in the streets somewhere and should have been at home."

"I know. It is his manner of speaking. Not to worry, I can handle it."

I asked him why he was there. He had to rush his wife to hospital, he said. He turned his head and looked out of the window. I decided not to press him.

"Is he always so unreasonable?" he asked.

"No," I said. "Only when he has an audience."

I was tired of his antics and was glad that he had left. I started praying for Derek and the children at home. Abdul and his wife promised that they would take care of them and I started to relax and felt more at peace. He looked vaguely familiar and I tried to recall where I had seen him before. I caught his attention and asked him where he lived. I said I was sure that I had seen him before somewhere.

He answered: "Most likely at Abdul's shop." Then he looked away again.

There was hurt in his eyes, I could see that. Was it because, like the rest of us there, he was waiting to hear about his wife?

It was after nine that evening when Derek was finally wheeled to his ward. The doctor told me that they had tried to do a skin graft with skin taken from his upper leg to cover the damage done on the lower leg below the knee. The rest of the leg was too mangled, but they had done their best to save most of it. The ankle, however, had been crushed.

"All we can do now is to pray that the skin transplant works. That in itself would take a miracle. And then we'd see what else we could do."

I sat at his bedside through the night until he awoke the next morning with the words: "So much pain, agony and frustration," he moaned. I was extremely upset to see my boy like this. I had to get away to vent my feelings.

They brought his breakfast and the sister and I helped him into a sitting position. At least there was nothing wrong with his appetite. I was glad of this as he would need all his strength. Pastor Ken walked in and knowing Derek well, he came to visit with something under his arm. He saw that I was extremely exhausted and he offered to stay with Derek until I returned, even if it took the rest of the day. Derek's smile gave me a boost and I agreed to go home for a much needed rest.

The next morning I told Ernie I had to go to school and fill them in on the details of Derek's accident. He insisted on going with. I wished I had kept my mouth shut as I knew that there would be another dramatic scene. I went to his class teacher and she called me into the classroom. I explained to her and the pupils about the accident and that Derek would not be attending school for a long time. The doctors could not give me a definite answer, but it would probably take about six months before he returned to school.

Ernie started up with his antics. In front of the class, he was at the point of fainting at any moment. The boys rushed forward to try and keep him on his feet. I took very little notice and some of them gave me looks of disgust. Kenneth, Derek's friend, was also standing there but did not take notice of Ernie either. He just shook his head.

It took two of the boys to support him and see him back to the car, each with one of his arms around their shoulders. Once in the car and around the first corner, he was sitting up smiling to himself. You are such a hypocrite! Always looking for attention. I stopped at the shop to bring them up to date. Ernie remained in the car. Abdul was happy that I had stopped by, and again offered any help I might need. I told him about the incident and Ernie's hasty retreat from hospital the previous night. I also told him that the guy who had confronted Ernie looked very familiar. Maybe he could find out who he was and why he had been at the hospital, as he had looked very worried.

"You know your shop. It is the local centre of gossip."

He just laughed and promised he would keep his ears open. He told me to get home and get some rest as I looked awful. Ernie had not come into the shop as he was too distraught.

The next morning, as Ernie was on permanent night shift and had not returned, I assumed he had gone directly from work to the hospital. The phone rang. It was Polly. Very curtly she asked me how Derek was. Without answering her I asked whether she had seen Ernie.

"Yes, the poor thing is sleeping. He is totally exhausted."

"From what?" I asked her.

There was no answer. Then she told me that Ernie was not to blame for the accident.

"You are something else, you know? Your children are never to blame for anything. It is always and conveniently someone else's fault. He is home during the day and he could have gone and collected his damned post himself. But no, he was too busy, so he sent Derek. I blame him and there is nothing you can say or do to change that. It was his fault." I slammed the phone down.

He was exhausted, I muttered to myself. He was too afraid to come home that was the real problem. Afraid of me, afraid he might run into that guy from the hospital again. His world was busy collapsing around him and he did not know how to handle it. There was more to it, I felt sure. I had my suspicions, but I kept them to myself.

The children had been fed and were just about ready for bed. I thanked God for the staff he had sent me. Everything ran like clockwork. I had a bath and told the children what had happened and promised that I would take them on Sunday to see their brother. He was going to be in hospital for a long time.

On my way I stopped in at the shop to get some snacks and drinks for Derek. Abdul told me that the bloke I had asked him about was indeed the husband of one of Ernie's victims.

"No wonder he was at his mother's place, too tired and exhausted to come home," I told Abdul. He just shook his head. He had prepared a parcel for Derek and gave it to me. Again I cursed the apartheid regime. I knew that both of these kind people would have loved to visit Derek. But they were Indians, and they were barred from such visits. On arrival Derek was his cheerful self. I supposed he had been given a lot of painkillers. The leg must have hurt very much, but he had decided to accept it and make the best of a bad situation.

We chatted, and at seven Eddie walked in and Derek was pleased to see him. He asked me where Ernie was and I just shrugged my shoulders. There was nothing to say. Sunday arrived and the children could not wait to see their brother. Greg was quite upset to see the brother he idolised laying in hospital. Kenneth, Derek's friend, also came. Derek was in his element.

Derek stayed in hospital for a month. I spent each day with him, reading, playing chess and other board games to help pass the time. He had some visitors, friends from school, but apart from Eddie and Alice, no other members of the B family came. After that first phone call, Polly did not phone again. Ernie, I believe, managed to go once. I did not witness it. Perhaps it was during one of my toilet breaks.

He was discharged and I took him home. I had to clean and dress the wound on a daily basis. The strain of travelling back and forth to the hospital had taken its toll, and I was relieved when I had him at home. After the first operation he had another nine operations. Pastor Ken helped me by taking us both to and from the hospital each time a follow up visit was required. Transporting him in his cast with crutches and all was difficult.

After one of these visits, Ken told me that he was no longer involved in Word to Africa. He asked me whether I would consider going back. I said I would like to do that, but I felt it was not right. I knew people would not understand me and think me stubborn, but for me, once God said no, it unfortunately meant no. It was time to move on.

"In fact, as I am sitting here, I can tell you it will not be long before we move away. Don't ask me how I know. I have a foreboding."

I recalled to him a dream of a white-painted house. In the dream I saw Polly and her kids approaching the house. In one part of the dream, Derek, not wanting to go through the garage, scaled the wall of the courtyard instead. It was completely walled in on the outside. Later, when we actually did move into this house that I had never seen before but in my dream, I had a gate put into this wall to make it possible to enter the courtyard without going through the garage.

"Do you really think Ernie will ever agree to move away from the plot and the animals?"

"That's what makes the dream so confusing to me. But if it is God's plan, then it will come to pass. Let's give it three months. If we are still here, I will come back to Word to Africa."

He smiled and said: "Jim has moved, as you know. But I'm convinced that they're not going to make it without you. The books you printed are nearly all gone and no one has bothered to try and print anymore and the office is in chaos. It seems you have a knack for organising things and bringing about order under any circumstances. I am not saying this merely to flatter you; it is simply how things stand. Unfortunately, though Jim is a very good speaker, he is not a talented manager."

"I told Jim not to move. Anyway, while Derek's leg is in plaster, I cannot consider any work, no matter how much I am battling financially," I said.

One day Ernie walked into the bedroom unannounced while I was dressing Derek's wound. I think it only dawned on him at that point how bad it really was. The blood drained from his face and he slowly backed out of the room. Not a word was said. I raised my eyes to see Derek's reaction and a flicker of pain crossed his eyes. Looking at his leg again, the thought crossed my mind that I should have opted for amputation. It would have spared him the physical pain of each skin graft, but I could not imagine my son with an amputated leg.

He had been through ten operations and was wheelchair bound for six months as they waited for the complete healing of the flesh wounds. Only then could the leg be placed in plaster. Kenneth his friend from school brought Derek his homework each Friday and this helped him stay abreast of his school work.

I was overjoyed when the leg was finally put in a plaster cast. There were two steel clamps screwed into the bones of his lower right leg, one below the knee and one in the ankle area with an external bridging rod joining the clamps. It looked utterly hideous. This contraption was meant to hold the leg together while the crushed bones beneath the surface healed. Now he could get out of the wheelchair and move around on crutches. He returned to school and completed his final year with good enough grades to enter university.

One more tragedy hit our family. My eldest brother, who was my icon, also committed suicide. I could not believe it, nor understand. His children were devastated. None of us could understand why? He had always been a pillar of strength in our family. What had triggered him to do such a thing would always remain a mystery. Chris one could understand. After his stroke, he had not been able to cope emotionally. But there was no explaining this suicide. The devastating pain and anger together with the flurry of needless and ugly comments from Ernie's family was too much. I had been emotionally battered so many times by now I had begun to move about like an automaton, mechanically making my way through each day. It was all I could do to keep from cracking up.

And there was high drama in Polly's house. As I understood it, both Polly and Maurice had decided years ago to save money for an overseas trip upon their retirement. They had opened a joint savings account and an amount had been deposited each month for I do not know how many years. Retirement day arrived and Polly was excited as she had been looking forward to this holiday with much excitement. She had worked her entire life, had raised eight children, and now deserved a rest. The moment of truth arrived. Maurice told her that there was no money. His children from his first marriage had needed help, so he had lent the money to them. They had not yet repaid him.

Polly was devastated. Eddie asked me whether Polly could come and stay with us for a week, just to get out of the house for a bit. Although she did not like me – she had made that obvious enough – I could not help feeling sorry for her. She really had worked her fingers to the bone. This was devastating. Fate had dealt her a cruel blow.

She was very quiet when she arrived at the plot. Eddie helped to get her settled. I did not pressure her and I kept quiet as she needed time to recover. Her lifelong dream had been shattered. What made matters worse was that she could not continue to work as her retirement papers had been finalised. Now she had nothing to keep her busy during the day and nothing to look forward to.

She had to share a room with Louise, but she did not seem to mind. Each morning I made her breakfast. After she had eaten, she would go outside and sit in the chair I had put under one of the trees for her. I had placed a small camping table next to it. I served her morning tea, and lunch outdoors as it was nice and warm, and the fresh air could only do her good. Supper was served mostly in front of the television with the children. It was different from what she was used to and she started to relax. A small flicker of a smile appeared on her face from time to time.

At least she could bond with the children. Due to all the animosity, I rarely went to their house except on special occasions. There appeared to be a momentary truce between us. She was a bit friendlier, and perhaps had no choice in the matter as Ernie was never to be seen and she mostly only had me for company.

Eddie came round and she complained to him about all the fuss. He told her just to sit and relax and enjoy herself. He had bought a house in Kensington. He was just waiting for the paper work to go through. Then she would have plenty to keep her busy with.

"You better have a good rest, as next week this time you will have enough to do," he said.

There was a half a smile on her face which was a good sign.

Two days down the line she was moaning again and I told her to pipe down in the nicest way I could. I reminded her that this was my domain and I would do here what I pleased.

"You will just have to accept and make the best of it while it lasts," I told her.

The week that she stayed gave her time to get over the shock a bit. Eddie was determined to get his mother away from Maurice and one could not blame him. I told him that I did not mind. She had stopped giving me "lip". He just smiled.

With the paperwork done and the key in his hand, he hired a truck and moved all Polly's furniture and belongings to the new house. He left Maurice with what he needed to get by until one his children came to the rescue.

The new house was also situated in Kensington and was not far from her daughter Gladys' place. A nice double-story house which she really liked when she saw it and it gave her a boost of energy. There was also a wee spring in her step, which was good to see.

We went through to help Eddie move in. First we stopped at Polly's old place to check up on Maurice. Getting out of the car, one could already hear his sobs. Then followed a wail so piercing, it was unnerving.

I went into the house and when he saw me he quieted down. He told me that they had taken his wife only because he had helped his children.

"Maurice, it has been nearly a week now, you must start thinking about getting some food into your body."

He had lost a lot of weight since Polly had left. He was really in a bad state.

"Why did you have to help your children?" I asked.

He looked at me as if I had doused him with ice-cold water.

"They asked me and I could not refuse," he said.

"With Polly's money included which she had trusted you with? She worked hard all her life, looked after you and her own children. She was looking forward to this trip for so long and you gave the money to your children. Apart from Patrick, it does not make any sense. He was the only one of your children who ever visited you. Michael only came when he needed money. I am sorry, but you had no right to do that. It was money that had been saved for both of you. She does not deserve this, and the worst of it all is that you have betrayed her trust. I don't think she will recover from this. You have let her down so badly. It is no use sitting here crying. You need to make new arrangements."

I heard footsteps; someone was coming up the stairs. It was Patrick, his son. He looked just as miserable.

"Patrick, I am glad I am not in your shoes. You have all my sympathy," I said. "It is over to you. Your father cannot sit here any longer. It is more than a week now. I do not think he has had anything to eat the whole time. Let me know what you decide to do. He is in a bad way and getting worse every day."

He walked with us to the car, and said: "Unfortunately it is his own fault. He will just have to suffer the consequences. The only thing I can think of is to place him in an old age home."

"That would be the best and the safest thing to do at this moment. I don't suppose you or any of your siblings would be able to take him in?"

He shook his head. Maurice started wailing again, so Patrick waved goodbye and went back into the house. Patrick did manage to get him into the Edenvale Old Age home, but unfortunately he never recovered and died not long after the separation. Ernie had not come with me into the house. I asked him why.

"I cannot handle rubbish like this," he said.

I looked at him in disbelief and said: "That's a bit rich coming from you. Let's rather go and see how Polly and Eddie are coping."

Arriving at their new house I was impressed as it was a very nice place. Polly, not having any obligations to anyone except Eddie, had applied herself to the task of unpacking and making the place liveable. She had made considerable progress. She looked really tired, and emotionally drained. I really felt for her. She had lost two husbands and with each her dreams had been taken from her.

I asked Eddie where the rest of the family was. There was no answer, so I asked where he wanted me to start. I was sent to the kitchen where some boxes with kitchen utensils waited to be unpacked. I found the kettle, some cups and tea bags and made them some tea. It was a welcome interlude.

Eddie was concentrating on getting the bedrooms ready so Polly at least could get a good night's rest. Ernie went to sit and Eddie told him to lift his butt and get the lounge furniture in place. By nightfall it looked more or less habitable. At least one could move around without falling over boxes.

When Ernie was done in the lounge, I asked him to flatten the boxes to take them to the plot as we would certainly find some use for them. He resented me telling him what to do, but grudgingly did anyway hat he was told. We left after eight that night with only a couple of boxes still to be unpacked. Polly expressed her gratitude, thanking me for the week, and for helping with the unpacking. I was really touched as it was the first time she had been this kind to me.

The children had been left at home. Ernest was at university and Derek in his last year at school. His leg was mending which I was glad of. Louise was also turning into a really beautiful young lady and at church she received many flattering looks from the boys. Greg was still at primary school.

Ernie seemed very unsettled and I asked him why. He told me he was overworked. I did not comment as there was very little to do during the night shift. The last flight normally left the airport at ten in the evening and then was very little to do and the staff, who were on standby anyway, took turns sleeping. There were always two on duty during the night shift. It is only when flights arrived at the airport that they had to go through to prepare the aircrafts for the next flight. So I could see no reason for him being especially tired. Since the day he had seen that guy at the hospital, he had been on edge. It was no use asking him, as he always gave evasive answers.

Now that Derek could manage, I needed to find a job again. Money was tight. Very little was contributed by Ernie unless I fought him hard for it. I asked Eddie if he did not know of any job openings. He said he would ask round. The following evening I received a phone call from Heather telling me she had recommended me to Edgar who owned a furniture factory, manufacturing custom-made furniture.

An interview was arranged and I was successful. I started at the beginning of August. The firm was situated in downtown Johannesburg, a block away from the Lower Court. I could see John Vorster Police Station from my office window. This was at a time when the ANC anti-apartheid campaign to free Mandela and achieve democracy escalated.

Early one morning I was sitting in my office when the peace was suddenly disrupted. I heard a tremendous explosion and as I looked out from my window, there were billows of smoke coming from three of the police station windows. I was still looking at that when from nowhere a rifle was pushed in my face. It was the police. They surmised that the bomb had been fired from the roof of our building. Before I could gather my thoughts, I asked him whether this looked like a roof to him. The weapon had shocked me. He apologised and followed the other men up to the roof. No evidence was found that the bomb had been fired from our building.

Another incident followed soon after. Another bomb blast occurred, twice as powerful as the one at the police station. It happened in the car park across the road from the Magistrates Courts, and two blocks away from our building.

The first, a minor explosion, had been a decoy. The second was more powerful and occurred a few minutes later.

The second explosion claimed the lives of three policemen and injured four others. Six bystanders were also injured.

It was so powerful it ripped the car park to pieces. Cars were piled up one on top of the other and some had fallen into a gigantic big hole that had been caused by the blast. Sadly there had been some casualties, too. One man had had his legs blown off. The noise was so loud that my ears rang and ached for a week. The only good to come of it was that we were all sent home early that day.

The previous night I had another dream about the unknown house. It was not a street-facing house, but one built sidelong. Polly with all her girls were walking toward it in a straight line. While I was watching them in my dream, I called to mind a mother duck, her ducklings trailing behind her. That was all. The following night I dreamt of the same house. Maybe a miracle was on its way. I pushed the thought aside, not daring to hope. It was weird.

When I arrived home earlier than usual, I found Ernie there. This was odd as he usually spent his days visiting neighbours. I told him about the incidents at John Vorster and the Magistrates court, and as usual, he just shrugged his shoulders. He showed no concern for my safety. I felt a bit deflated, but what was new? I asked myself.

He told me we might move. I must have given him an unbelievable look, and he hastened to add that he had found out that the SAA was assisting staff members with home loans. He had applied and his application had been approved.

That weekend we went house hunting in the Edenvale area. On hour return home, he seemed to be in a hurry to get to work, and he left soon after. He would explain the next day. I was over the moon. Then I remembered the dream and I knew exactly which house we were to buy. I was dancing for joy. The children wanted to know what it was all about, but I told them they would have to wait and see. Miracles still occur, it seemed. Sadly, given my experience with Ernie, I was not ready to believe anything until I saw written proof of it.

I went to Abdul as I needed to speak to someone. I told him what Ernie had told me and asked him if he knew anything that might have caused this sudden change in Ernie. I told him about the incident at the hospital where a man had confronted him. Since that day, Ernie had not been himself. He was always on the lookout, restless and was spending far too much time at home, something uncommon for him. Maybe the men in the neighbourhood are on his case regarding the frequent visits to their wives when they are not at home?

Abdul confirmed my thoughts. He told me that Ernie was indeed hiding at the moment. He was standing on very thin ice. It would be best for him to get away as soon as possible.

"I am overjoyed, but I am going to miss you guys," I told him. "It seems to me every time I get comfortable and accept my lot, I get uprooted, but this time I do not mind."

Abdul said: "We have to wait and see what happens. If you move, we will miss you very much, and the children even more."

I suspected there was much more that Abdul could tell me, but he was reluctant to talk, and I did not pry.

I could hardly sleep that night. I just lay on my bed thanking the Lord for answered prayers. My eleven years of sheer hell on the plot were over. Ernest turned twenty-one, and was still at university. He lived in a rented apartment in Braamfontein near the university. I arranged for a party at the plot and all his friends and the family came to celebrate with him.

Derek graduated from high school that year, and he applied for a position in a bank and was successful. He would commence work at Standard bank Hillbrow on the first of February the following year. I bought him a secondhand car, too, as the plan was that he would share the flat in

Braamfontein with Ernest and commute to work. But the best news of all was that we would move to the city. How good could life get? Thank you my Father.

The following day Ernie phoned to confirm the approval of the loan. We could go and look at houses. I was in two minds. It seemed to me he was blundering ahead again without planning things out carefully. He always did things like this, impulsively. I felt excited, though, and I truly wanted to move. But what about the farm help and all the animals? Had he considered their future? "We need to talk," I said. His reply was that we could discuss it all later. The important thing was to find a house.

Driving home that afternoon, I mulled over all these new developments. Again I had to declare that I did not understand Ernie. I doubted that a Psychiatrist would have been able to make head of tail of his behavioural patterns. He was like a Klip Springer, jumping from one place to another with no thought given to planning, or any consideration to the consequences of his actions. It was enough to make anyone nervous. The next day, Saturday, we would go and view some properties. When I arrived home, Ernie was there just long enough to tell me that there were a few houses he had already seen, but he wanted me to view them first before deciding. I was astounded that, this time, my approval was being requested before he had made a decision.

I asked the children whether they wanted to come with us. Derek told me that Kenneth was coming over. Louise wanted to go horse riding and Greg also decided to stay at home. So I would have to face the ordeal alone. I asked Jesus to be with me, to give me guidance, as I was so very tired of the conflicts between Ernie and I. I was determined that this time it would be my choice of house. I would not be forced into a decision. I would take the house that appealed to me. I already had an image in my mind brought to me in a dream.

We met with the realtor and the first house we looked at was a big no. So was the second one, but when we arrived at the third, it turned out to be exactly as I had visualised it in the dream. Ernie gave me a sideways glance. He could see that I was keen. As we walked through the house, I could feel that this was it. The outlay of the rooms was perfect. There were a few things I would change, but for now it was just right. Ernie gave a big sigh of relief, and so did the realtor. With the loan pre-approved a lot of time would be saved. All we had to wait for now was the transfer of ownership and that would take the best part of three months. It was perfect timing as we would be able to move in by the end of the year, perfect for changing schools. God is good. Everything, even the timing, was just right. The most amazing thing was that it resembled the house that I had dreamt about.

I came back alone. Ernie stayed behind in Kensington with the excuse that it was too late – he would have to start work in a few hours. It was understandable, but strange, as normally he would not have hesitated about going to the plot and then back to work.

On arrival back home, the children wanted to know about the new house. I told them about the layout. In addition, the new house had a big swimming pool. They were very excited. They wanted to know when we would move.

"We are moving on the first of January. The good thing is that you will begin at the new school right at the start of the next school year."

I was very happy. My thoughts flew to the enormous task that lay before me. I was still trying to absorb the shock that I was included in choosing a new house. There was no chance that he would help me with the packing.

The next day when I arrived home from work, I called the staff and told them about the move. They were sad, but understood the situation.

I told them that they would all be welcome to stay on as long as they wished. We would not be selling the plot. Eddie, his brother, would come round from time to time to see that everything was running smoothly. Ernie did not want to get rid of anything. He just did not want to stay there anymore. I told them not to worry; they still had a roof over their heads and would still get paid each month. With that they were very pleased.

Edenvale

With much relief we arrived at our new home in Edenvale. Back to civilisation. But I could not help feeling a bit nostalgic. I longed for the openness and I missed the quiet. Here there was a constant stream of traffic. The farm was an idyllic place in general where people cared for people. Even when they lived far apart, when one needed help, it was always at hand. Living in the suburbs with your neighbour a mere ten to twenty metres away, no one was interested in what happened to you. I found suburban life selfish and cold after eleven years in the country.

I was still employed at Young World, and the boss had taken on a new partner who specialised in kitchens. Am I blessed or what? I thought. As the kitchen cupboards were a bright orange colour, I soon had them replaced at staff prices which were just about half the selling prices.

It was not long before I heard the splashing of water followed by squeals of laughter. Who could resist it? It was extremely hot, and a dip in the pool sheer magic. It was so encouraging to hear their laughter and I could not help but thank the Lord for this blessing.

There were moans from Ernie, Eddie and Alan, as they had to do most of the offloading. But I ignored them and they knew better than to complain. The era of child labour had long gone. The children had worked a lot on the plot helping to feed the animals and cleaning cages while father sat about giving out instructions.

"They can swim for as long as they like," I said. "Later they will have to come in to unpack their stuff, make their beds and tidy their rooms."

By nightfall everything was in place and we could relax and start living, hopefully as a close family unit. I still had dreams of Ernie taking an interest in the family. He also seemed much more relaxed, but I could not help smiling as I recalled how anxious he had looked this morning while they were loading the furniture onto the truck. He had left with Alan and the children and I had followed with Eddie and a car load of linen and kitchen utensils.

I suggested to Ernie that he should get people to stay in the house for security reasons.

"All the animals are still there," I argued.

But he refused, as he wanted to go there on alternate weekends to see if everything was in order. He had his own mind and would never listen to a bit of logic, so I left it. I would not have to go there and that thought was enough to console me. They could carry the cottage away rock by rock for all I cared. One glorious advantage of the home loan from his employers was that the bond payments would be deducted from his salary each month −one less worry for me.

Between the house and the garage there was an area with a patch of lawn and rose bushes that I had paved. It was perfect for Sunday lunches during the summer months.

In the back corner of the property I had a "lapa" built. A lapa is a structure popularly used for outdoor entertainment in South Africa and known abroad as a pergola. It usually consists of a thatched roof supported by four or more thick wooden poles, depending upon the size of the structure, and the floor was paved. With a wrought-iron table and chairs, it was used extensively for outdoor entertainment. It was next to the pool, so it was ideal, as one could supervise the children swimming.

I took two weeks leave to give me ample time to unpack and prepare for the school year. We had to go shopping for new school uniforms. Louise, now in high school, was destined to attend Edenvale High School and Greg was enrolled in Hurleyvale Primary School.

Louise was not as keen on the move as it meant she had to leave her friends and her beloved horse Vicky. She had to make new friends, and this worried her. Greg, who was born on the farm, might have resisted the move to the city. But he surprised me, in fact both of them did. There was no need for concern. At the beginning of the new school year, they were enrolled and settled down quickly into their new routines.

The Edenvale Baptist Church was God's choice for me. When we were certain about the move, a few members of the Walkerville Baptist recommended it to me and gave me contact names and numbers. I met Martin Pholmann who was the pastor of the church and soon got involved in some of the multitude of ministries and outreach programs. As I had been involved in similar work at the Walkerville Baptist church, I soon became a member of the mission committee. Each year during August and September we had "mission week". I also had the privilege of accompanying a group from the church to Malawi, as we supported a family from Port Elizabeth who has been working with the Yao people for the past fifteen years.

The ladies mainly helped the missionaries to prepare materials needed during the year. We actually resided in the village itself and it was an awesome experience. We joined in their everyday routine by fetching the day's water from the waterhole, and cooking over an open fire that was outside the hut. The Yao people were happy, contented and friendly. It was a very safe place to live as any mischief done was immediately dealt with by the chief of the village according to the tribal laws. If it was something more serious, like murder, the case would be referred to the High Court in Blantyre. As we were accustomed to the high crime rate in our country, I hesitantly accepted their word that here crime was just about non-existent. The biggest crime in recent years was the disappearance of the zinc used for the church roof. We slept in sleeping bags on straw mats, no such luxury as a bed. The men attended to the physical labour side of the operations. A new church was built but lacked steps, and that was their project. Permission was granted by the Chief of the village and we showed a film about Jesus. At the beginning there were a few sniggers, but as the show progressed, the crowd became increasingly subdued. Each one returned to their hut with a lot to think about. Another treat we enjoyed was a weekend trip to the banks of Lake Malawi. It was a magical experience. On our way we had to cross a bridge and at times, especially when there were foreigners in the group, tolls had to be paid. None of us had any money with us, so they asked for a bible and I gave them mine. They were jubilant.

On arrival we were shown to our chalets, two people sharing. The following morning we all awoke refreshed. We had had early morning devotions with a nice breakfast prepared for us which we ate, after which we were free to do as we pleased. Just being there in the fresh air and good company where we all shared the same goal, was an awesome experience. Malawi is a beautiful country and the lake is a magical place. Just to sit there in the stillness, and contemplate life, is wonderful. This is how life should be. No stress, no rush, just a relaxed existence in this tranquil paradise.

There was a colossal hotel nearby. We were told that they were kept busy all year round with a steady flow of tourists. It was difficult to get a booking, and very expensive. It was mostly oversees travellers that kept the cash flowing in. Amazingly, in spite of all the hotel guests and campers, it was still peaceful. Lunch was just sandwiches, with a nice barbeque in the early evening, followed by a scripture reading and discussion. The two weeks passed so quickly. I was astonished that one never got bored and stayed busy at all times. It was time to pack up for the trip down south and back to everyday stress again. It was a good interlude. Good memories I could store for the rest of my life.

Once more reality hit me extremely hard because I was married to a man who only considered his own desires and feelings. I could not believe my eyes when I entered the property and found that the garage was no longer a place to park the car. It had been taken over by his show chickens. The farm was too far away and they were not looked after properly there, according to Ernie, who had never looked after any of the animals when we were staying on the plot. There were rows upon rows of dilapidated cages and one could hardly move in between them in the garage. But that was not the end of it. There were cages stacked up all along the fences, too, one on top of the other. And besides the chickens, he had also decided to bring the rabbits. It was a sight to make one's eyes sore.

Louise and Greg were very upset. It was humiliating. They could not bring friends to a place like this. And we had to endure the neighbours' scorn. All the beauty that had been there was destroyed, the garden a mess. You could not swim or sit in the garden. All one smelled were the stinking animals. Polly wanted to know how I dared to complain, where had I thought he would put his show chickens? I responded by suggesting he moved in with her and Eddie, taking all the animals with him.

I asked why he had brought them there. His reply was that it was too far to travel when the shows were on. There would be no time to wash them and get them ready for exhibitions. To garner support, he told me that William and company did not care to help him prepare them for shows, seeking sympathy in this way.

"Look," I said. "I do not care a damn about your chickens. What about us? Did you ask me how I felt about it? No, you did not. Instead, like a coward, you waited until I was away and then you sneaked them in knowing that your family would support it. Yet, they would not allow their husbands to do these things. What about the children and their friends, how can they swim with this smell coming from the animals? And who is going to clean the cages? For all I care you can move back to the plot."

Again the answer came: "I cannot do that. It is too far to travel."

"That is not the reason you cannot move back, is it? Be honest with yourself just for once. The real reason is that the husbands are after your hide because of your philandering. You were the stud bull and you cannot deny it as it was common knowledge. I was the laughing stock of the whole neighbourhood, but in the end you came a cropper. Where may I ask are you going to wash and groom these birds? In the house? Sorry, I will not allow it."

He turned around and left without giving me an answer. It was so frustrating. Could he not see what he was doing to his family? Would he ever care at all?

Not long after this conversation, I received a call from Polly about the state her son was in. I asked her whether she had thought about the state we were all in.

"I have just arrived back from a trip to Malawi, and as usual he waited until I was not around before underhandedly bringing his chickens and rabbits to the house. The children cannot bring their friends here any longer as the place smells like a sewerage farm, even the neighbours are complaining about the stench. Are the children's feelings taken into account? No, they are not, and what about my feelings?" I asked her.

On the plot I had lived like a recluse for the same reasons. I was not, under any circumstances, going down that road again, and neither would our children.

"The children will never again be subjected to the embarrassment caused by the selfishness of your son. He can move back to the plot. I want to make myself very clear. It is about time that your poor son grows up and behaves like a decent human being should."

Sadly, with the heat in the garage, the chickens started to die one after the other. Those that survived were moved into the backyard. Needless to say the garden was destroyed. The neighbours reported him to the Edenvale Council's Health Department. He ignored them. He was a law unto himself.

As if the chickens were not enough, he started to bring scrap cars to the house. They were pushed into the ally between the wall of the garage and neighbour's fence. Not long afterwards, the place became rat infested. We all had to endure the embarrassment of the complaints and snide remarks of the neighbours. At times it was too much to bear. One neighbour erected a six foot wall between our properties. The neighbours at the back put up pre-cast walling. It did not get rid of the smell, though. They complained about this bitterly but it fell on deaf ears. Again they called the health inspector, but Ernie took no notice.

Around this time, the SAA gave employees with a service record of longer than 10 years the opportunity to apply for a free international flight ticket for a close relative in addition to this annual benefit provided to spouse and children. I told Ernie to apply for his mum as we were going to England in July, and we would present it to her at her next birthday party in May and it would also give her time to prepare for the trip.

He was excited about the prospect of taking Polly, but alas I had to nag him to get the ticket. In the end I had to threaten him that I would phone his boss if the ticket was not in my hands that evening. He did not want to take that risk and the threat paid off as he finally remembered to apply, and brought the documents home the following day. Why do I bother? I thought. I put myself through so much stress for a woman who has never cared whether I lived or died. With the ticket in hand, I could arrange her birthday party. All was in place to realise her lifelong dream of traveling to England.

She was overjoyed, but again her son got the pat on the back. Polly, Ernie, Louise and Greg set off for London, and I followed a week later as I had had to oversee an audit of the company's accounts. The Friday night I was due to leave, all passengers boarded and the plane was ready to take off when we were ordered off the plane. They had received a message of a possible bomb on board. All luggage was offloaded and we had to identify our own luggage. After that initial scare, we departed with a two-hour delay.

Once in London I learned that Polly had visited her Aunt Beatrice and met her mother's sister and husband Edward for the first time. She had a wonderful time in York, Scarborough and London. We were only there for two weeks and with such a lot to see. We managed to show her the most important sights. Overall I think Polly had a great time and I was truly glad that she had had the opportunity to fulfil her lifelong dream.

After we came back from our trip, Ernie had a heart attack. This led to four-way bypass surgery and early retirement. After seventeen years of service, he only received a measly disability pension of R 834.00 per month. There was a significant difference between retirement and disability pensions.

I took the opportunity of his absence to get rid of all the chickens and rabbits on the property. The relief of the neighbours was palpable. However, so was the dismay of his family. I told them they were welcome to have them and look after them as I had no inclination to do so. There was no money for their upkeep. Not only did I become even more unpopular with the B family, I was branded the most heartless soul on planet earth.

They had declined my offer and possibly thought I was bluffing, but to their surprise when they came to investigate, the property and garage were spotlessly clean. They wanted to know what I had done with the animals and I told them I had put them on the pavement and many black families had had lovely dinners. There followed some obscene and unprintable abuse.

I had enough to cope with. Derek decided to have his leg amputated just below the knee and I was actually amazed at how well he handled the whole ordeal. I had to marvel at the positive attitude of this child. He was back at work in no time. That evening he demonstrated to us what he did to poor Molly, his boss at the time. He drew a smiling face at the bottom of his stump, lifted it up and played puppet, telling her he was watching her. Molly ran from the office, and afterwards told him he was never to do that again. He was remarkable, but I did not appreciate it myself. Apart from Heather, who had visited him once in hospital, no one else from the B clan even bothered to phone to enquire about his wellbeing or how he was coping with the loss of his leg.

Ernest had been called up, like all young South African white men during apartheid, to do his 2-year compulsory military service. After a time, he had had enough of the army and had decided to abscond. I kept in contact with his immediate superior, Sergeant Potgieter. The struggle for emancipation led by the African National Congress was escalating during this period.

Louise and Greg were still too young to take any a real interest in the politics of the country. Ernest went missing for a year. I did not know where my child was, and it added to the normal stress of each day. In addition, a court case was pending regarding Derek's accident. The fault lay with a driver employed by the municipal authorities. After several years, the case ended and the court awarded Derek a financial compensation with which he started a business. He opened a toy shop called "Ball & Duck". I was running the shop while he and his friend Chris operated another business. The shop was not doing too well and Chris decided to go back to his native country, Germany, and it was not long afterwards that Derek followed.

With the shop closed, I had to look for another job and found one at an Optometrist in Eastgate shopping centre where I worked as a bookkeeper. Lacking funds, I was unable to enrol Louise in college to study photography which she so much wanted to do. I fell behind with my car payments, and the bank came round to repossess the car. I asked Ernie to help me to pay the two months arrears and he stood there laughing and told the men to take the car as I did not have money to pay for it. Afterwards he made the gallant effort of purchasing a nineteen-eighty-four Ford Cortina for me. I asked him why he had done this. It would have been cheaper to simply give me the money for the two outstanding payments on my new car. Instead, he bought me a secondhand car. He just shrugged his shoulders. It only made me angrier.

My natural inclination to see the funny side of things died. I was told to relax and become my own laughing self again. I lay in bed that night but could not fall asleep. I tossed and turned. My mind was whizzing round, thinking about the physical and emotional pain Ernest must be feeling. No one could convince me that hiding from the army and everyone he knew did not bother him at all.

I could not sleep and went to my comfort patch on the carpet in the lounge. I laid there sobbing. After I stopped sobbing, I started to relax. I could feel a calmness come over me. I so much wanted someone to hold and comfort me physically. Over the years I had conversations with Ernie about how a family structure should work, that we should be there for each other in time of need, but all I ever met with was hostility from him and his family, which I could not understand. What had I done to deserve it? I really tried to fit in and all the time everything I did was never acknowledged. Ernie took centre stage and took all the praise.

In December Ernie, Gregory and I went on holiday and upon our arrival back home we found Ernest was there. I was overjoyed. I was going to phone Sergeant Potgieter the next day to try and sort this mess out. But before I knew what was happening, there were about six military policemen bursting into the house. Ernest tried to make a run for it, but they got hold of him and he was kicked in the face, two guys had a leg each which they pulled apart, with a third one kicking him between the legs and calling him names. The other two each had a baton in the one hand and an arm in the other, and they were hitting him in his face and upper body. I was standing at our front gate witnessing it all and I was powerless to do anything. One of them just walked beside him and he looked back and saw me, and he signalled to them. As they looked up, they stopped, but then they dragged him across the tarred road by his hair. I had never seen such brutality in my life and was appalled at the way these youngsters behaved.

I went inside and asked Ernie why he had called the military police as he knew I was in contact with Sergeant Potgieter who I was going to phone the following day. His answer was that it had been his duty.

"You say it was your duty, and you stood there enjoying seeing them kick your son? I cannot understand you. You are just as sadistic as those mongrels. Your duty lies with your family. I told you once, when you carried on with Chris and had no feeling for him, your day will come. Just remember that." He did not answer me.

I went into the bedroom and sobbed uncontrollably. My heart was broken. I complained bitterly to God about this road he had put me on. I do not know how long I was there next to the bed on my knees before I became aware of myself again. I got to my feet, had a bath, and went to bed.

There was a military hearing and Sergeant Potgieter attended. Because we had worked closely together through the year of his disappearance, he was only sentenced to three months in solitary confinement instead of six months. After completing his sentence, he still had to go back to finish his military training which consisted in standing guard. I had an interview with Sergeant Potgieter and I also told him what the MPs had done. I explained Ernest's background, that he had studied Physics, Computer programming and Psychology at Wits University, just to be reduced by the army to the empty shell he had become, just staring into space.

"I wish I had all this information back then, and do not worry about those military police; I will take care of them. They should be stripped of their ranks for starters."

I did not reply as my hatred towards the apartheid regime blurred my judgment, but I knew that he would take action.

Thanks to the Sergeant an arrangement was made such that I could take Ernest home on a daily basis from the army base in Pretoria and bring him back each morning. This I did for six months. At the end of those six months, I was told by one of the military doctors that he would be discharged. I was advised to seek private medical treatment as there was something seriously wrong with him. I asked them what it was and he politely told me he could not tell me more due to army policy.

"I see," I told him. "They took my child, ruined his life, and now I must deal with the aftermath of it all."

I was very angry and more so with Ernie who was the cause it all.

I took him to a doctor, but according to him he could not find anything wrong with Ernest. Derek was in London at the time and I thought that if Ernest joined him, it might help. At the time they were close. Unfortunately, it did not work out. They had a fight and Derek banned him from his apartment. Ernest would turn on a tap and close it again, the same with the stove, switch it on and leave it.

We went to London to see if we could locate Ernest and to my embarrassment Ernie stopped every Bobby to ask whether he had seen our son. Tearfully he told them that he was missing and somewhere here in London. Ernie became so emotional, it was actually nauseating. I said to him that he was truly something else, a real marvel. He had never cared for any of his children, and now he was performing again in such a melodramatic way. It had been the same when Derek had had his accident. I begged him to stop.

The constable had advised him to look in all the parks in and around London as there one often found these children, coming from different countries, who had no money to get home. We looked but with no success. Then it was time for us to go home.

On our arrival I found him at home. As I walked in, he came out of the bathroom. He had a look of total confusion in his eyes. He was so bedraggled, like a real homeless creature, with a long red beard down to his chest. When he saw me, he threw his arms around me and started to sob, real heartrending sobs. I comforted him and after a while he became calm. I asked him how he had gotten home and he could not tell me.

The phone rang and it was Eddie. He told me that the only number Ernest could remember on his arrival at Jan Smuts Airport was his friend's telephone number. The friend had gone and fetched him from the airport and taken him to Polly's place, who, in turn, told Eddie to take him home, despite knowing that he was in such a state that he could not take care of himself, and to leave him there as it was not her problem. I was disgusted but did not say a word. He also told me that Michelle, Clive's wife, had died while we were in London. Life seemed so unfair. Here was one child of Polly that had found real happiness in his marriage and now his wife had died. They had two daughters and a son.

I asked him why he had just dropped Ernest at home and I was told that Polly had not wanted to take responsibility for him.

"Can a Bezuidenhout take responsibility for anything?" I asked. "Did it not bother anyone that he had nothing to eat for the week we were gone?"

There was no reply and I put the phone down. It took months and with the help of a psychiatrist we slowly brought him back to reality again. I did meet Sergeant Potgieter again by chance and asked him if anything had ever been done about the violent MPs. He smiled and replied that he had made sure that they were stripped of their ranks. They had become rookies again. More than that he could not have done, but rest assured they had not gotten off lightly. That, at least, brought some closure for me.

To crown it all Ernie had a heart attack and a heart by-pass operation was recommended. Polly called to berate me. I was so very tired of these people that always found fault with whatever I did. I listened and when she was done, I said:

"Polly, a person can only take so much and I've had about as much as anyone can take. This has been going on now for twenty-three years. Give it a break, will you."

No answer but at least I had gotten rid of all the tension that had been building up within me. I felt much better, but it did not take the heartache away. I told Ernie that I was very tired of Polly's accusations and his lack of concern for any of us. What Polly said was law for him, but not for me.

Once again I could not sleep and went to my favourite place on the carpet in the lounge. I laid there sobbing.

I took Ernie to a heart specialist for his post-op examination and he was referred for follow-up treatment to a doctor in Kempton Park. At least it was only fifteen to twenty minutes' drive from our place and there was much less traffic to contend with. I was still working and needed to get back to my daily routine. Ernie was at home recovering now. His measly pension was insufficient to cover our expenses.

I had had to apply for a loan from my bank and it had been granted. This helped us to bridge the financial gap for the time being and keep a roof over our heads.

Again I stood amazed at God's goodness. I needed most of all to know that my children would not have to suffer any disruptions in their daily lives. What would we have done if I had not secured the loan?

God had provided thus far and now I had to learn the important lesson of how to let things go and concentrate on what God wanted me to do with my life. I promised myself that I would take one day at a time and cultivate the habit of not thinking about what tomorrow might bring and keeping in touch by prayer, asking for directions each day.

If only it was as easy as it sounded, but it was not so. In fact, it was the most difficult lesson I had to learn as I was very much inclined to stumble forward, doing whatever came to mind, instead of standing still and allowing the Holy Spirit to direct my thoughts. One is naturally inclined to worry: "What if?" we constantly ask. The "if" might not even materialise. Derek had once told me that one should learn to accept the things one cannot control. He left out: AND LET GOD. He had very much been on fire for God as a teenager, but since his accident he had sadly turned away from Him.

Money was my main issue. I discovered that every disability or insurance policy we had ever taken out had either lapsed due to Ernie not meeting payments or cancelled, usually for the same reason or upon Polly's insistence. She did not believe in insurance. Why make other people rich? She had said.

"How am I to provide for the children and Ernie? How will I pay the bills that the medical aid refuses to pay, and the school fees? Are you going to help me? It is for times like these that the money would have come in handy."

Her answer was that I had placed too much responsibility upon Ernie. That was why he had had a heart attack.

"If that's how you see it, this is the end of our relationship. I am tired of your accusations. I will not keep your son from seeing you, but count me out, I will never, ever, set a foot into your house again. I am very disappointed about the policies that were cancelled by him without my knowledge and at your insistence. And you blame me for his illness? This is too much, this is the last straw."

That evening, I pleaded: "Father God, how much more can a person bear? I am only human and I cannot take any more of this deceitfulness. I am so tired."

What should I discover that night as I read my bible?

The reading was Two Corinthians 12 verse nine. 9 "My grace is sufficient for you, for my power is made perfect in weakness."

I took this to mean that I should boast all the more gladly about my weaknesses, so that Christ's power would come to rest upon me. The time to leave Ernie had not yet arrived. Again I was filled with the peace of God and I fell into a deep, peaceful sleep. I did not have time to mull over the proceedings of the day, and this in itself was a mighty blessing.

Another verse that boosted my energy was: "I can do all things through Christ who strengthens me." Philippians 4 verse 13. I had no choice, my destiny was in the hands of almighty God, and the road up to this point had been lined with thistles.

With the money crisis, cancelled policies, and Ernie at home, life was difficult. He made a slow but certain recovery. Once fit enough to work again, one of his friends advised him to apply for a job at a private airline, Safair. He would have a steady income and they would very likely prize the long years of experience and training he had received at the state airline, SAA. He applied and succeeded. Of course, once again it was regarded as his money as he had worked for it.

When Polly's next birthday came around again, I vowed not to do anything and not to go. To my surprise, Clive approached me and asked me whether I would help him arrange Polly's seventieth birthday celebration. Clive explained that he could see that the rest of her children had no inclination to do anything special for her with the exception of Eddie, as usual, who was anyway taking care of her as they lived together. At last someone appreciated me and acknowledged what I had done for Polly in the past. It made me feel good.

Laying on the lounge floor the words: "Never will I leave you; never will I forsake you" from Hebrew 13:5 entered into my mind. This time I was too distraught to take comfort in them and dissolved in tears, a real one-woman pity party. At some point I must have fallen asleep, as when I opened my eyes again, it was morning and I was still lying on the lounge floor.

As another day full of difficulties ended, I crawled into bed. Laying there the only things that filled my mind were the problems facing me. Even if these problems could be solved, the mere fact of being around him and his family was enough to make me want to throw in the towel. I felt so tired. I knew I would never get him to leave even if we actually got divorced. And waiting for him to take responsibility was wishful thinking. I could not fall asleep. I tossed and turned. He seemed as happy as could be, fast asleep and obviously quite pleased with himself.

I experienced the most awful feeling spreading through my body, my mind was racing, and I could not breathe. My chest felt tight, and I started to shake uncontrollably. I panicked, got out of bed and went to the lounge. What I was looking for I could not say. The doctor had prescribed tranquillisers, which I was taking, but they did not help. I looked at the tablets and threw them against the wall. I said to God: "Please just take me, take my life as I am not going to take this medication any longer, it is not helping. I need your help, Father God, I have had enough and I cannot continue. Just take me home," I wailed. Instead of taking me home, God gave me the peace that surpasses all understanding. The tightness in my chest disappeared, and disappointingly, I was still on this side of the universe.

Derek had joined his friend Chris in Germany. After trying to get a job there but failed and Derek had left for London. There he held several part-time jobs including a dustman. (It was during this time in London that Ernest joined him.) With the Berlin wall down, Derek had the idea of taking a course in teaching second language learners how to speak English. With the fall of communism, teachers of English were very much in demand. Soon after he graduated, he applied for a teaching post in Poland and was successful. Leaving England by a bus bound for Poland he met a Professor from the Olomouc University in the Czechoslovakia. He asked Derek where he was heading and he told him. The Professor convinced him to come to Czechoslovakia instead.

"You are destined for our university. Our country is also in desperate need of English tutors," Derek the opportunist accepted.

I was very worried about him, so far from home. But Father God knows our needs and He opened the doors for Derek. With only his diploma in English and no experience, he was employed to teach at the University of Olomouc. He received a good salary that included accommodation. On receiving the news, I was overwhelmed and filled with joy. Everything was falling into place for him.

Now back to Ernest's story. After his disastrous adventure in London and my returning from visiting Derek there and then finding him in such a sorry state back home, I took him to see many doctors. Eventually he was referred to a psychiatrist for tests. I could see that there was definitely something the matter with Ernest. Dr. Smart diagnosed him with schizophrenia. He was placed on medication and over the years he has improved incredibly.

Ernie had started working again, this time at Safair. At first he was working under revolving short-term contracts, but it was not long before they offered him a permanent position as foreman. This was a Godsend. I insisted that he contribute half of his salary to the household budget which included his upkeep.

"I refuse to feed and clothe you while you spend your own 'well-earned' money on yourself. It is about time that you chip in. If you should find this unacceptable, you are free to go back to your mother. I will personally pack your things and deliver you to her door. I also want you to spare a few thoughts for your son. You will have to support him financially, too, for the rest of your life. It is your fault he is in this state today," I said.

Polly was furious when she heard what I had said. She threw a tantrum and demanded to know how I could accuse him of Ernest's illness.

"Just as easily as you blame me for each and every thing that has happened to your son despite the fact that it has never been my fault. But what he has done to Ernest is his fault, and you did not even have the decency to look after him until we arrived home. You literally dumped him in his terrible state at the door of this house *no* food had passed his lips for more than a week. You abandoned him, you are disgusting," I retorted.

I told her that I had had more than enough of her interference.

"There are only two options. Either you take your son back and look after him, or he accepts blame and responsibility and acts accordingly," I said.

Silence descended on the telephone and a few seconds later I heard a click. A little later Heather called a family meeting at our house to try and stifle the animosity that had flared up between Polly and me. They wanted to know what the story was. Was it true that I had said I would not set foot in their mother's house again? I told them it was true.

"All of you stand on the side-line screaming abuse, but not one of you, with the exception of Eddie, is prepared to stick his or her neck out and offer some help. I am tired of the whole situation. It is not my fault he had a heart attack, it was his lifestyle," I said.

"But you must understand that people sometimes say things they do not mean when they are upset," Evelyn said.

"Would you stand for it when people say hurtful things, especially if they are not true?" There was silence. "Who arranged her parties, who suggested the overseas trip, who pushed your brother into getting her a flight ticket?"

Heather said something about supporting one another as members of the same family. I cut her short and asked her whether anyone had supported me. Silence followed.

"No, there was no family support. Only verbal abuse and false accusations," I said.

"Your cousin Jenny phoned, and before she could say anything I told her how Ernie was and how he was progressing. She cut me short and told me that she did not phone to hear about Ernie, she wanted to know how I was coping. Well, I was literally gobsmacked. I could not believe that someone could phone me to find out how I was coping. I told her that I was fine. Now that is what I call family. It is amazing what one phone call can do for a person's morale. As I told your mother, I'm done with it. I think that after twenty-five years I must concede defeat. I have lost the battle. You are welcome to visit your brother, but as for me, I will not set my foot in your mother's house ever again," I concluded.

Unfortunately Polly suddenly took ill and died. She had suffered a heart attack in the middle of the night and Eddie had taken her to hospital, but alas she had died before they got there. Having not yet been informed, when the phone rang at 5a.m. the next morning, I had a premonition. I told Ernie he should answer the phone as it was about his mother. I told him that she was no longer with us. He looked at me as if I was mad. After answering the phone, he came back and crawled into bed again. I asked him who it had been and he answered that Eddie had called to report his mother's passing. The next minute he was fast asleep again, seemingly without a care in the world. I did not understand him.

Derek decided to study for an English degree through Unisa, a distance university. After obtaining his goal, he continued his studies and in the end achieved his Doctorate in English Literature. He met Marketa in Prague while teaching English and they came to South Africa for their wedding. I was happy that he found happiness after all he had suffered. After the wedding they settled in Vienna.

One day Ernie came home with a motorbike and I asked him what it was for. I was told that he had a new lease on life and he intended to make the most of it. He had always wanted to get a motorbike again and now he had joined a motorbike club.

My thoughts were: Here we go again. I was right in a sense as, once again, he was almost never at home. Every weekend there were motorbike rallies and once he suggested that I join, too. He had an outfit for me. It consisted in a skimpy top and some tight pants to go with the rest of the bike paraphernalia.

"What kind of club is this?" I asked. It turned out to be one of those clubs where everything was permissible.

"You really want me to join you?" It was insulting. He expected me to lower myself by joining in such amusements.

"Yes," he replied. "Stop being such a prude and start living life. Life is there for the taking," he philosophised.

"Life might be there for the taking in your view, but not for me, thank you."

Every weekend he was out on his bike. Sometimes there were street parties. During this time, I had to wait up for him. He would come home at all hours, sometimes "high." I-could-not-tell-you-what drugs or alcohol and leave gates and doors unlocked or even open. Sometimes he would not make it as far as the bed, and sleep where he fell. There was just no end to his escapades and well into his sixties?

To celebrate the 1999/2000 turn of the century, our family got together in Simonstown in the Cape Province. Derek and Marketa and their daughter Kayla also joined us. We had a wonderful time together. The only one under the weather was Ernie, as he wanted to be with his club buddies. A big rally had been organized for the year-end party, but with all the children there, he could not get away without revealing this side of his private life.

Alas, with the celebration over, it was time to go and Derek departed for Vienna. Marketa would join him later, and she returned with us to Johannesburg as there was the possibility of adopting a little coloured boy. The mum was looking for an overseas adoption. The B family was not in favour of it, but by now they had learned to keep quiet.

With a few trips to Pretoria, and all the paperwork in order, little Joshua and Mum departed for Vienna. Now they had two children, Kayla and Josh. I visited them a lot in Vienna. Ernie went once or twice, but for years I went by myself and watched them grow.

The Head Hunter motorbike club was the last straw. I filed for divorce. He did not even bother to come to court. The sad thing was, however, that I still could not get him out of the house. I tried everything. I threw all his clothes onto the pavement. The divorce settlement gave him the Walkerville plot and me the house in Edenvale. However, the plot being too far out of town for him, he refused to go.

On 2nd December 2000, I was shopping at Woolworths when I received a telephone call from Safair telling me that Ernie had had a stroke. They were transporting him to the Arwyp hospital. I informed the family, but there was no real interest except on the part of Eddie. Luckily there was no paperwork as they had all his medical history in their files.

On my arrival, I was told that he was still in the operating theatre. A call came through on his mobile phone and when I answered it, a voice began yelling at me. The voice complained loudly that Ernie was holding them up. The whole club was waiting for him. The planned weekend rally was set to begin. The voice reminded him that there was a penalty to pay for not arriving on time. It took a minute before I regained my senses. I started to yell back and informed the caller that Ernie had had a stroke. They were free to go and need not wait on him. In fact, they probably would do well not to count on him in any future activities, as he was unlikely, even if he survived, to ever ride a bike again. The caller was stunned and mumbled "sorry". He asked which hospital he was in. They would come around on Sunday afternoon after the rally. I just switched the phone off.

After the operation, the doctor explained to me that he in fact had had two strokes: one large one followed by a small one. Only time would tell. He told me, too, that Ernie was lucky that he was still breathing. I phoned the family to tell them and as usual I was blamed for it. It was so infuriating.

The Head Hunters arrived on Sunday. I think they were a bit taken aback. They did not stay long. They told him that they had drunk a "poison" in his honour. Fortunately, the club was soon disbanded. Their club house was situated next to our church. It closed down soon after, and I heard that the leader of the pack had returned to his native country, England.

The diagnosis was bad. He pulled through and after a month in hospital, he was transferred to a convalescent care home in Boksburg. He was unable to walk or use a bedpan and had to use nappies, which also cost a lot of money. Every night I had to drive through to see him. Why I actually bothered to do this, I do not know as we were no longer married. I actually owed him nothing. I left Eastgate each day at four thirty only to arrive back home at nine. It was a long day, not to mention the cost of it all, and all because some people were so selfish all they could think to do was to live their lives without regard to others. The home cost me three thousand rand per month. This represented a sizeable bite out of any salary in those days and I was the only breadwinner.

The room at the home came without furniture. One had to supply one's own. My family helped me to furnish it. Not one member of the Bezuidenhout family bothered to go and visit him there, again with the exception of Eddie. He was the only one. We agreed that he would go on Mondays, Wednesdays and Fridays and I would do the runs on Tuesdays, Thursdays, Saturdays and Sundays.

One evening there was a knock on the gate. It was one of his co-workers with a huge box for Ernie. I told him the stroke was so bad, that there was no way that he would ever be able to go back to work again. On his way out, he asked me whether he could say something. I told him to feel free to say whatever it was that bothered him.

"We are all sorry he had a stroke, but Mrs. Bezuidenhout, but we are all glad that he is not coming back."

He looked at me, not sure how I would respond. I told him that I fully understood. He had a temper that he could not control. When something went wrong, he would put the blame on his co-workers, it was always their fault.

"His temper was unbearable," he remarked. The huge box, and I mean huge, was filled to the brim with pornographic filth. Even at my age, it was an eye-opener. On the farm, I had known him to bring Playboy magazines home. Examining the contents, I had never come across anything of the kind. Even a Playboy playmate would blush at this filth. He had no respect for himself let alone anyone else. In the box, too, there was some paperwork discussing a charge against him of sexual harassment at the workplace.

During the bike period, I had moved Ernie into the garage. He converted it into a kind of boy's club room. After the stroke, Greg came to the house to help me clean it out. In a way I was sorry to have him there as the filth that came out of those cupboards was disgusting. In addition, there were photos taken at the rallies, women riding topless around on the back of motorbikes and the like. What else did they do at those rallies? I wondered. In the end, Greg got so angry that he just took the heaps of magazines and threw them against the wall.

After the garage was cleaned out, I could park the car there. Not for long, though. Glen, the son of Uncle Dick and Aunt Hetty, asked me whether I might agree to look after his aging parents. Their plot had been sold. They were now too old to run it. Glen had built quarters for them on his property, but arguments had flared up. I offered to turn our garage into a small flat for them. There they lived very happily for almost two years.

Uncle Dick was a quite a difficult person to live with. Everything had to be done exactly according to his specifications. Aunt Hetty was used to it, but I was not. In addition, I could not take his screaming at Aunt Hetty. She began to exhibit signs of Alzheimer's disease. She would forget herself in the middle of a sentence, or forget where she was or what she was doing. This was unacceptable to Uncle Dick. If she put a knife or fork a bit askew, she would be screamed at. Towards the end it seemed she had simply given up. One day he pushed it a bit too far and I flew into their room and told him where to get off. I also said to him that if he ever raised his voice to her again, I would send him back to live with his son. Not long after, Glen came to pick them up. On the day of the actual move, Aunt Hetty came to me and told me not to worry, I had done my best.

Eddie went to visit them once after the move back. He later reported that Uncle Dick regretted the move. Living with Marie had been better.

"That's a feather in your cap," he joked.

Soon after, Aunt Hetty passed. Uncle Dick was placed in Jafta, a Government run old age home in Johannesburg, where he later died, a sad and lonely old man.

Ernie had recovered sufficiently and was home again. We were divorced, but his family refused to look after him. According to them, it was my responsibility. At times I wished I had their sense of responsibility as none of them would look after their ex-husbands. It took a while before he could walk properly again.

I converted the garage-flat into an office for me and an extra bedroom for visitors. I had racks installed for all my books and kept my sewing machine there. I called it my hobby room. Little did I know it would come in handy just two months down the line as the building we worked in was sold. We were going to share offices in a house rented in Edenvale. I asked my boss if I could work from home. He would save on rent and so he consented. It saved me money on fuel, but I soon found that I had made a huge mistake.

Ernie found a new pastime. He started to eavesdrop on my phone conversations and whenever I had visitors. I caught him many times standing where he thought I could not see him. My daughter Louise phoned me and told me I must be careful what I say and to whom I say it. That confirmed it and I confronted him. He fervently denied spreading rumours. Now I understood why the family did not come and visit, except for Eve, his sister. I felt so resentful because I had taken him in, and he had once more violated my trust. He had no decency nor showed any appreciation for what I was doing for him. He even wrote to my sister in Limpopo telling her that I did not look after him properly. She nearly fainted.

Just to get some peace, I began taking him on Wednesdays to the shopping centre in Edenvale. While wondering around there one day, he had befriended the owner of a stamp shop. Now he spent his time there sorting out stamps that people had donated, usually boxes and albums from someone's estate. It gave both Ernest and I a break. Ernie was in the habit of nagging him to type out letters for him as he had lost the use of his good arm. I had refused to type out his irrelevant drivel. It would drive Ernest half crazy, but he did it because the nagging drove him crazier still.

I was getting uptight. Ernest got upset by his father and, unlike me, could not refuse him his requests. When he did not get his way, Ernie would send text messages to everyone in his contact list complaining about how we were treating him. I no longer cared, but it worked on Ernest's nerves. Ernie was unhappy, but what had he expected? Everything that had happened to him was the result of his own lifestyle choices. And if he had been a caring husband and father, our attitudes would certainly have been different. Now he would just have to suffer the consequences of all his years of living like a bachelor without a care in the world. I told him that he was very lucky to still live here at all. That annoyed him and mercifully made him retreat into his room and leave us in peace for a while.

I was getting close to retiring age. I had always wanted to retire to the Cape Province. Greg and his family had returned from Europe and had settled in Cape Town. He reminded me that I am nearing retirement age and wanted to know whether I was still planning to move to the Cape. I confirmed that I was coming. He and his wife, Melissa, set out looking for a suitable place and found a two bedroom townhouse that met with all my requirements with the exception of being literally at the seaside. But with the house situated in Blouberg Strand and across the road from the sea, it was nevertheless fabulous, and the walk to the beach would do me good.

When it came closer to the time of the move, I asked Ernie whether he wanted to come with or whether he wanted to go to an old age home. His decision was to stay in Johannesburg with his family and friends. A suitable home was found and he happily retired there. The family was up in arms because he was placed in an old age home and again I was called all the names under the sun. I was told how dreadfully selfish I was to leave him there and move to Cape Town. They even ranted and raved about all the money I had taken.

What money? I wondered, but with time one learns just to let them go on as they please. It was not worth the energy or trouble. Sadly no one except Eddie visited him once he had moved there. Where was the great love this family had for each other?

Louise told me that she hoped that I would not begin to feel sorry for him and take him back again. I told her I would most definitely not do that. There was no way I was going to give him yet another chance after all the drama he had caused me.

In January 2011, I started painting and cleaning out the house, preparing it for the sale. It was hard going, as over the years Ernie had gathered up a lot of junk: old car parts, unidentifiable rotting junk as per usual, pieces of this and that. Whatever was in good enough condition to sell, I sold. His sewing machine was sold, as well as old tools and other re-reusable items. It took some doing, but we finally had the place cleaned up.

I retired in September 2011 and was ready for the move. One evening, feeling very tired, I went to bed. I fell asleep very quickly and had a dream about Polly. She looked very tired and exhausted. Her eyes were big and they were extremely sad. She was bent over as she stood there looking at me. I wondered: what does she want from me?

I stared at her, waiting for some response. I could sense that there was a reason for this visit and finally it came.

"Please tell my children there are only two options," she said, echoing my words of years before.

I was so shocked at the message. I shook my head in disbelief. With a sad smile, I told her that it was impossible. Her children would never believe me.

"When I tell them what you have just said, they will ignore me. You have trained them too well. When you told them that there was no God, they believed you."

She turned around and slowly went on her way. Of all the visions I had had in my life, this one was the most incredible.

"How can this be? Your word states clearly that the dead cannot come back and ask their relatives to repent. It was written in your word where Jesus was teaching his disciples:

LK 16:19 "There was a rich man who was dressed in purple and fine linen and lived in luxury every day. [20] At his gate was laid a beggar named Lazarus, covered with sores [21] and longing to eat what fell from the rich man's table. Even the dogs came and licked his sores.

LK 16:22 "The time came when the beggar died and the angels carried him to Abraham's side. The rich man also died and was buried. 23 In hell, where he was in torment, he looked up and saw Abraham far away, with Lazarus by his side. 24 So he called to him, 'Father Abraham, have pity on me and send Lazarus to dip the tip of his finger in water and cool my tongue, because I am in agony in this fire.'

LK 16:25 "But Abraham replied, 'Son, remember that in your lifetime you received your good things, while Lazarus received bad things, but now he is comforted here and you are in agony. 26 And besides all this, between us and you a great chasm has been fixed, so that those who want to go from here to you cannot, nor can anyone cross over from there to us.'

LK 16:27 "He answered, 'Then I beg you, father, send Lazarus to my father's house, 28 for I have five brothers. Let him warn them, so that they will not also come to this place of torment.'

LK 16:29 "Abraham replied, 'they have Moses and the Prophets; let them listen to them.'

LK 16:30 " 'No, father Abraham,' he said, 'but if someone from the dead goes to them, they will repent.'

LK 16:31 "He said to him, 'If they do not listen to Moses and the Prophets, they will not be convinced even if someone rises from the dead.'

At this moment I woke up in a sitting position in my bed arguing with God, as I did not want to go and tell the Bezuidenhout family about this dream.

Then God directed me to Acts where he told Peter to go to the Roman Centurion and read what was written there. Here he was talking to me and my rebelliousness:

AC 10:1 At Caesarea there was a man named Cornelius, a centurion in what was known as the Italian Regiment. 2 He and all his family were devout and God-fearing; he gave

generously to those in need and prayed to God regularly. ³
One day at about three in the afternoon he had a vision. He
distinctly saw an angel of God, who came to him and said,
"Cornelius."

AC 10:4 Cornelius stared at him in fear. "What is it, Lord?"
he asked.

The angel answered, "Your prayers and gifts to the poor
have come up as a memorial offering before God. ⁵ Now send
men to Joppa to bring back a man named Simon who is called
Peter. ⁶ He is staying with Simon the tanner, whose house is
by the sea."

AC 10:7 when the angel who spoke to him had gone,
Cornelius called two of his servants and a devout soldier who
was one of his attendants. ⁸ He told them everything that had
happened and sent them to Joppa.

AC 10:9 About noon the following day as they were on
their journey and approaching the city, Peter went up on the
roof to pray. ¹⁰ He became hungry and wanted something to
eat, and while the meal was being prepared, he fell into a
trance. ¹¹ He saw heaven opened and something like a large
sheet being let down to earth by its four corners. ¹² It
contained all kinds of four-footed animals, as well as reptiles
of the earth and birds of the air. ¹³ Then a voice told him, "Get
up, Peter. Kill and eat."

AC 10:14 "Surely not, Lord." Peter replied. "I have never
eaten anything impure or unclean."

AC 10:15 The voice spoke to him a second time, "Do not
call anything impure that God has made clean."

AC 10:16 This happened three times, and immediately the
sheet was taken back to heaven.

AC 10:17 While Peter was wondering about the meaning of
the vision, the men sent by Cornelius found out where
Simon's house was and stopped at the gate. ¹⁸ They called out,
asking if Simon who was known as Peter was staying there.

^{AC 10:19} While Peter was still thinking about the vision, the Spirit said to him, "Simon, three men are looking for you. ²⁰ So get up and go downstairs. Do not hesitate to go with them, for I have sent them."

^{AC 10:21} Peter went down and said to the men, "I'm the one you're looking for. Why have you come?"

^{AC 10:22} The men replied, "We have come from Cornelius the centurion. He is a righteous and God-fearing man, who is respected by all the Jewish people. A holy angel told him to have you come to his house so that he could hear what you have to say." ²³ Then Peter invited the men into the house to be his guests.

The next day Peter started out with them, and some of the brothers from Joppa went along. ²⁴ The following day he arrived in Caesarea. Cornelius was expecting them and had called together his relatives and close friends. ²⁵ As Peter entered the house, Cornelius met him and fell at his feet in reverence. ²⁶ But Peter made him get up. "Stand up," he said, "I am only a man myself."

^{AC 10:27} Talking with him, Peter went inside and found a large gathering of people. ²⁸ He said to them: "You are well aware that it is against our law for a Jew to associate with a Gentile or visit him. But God has shown me that I should not call any man impure or unclean. ²⁹ So when I was sent for, I came without raising any objection. May I ask why you sent for me?"

^{AC 10:30} Cornelius answered: "Four days ago I was in my house praying at this hour, at three in the afternoon. Suddenly a man in shining clothes stood before me ³¹ and said, 'Cornelius, God has heard your prayer and remembered your gifts to the poor. ³² Send to Joppa for Simon who is called Peter. He is a guest in the home of Simon the tanner, who lives by the sea.' ³³ So I sent for you immediately, and it was good of you to come. Now we are all here in the presence of God to listen to everything the Lord has commanded you to tell us."

AC 10:34 Then Peter began to speak: "I now realize how true it is that God does not show favouritism [35] but accepts men from every nation who fear him and do what is right. [36] You know the message God sent to the people of Israel, telling the good news of peace through Jesus Christ, who is Lord of all. [37] You know what has happened throughout Judea, beginning in Galilee after the baptism that John preached-- [38] how God anointed Jesus of Nazareth with the Holy Spirit and power, and how he went around doing good and healing all who were under the power of the devil, because God was with him.

AC 10:39 "We are witnesses of everything he did in the country of the Jews and in Jerusalem. They killed him by hanging him on a tree, [40] but God raised him from the dead on the third day and caused him to be seen. [41] He was not seen by all the people, but by witnesses whom God had already chosen--by us who ate and drank with him after he rose from the dead. [42] He commanded us to preach to the people and to testify that he is the one whom God appointed as judge of the living and the dead. [43] All the prophets testify about him that everyone who believes in him receives forgiveness of sins through his name."

AC 10:44 While Peter was still speaking these words, the Holy Spirit came on all who heard the message. [45] The circumcised believers who had come with Peter were astonished that the gift of the Holy Spirit had been poured out even on the Gentiles. [46] For they heard them speaking in tongues and praising God.

Then Peter said, [47] "Can anyone keep these people from being baptized with water? They have received the Holy Spirit just as we have." [48] So he ordered that they be baptized in the name of Jesus Christ. Then they asked Peter to stay with them for a few days.

I told Eve and Gladys, but they just scoffed at the dream. Eve insisted her mother had always told them there is no God.

I did not manage to speak to any of the others, as they never came to visit me.

I placed the house on the market. My plan was to leave on the first of November 2011. The realtor advised against an immediate sale: the market was bad. She suggested a six-month rental agreement and to monitor developments for a while. The house would remain listed to be sold. A suitable tenant was found who moved in on the day that we left for Cape Town. The market improved and we managed to sell the house. Finally, I closed the book on all the difficulties I had experienced until then, and started a truly new life here in Cape Town.

I had seen the outside of the townhouse once when I had been in Cape Town for a weekend visit. Entering it now, Ernest and I were in heaven. We would really enjoy it down here, away from the stress caused by Ernie. .

The journey was one thousand four hundred kilometres long and took three days. We stopped along the route at Beaufort West, Laingsburg and Matjiesfontein. It is a long road, but breathtakingly beautiful.

We arrived on a Friday and they were still busy cleaning the place after the previous tenants had vacated it. But it was beautiful inside already and I could not wait to settle. At the time Ernest did not say much. Now he enjoys his routines. He never misses a day walking to the beach and he never mentions Edenvale.

I now understand why they call it the "wild" coast. The environment is forever changing. The sea washes over the beach each day, reshaping it anew. Speaking for myself, I would not change the peace and tranquillity of it for anything.

I found a Baptist Church in Melkbos where I attend services. When I first started going there, they were organising a ladies retreat, a weekend away, and I applied. We would share chalets and transport and I was teamed with a lady called Johanna. I just had to go. On our arrival and settling into each of our cottages, we had a meeting to inform us of the weekend program.

With the few daylight hours left, we got acquainted with our fellow travellers and after supper and a short devotion, we were ready to settle in bed. The following day there were some baptisms in the sea and Johanna was one of the ladies who got baptised on that day. In evening there was a gathering and we were told that Pastor Rob and some of his prayer warriors were praying through the night and there were some messages for some of the people present.

To my surprise I was called up. It was the first time that the pastor had spoken to me directly and he told me that, while he was praying, the Lord had given him the following message for me:

"Maria, the Lord said that it was a long and difficult journey, but it is over. He will restore everything that the locusts had eaten over the years."

Then a lady added that I do not have to worry, as all my children and their children will serve the Lord. Unbeknown to the pastor, his message contained more or the less the same words that had been spoken to me in my dream forty-seven years before.

It was absolutely amazing as none of these people knew me, and certainly could have no idea about what had happened to me in the past. I was overjoyed to say the least. I felt very battered by the storms of life, but now after two years I can say that I am much stronger and the restoration is beginning to show. I can only praise the Lord for what he has done in my life, the strength and the ability He has given me to weather each storm. Do not get tired of waiting and never give up. My journey took fifty-seven years, but we serve a faithful and just God. The storms have ceased. One difficulty I have is learning how to get used to it.

Thank You Father God for your faithfulness and Jesus for Your love and assurance that you will never leave me nor forsake me and the Holy Spirit for Your guidance.